TRADERS AND TINKERS

CULTURE AND ECONOMIC LIFE

TRADERS AND TINKERS

Bazaars in the Global Economy

MAITRAYEE DEKA

STANFORD UNIVERSITY PRESS
Stanford, California

Stanford University Press
Stanford, California

Printed in the United States of America on acid-free, archival-quality paper

ISBN 9781503635333 (cloth)
ISBN 9781503636002 (paper)
ISBN 9781503636019 (electronic)

Library of Congress Control Number: 2022048478

Library of Congress Cataloging-in-Publication Data available upon request.

Cover Design: Lindy Kasler

Cover Photographs: Shutterstock

Typeset by Newgen in Minion Pro 10/14

For my father

Contents

List of Illustrations   ix
Acknowledgments   xi

Introduction   1

1 Bazaar Aesthetics, Commerce, and Commons   38

2 Bazaar Pricing and Bargaining   71

3 Bazaar Tinkering, *Jugaad*, and Popular Knowledge   100

4 Bazaar Ethics and a Common Human Condition   129

5 Bazaar Platforms: Encounters with a New Competitor   154

Conclusion   173

Notes   187
References   201
Index   217

List of Illustrations

Figure I.1: A box of a street vendor's stock of pirated games on a table in Nehru Place   3

Figure 1.1: View from the main entrance staircase of Palika Bazaar into the inner circle   53

Figure 1.2: A repair person's desk at Palika Bazaar   60

Figure 3.1: A locally assembled wooden PlayStation console in Lajpat Rai Market   107

Figure 4.1: A pillar covered with images of Hindu gods in Nehru Place   143

Acknowledgments

INEVITABLY FOR A BOOK about bazaar sociality, this book would not have been possible without the generosity shown by strangers, visitors, and, notably, traders and street vendors of video games in Delhi's Lajpat Rai Market, Palika Bazaar and Nehru Place. This book is, first and foremost, theirs. To the city of Delhi that obscures an outsider's immediate intimacy but goes on to intrigue and eventually excite, this book is about the spirit of Delhi and its many faces.

I initially trained as a social scientist at the Delhi School of Economics. I am grateful to Yasmeen Arif, Roma Chatterji, Deepak Mehta, Rajni Palriwala, Rabindra Ray, and J. P. S. Uberoi for being brilliant teachers and scholars encouraging a critical sociological imagination. Rita Brara, thank you for being a mentor. When I was a master's student at the Delhi School of Economics, Meenakshi Thapan trained me to conduct fieldwork in a school in Delhi that would be a good base for a future ethnography in the city. I am thankful to her for being an intellectual mentor, guide, and friend all these years. I thank Tara Basumatary, Ashawari Chaudhury, Ishita Dey, Yoonjeong Cheong, Ransaigra Daimary, Syed Mohammad Faisal, Bonojit Hussain, Amrita Kurian, Vineet Rathee, Subhadeepta Ray, Ishani Saraf, Haripriya Soibam, William Stafford, Mohammad Sayeed, Prasenjeet Tribhuvan, and Praveen Verma for many fantastic discussions at JP tea stall and for being exciting thinkers.

During my master of philosophy study in Delhi, as part of the European Studies Programme, I was at the École normale supérieure in Paris doing brief fieldwork among Algerian immigrants. I am thankful to Éric Fassin for his guidance in developing field sites critically and for giving me the confidence to study a new context. As a PhD student and later as an EU FP7 P2PValue postdoctoral fellow at the State University of Milan, I was part of a stimulating network of digital studies and critical theory. Milan, as a city, continues to fascinate me. From the outside, it is the fashion and design hub. Underneath are the hidden courtyards, passages, and the quiet corners of Feltrinelli bookstores where one can brood and write. I am thankful to Massimo Airoldi, Carolina Bandinelli, Tiziano Bonini, Carlo Burelli, Alberto Cossu, Alessandro Caliandro, Alessandro Delfanti, Alessandro Gandini, Alessandro Gerosa, Vincenzo Luise, and Valeria Piro, with whom I have had many spirited conversations. They continue to be friends and collaborators. I thank senior colleagues Enzo Colombo and Luisa Leonini for being wonderful mentors. I am indebted to my PhD examiner Celia Lury for her support and encouragement when I needed it the most.

This book found an intellectual home at the Centre for the Study of Developing Society (CSDS), Delhi. From browsing through the media archives to conversations with colleagues over seminars and talks, CSDS provided me with a unique insight into the media aesthetic of Delhi. I am thankful for the journal *Bioscope*'s editorial team, especially Lotte Hoek and Ravi Vasudevan, who gave me the platform to publish my first academic article. I especially want to thank senior colleague Ravi Sundaram who has been a constant support and mentor. In many ways, his work on Delhi's media urbanism inspired me to think differently about ordinary practices. His work has been the most profound influence on this book. During the fieldwork, I had fruitful discussions with Sumandro Chattapadhyay from the Centre for Internet and Society about the media economies of Delhi.

At the University of Essex, I am fortunate to have engaging colleagues with whom I have discussed this book at various stages. I thank Shaul Bar Haim, Boroka Bo, Andrew Canessa, Alexandra Cox, Pam Cox, Isabel Crowhurst, Neli Demireva, Roisin Ryan-Flood, Carlos Gigoux, Sandya Hewamanne, Mark Harvey, Laurie James-Hawkins, Tara Mahfoud, James Allen-Roberston, Johanna Romer, Anna Sergi, Darren Thiel, Nigel South, Jason Sumich, and Katy Wheeler for their support. Special thanks to Michael Halewood for pointing me toward the literature on medieval tinkers. Anna Di Ronco and Linsey McGoey, you have been incredible colleagues and friends, and I could not see myself having completed this book without our lunches in person and on Zoom. I have shared ideas from this book with my students of social theory at the undergraduate and master's levels, and I benefited a lot from those discussions. I am thankful to the library staff at Essex, particularly

Sandy Macmillan, for being swift in providing urgent resources, and to the British Library, where I have spent days working on the book. In London, special thanks to Scott Lash, with whom I have discussed this book on many occasions and always come away enriched by our conversations. I acknowledge Maitrayee Basu, Jane Hindley, Carolyn Laubender, Sean Nixon, Holly Pester, Colin Samson, and Robin West for including me in their world of art, birds, poetry, composting, allotments, Red Lion books, and walks.

This book has benefited from conference presentations, talks and seminars on campuses, and online interaction. I am thankful to the participants and organizers who engaged with my work and gave genuine comments to work with. I am grateful to journal editors and reviewers whose comments on my published pieces helped me to reframe ideas in this book.

I want to thank the editorial team at Stanford University Press, particularly the fantastic support offered by senior editor Marcela Maxfield. This book would not have been possible without her guidance and her being so accommodating of my needs. I want to thank Fred Wherry, who showed trust in the manuscript at the initial stage and put me on a steady course of writing. I want to thank the two anonymous reviewers whose comments were invaluable in revising the manuscript for their generosity and time.

Adam Arvidsson, Raisa Choudhuri, Matteo Miele, Kakoli Mukherjee, Felix Schnell, and Zeenat Saberin, thank you for being wonderful companions and my support system. Other friends in India, Italy, the UK, and the US, you know who you are, and I want to thank you for lending a patient ear, regaling me with your stories, and instilling new energy into my academic life. I want to thank my maternal aunt Madhavi Kalita for being an early feminist inspiration and a dear friend. The extended Deka-Kalita family, thank you for being there for me.

My mother, Kalyani Deka, is one of the strongest influences in my life. Her humor, community service, and integrity inspire me. My brothers, Angshuman and Dhritiman, thank you for your unwavering support and love. You both are such wonderful human beings, and I am happy to grow old with you, hearing about your adventures with food, books, places, and people in North East India. I recently lost my father, Dhireswar Deka, and I owe him anything to do with creativity, ambition, and a passion for life. My interior life would not have found any expression if my father did not encourage me to philosophize life, from birds to books, trees, and stars; he and I could chatter for hours about nothing. His absence has been challenging, and his slow attention to life has gotten me to pause, observe, wonder, and be kind.

I wrote parts of this book in the idyllic countryside of Assam, and it continues to be the most crucial element of my life; the rolling hills, the rivers, the music, the people, and the ecology have kept me grounded. Love to my stray pet dogs, Bhotku, Chotku, and Chutki.

TRADERS AND TINKERS

Introduction

WHAT DOES A VENDOR in Indonesia selling vegetables at a kiosk have in common with a street vendor selling electronics on India's roads or pirated music in Mali? Or what does a repair person in Santiago, Chile, share with a Shenzhen repair shop? To ask more broadly, what does an Iranian carpet trader have in common with an African cell phone trader? On the surface, the answer would be nothing significant, as they all belong to different cultural contexts and deal with varying types of goods. But suppose we get past these noticeable differences in locations and trade specifics. In that case, peeling the layers, we will see many similarities suggesting that they have the same essence of commerce. For instance, these varied groups of actors acutely share the urban experiences of living on the margins. They operate under duress of some sort, either threats from local authorities and sudden evictions from their place of work or being targeted for selling illegal and pirated products as a bourgeois aesthetic of clean, orderly, and "smart" cities dominates our urban visions. They also face stiff competition from e-commerce platforms that are shifting these vendors' longtime clientele base, and they increasingly feel that their way of life is on its way out. These actors' similarities do not end in sharing the predicament of being less powerful actors in the urban economy. Street-level businesses have a similar routine and pace of commerce. The actors are likely to bargain to settle prices for their nonstandardized goods, and they often depend on rudimentary infrastructure to display them—tarpaulin sheets to get cover from the rain, everyday tools, and furniture pieces such as wooden

1

benches, chairs, and bamboo sheds (see Figure I.1). To different degrees, all these actors are part of transnational commerce, dealing in cheap consumer items and knock-offs that arrive in ferries from China or trips taken to Hong Kong or Dubai by air by so-called suitcase entrepreneurs. Is there a word to describe the routines of trade and experiential reality of this motley group of urban economic non-elites primarily working with household capital? Perhaps we need an equally traveled word—bazaars.[1]

In Eric Raymond's (1999) classic, *The Cathedral and the Bazaar*, he uses the image of the bazaar to invoke a radical alternative to the hierarchical corporate version of the information society: he describes Linux software as looking like a "great babbling bazaar of different agendas and approaches." Ever since the origins of modern consumer society, bazaars have been part of an orientalist imaginary as home to goblins and sorcerers from the "East," a vision intrinsically related to European colonialism. While divergent, both these definitions show why we, as modern minds, cannot shake off our fascination with the term and introduce bazaars as an emancipatory metaphor for change or to hearken back to a mythical time. In fact, there are countless renditions of the word "bazaar," from animated movies to posters and magazines that seek to capture an entity that is real but so out of sight as to awe and shock in equal measures. It is perhaps the magic that this word conjures in our imagination from fairy tales, myths, and European colonialism that somehow we feel bazaars can be anything, quietly revolutionary or decadent or frightfully alien.

Like all exaggerations, there are some truths to them. In the case of Raymond's comparison of Linux software with a bazaar, indeed the latter is open, but it is not exactly open the way he saw it as some form of subversive instrument. Physical bazaars are not open as a result of an ideology. They are open in their sociality, posing fewer entry hurdles, whether with new commercial actors or an itinerant group who quickly become part of the bazaar environment and would not be so readily welcomed in elite consumer spaces. Similarly, modern bazaars display a muddling variety of new, old, and stolen products. Yet they do not represent the strange cultures conjured up by the colonial mindset. In fact, far from the exotic and regressive ideas of colonial bazaars, contemporary bazaars are as real as it gets in providing wares to the lowest level of consumers globally. Their great assortment of goods caters to lower-end buyers whose economic constraints push them to look for cheap and wide-ranging alternatives to high-priced consumer items. Physical bazaars

Figure I.1 A box of a street vendor's stock of pirated games on a table in Nehru Place (author's image).

cast their networks wide when it comes to aggregating different types of products—stolen, secondhand, pirated, counterfeited, and originals—nobody knows for sure with what demand the next consumer comes. Or, more importantly, who enters the shop next. It can be a new migrant to the city looking for a job. Or an architecture student who could not afford the latest AutoCAD software and is in the bazaar looking for a cheaper, pirated version. Or it could be a rickshaw puller who wants to replace his old phone with a new one. There are also consumers who are looking to make extra money selling their used electronics and other household items for a good price. And a large pool of ordinary consumers want to be dazzled by the experience of owning the latest trending product on their social media feeds.

To be a dealer in a bazaar is to trade in nonstandardized goods, using semi-legal to illegal distribution networks, and in the absence of institutionalized trust, dealers use bargaining and build clientele relationships to settle price. A lot of the characters discussed in the book—street vendors and traders—operate in an economy of face-to-face trade. Although this work provides their lifeline, it also means that these street vendors, small-scale traders, and peddlers in global cities face the grind of being in a competitive urban environment and may be penalized for selling illegal, semi-legal, and often pirated commodities. The stories of places of business destroyed from one day to the next appear in major news portals in the world, how such and such temporary and permanent establishments had to be removed to make way for new roads and construction sites for a sporting venue, housing, urban mall, or other urban redevelopment. One also hears the simple moral argument that bazaars and street businesses are depraved places giving rise to all kinds of antisocial and unhygienic practices, from violating copyrights to serving food with dubious health standards; the latter has been in the news especially when it comes to food hawkers.

However, this book is also about the tenacity of street-level commerce and how small-scale traders, vendors, and peddlers continue to pepper the streets and small shops of global cities despite challenges of different types. This they do by activating personal and familial networks for commerce as well as optimizing most opportunities that come their way, and importantly having a strong sense of the pulse of the ordinary buyer, the aspirations and constraints that are taken into consideration before buying a consumer item. Most actors absorbed in the bazaar economy globally are not from the elite section of society: they are school dropouts, refugees, and migrants to cities looking for new opportunities. In fact, if it were not for bazaar-like places, many of these people would not have found a foothold in a new city. Part of this absorption happens by resorting to existing contacts from village and family ties, but a lot of contacts are also accidental friendships made in a new city. Depending on the skills and the resources one can arrange, traders, peddlers, and vendors take up different positions in the bazaar economy. Usually, people with the least capital and skills would take up odd jobs as loaders and pullers, or as street vendors having their mobile business on the streets. Those who could accrue a little more in the form of household capital, savings, and money borrowed from friends and family would likely be small-scale traders as they have the network and household capital to acquire goods and pay rent and fixed costs. Although status and income differ among the different actors of a bazaar economy, the overall rationale of trading, and the pressures from civic and legal bodies and increasingly from e-commerce businesses, are comparable.

The various chapters of this book expand on the features of an urban bazaar economy to highlight what participating in a bazaar economy entails for a diverse group of non-elite economic actors. Examining these features becomes a way of understanding the legs of a bazaar economy; how do bazaars continue to be in our midst despite not receiving enough attention or support from elite quarters? One answer, discussed in Chapter 1, lies in their aesthetic composition, how bazaars have managed to carve a space in the interstices of visible structures, whether that be the narrow alleys leading off of main roads or dilapidated architecture, and how they host an excess of bodily and commodity forms. It is as if the cracks and fissures of urban cities are the natural homes of marginalized groups whose futures are not always taken into consideration when making changes. In fact, bazaars take hold of parts of state infrastructure and the streets that are not brand-new. They are found in dilapidated edifices only just functioning that let non-elites take their chances but that are not good enough for elites who have moved into new, flashier spaces. As Chapters 2 and 3 show, dealers at bazaars are able to experiment with existing knowledge structures and embodied and traditional crafts that then compensate for their lack of access to formal market devices such as advertising, marketing teams, and computer-generated datasets. Instead, bargaining is where the battle of price and profit is set. Of course, at one level, the pressure of finding a way against all odds, having to constantly innovate and be on the alert, takes a toll on bazaar actors. Still, a few things work in their

favor in a competitive urban environment when it comes to collective negotiation for desirable changes and navigating the power corridors of global cities.
Chapter 4 , on ethics, elaborates on the physical and emotional toll on bazaar
actors operating in a hostile urban environment, as well as on the personal
ethics providing solace in the most grueling business hours. Chapter 5, on
the interaction between e-commerce platforms and bazaars, shows the latter's
resilience in facing different challenges. This chapter elaborates on how the
technological question varies for different groups. For e-commerce platforms,
it has more to do with centralizing exchange through shopping, digital payments, and delivery managed through a single portal. In the case of bazaars,
digital technologies rub shoulders with bargaining routines and face-to-face
commerce, thereby combining new technologies with age-old tricks and practices of commerce.

While historical and anthropological writings inform the layers of a
bazaar economy, the heart of this book is small-scale traders and street vendors I met in Delhi's electronic marketplaces—Lajpat Rai, Palika Bazaar,
and Nehru Place. I started with a year-long ethnography of these bazaars
between September 2012 and 2013. I spent large parts of 2012 acclimatizing
to the places, and it was well into the first months of 2013 that I started visiting the marketplaces daily to get an in-depth understanding of the routines
of trade. As I was investigating mainly vendors and traders of video games,
the trade-related information also became a way to understand the ordinary
use and exchange of media products. Some of the information covered in the
book pertains to video games. Yet these dealers share with other marketplaces
the predisposition to rely on common resources and interpersonal networks
alongside bazaar shenanigans to get through their everyday minor to significant crises. Even after my 12 months of fieldwork, I visited these marketplaces
once or twice yearly. The last visit was in April 2022. Apart from the pandemic
years (2020–21), I was back in the marketplaces talking to my initial contacts
and expanding to new people, trying to see where and what kind of changes
these bazaars underwent. The longitudinal study gave me a grounding to understand the permanent features of these marketplaces and examine change
and adjustments. I spoke at length to traders of video games in Palika Bazaar
and Lajpat Rai Market and street vendors in Nehru Place. These were men between the ages of nineteen and sixty-five selling consoles of video games and
pirated CDs and DVDs from small shops and pavements. Many were from
middle-class business families whose other members were trading in different

marketplaces in the city. In the case of the street vendors, they were mostly from slum redevelopment colonies in the vicinity of Nehru Place.[2]

I use the term "tinker" to talk about the motley group of small-scale traders and street vendors in the field. It is clear that the bazaar actors were not just selling video games. They are also innovators and creators in their own rights. "Tinker" connects earlier marginal groups such as Roma and Irish tinkers with tools and tricks similar to those of the electronic tinkers in Delhi's bazaars, the latest group getting by with an ingenious use of available resources, a sense of the theatrical followed by innovative use of the body. Using "bazaar" and "tinker" side by side is a way to see if we gain something by reintroducing these concepts to our everyday understanding of economic systems. Of course, "bazaar" has had different meanings attached to it, some emancipatory and others problematic. A part of the exercise is drawing from sources and saying something about urban bazaars that share similarities with peasant marketing, souks, and colonial bazaars. Sometimes, such analysis may be at the cost of losing a certain definitional rigor and running the risk of generalization, but in the possible lapses also emerge new ways of gazing at existing and past connections. I take many such liberties in this book, like comparing street repair scenes in different contexts and analyzing them side by side with fairs, carnivals, marketplaces, and bazaars, or talking about magicians, street performers, hackers, and tinkers in the same place.[3] Of course, individual contexts carry specificities that may not extend to their comparative cases. It is fulfilling to see what comparisons allow rather than what they dissuade. Perhaps economic non-elites have been invisible in mainstream life for too long as there is no single category that directly addresses their predicament. By extending categories like bazaars and tinkers, this book makes a case for centering the affect and the everyday realities of economic non-elites whose sense of precarity often overshadows other experiences of being in a city.

Where Bazaars Depart from Capitalism

Apart from detailing the life of urban bazaars, this book has another imperative. The features of a bazaar economy show that the actors are not in their day-to-day life strictly capitalist. They partake in trade and profit, but such pursuits don't take on a character of incessant accumulation at the cost of social and moral values. This is where the theoretical lineage of the book comes to the fore. It is not arguing bazaars to be outside of capitalism or the opposite of capitalism. By showing the everyday workings and features of a bazaar economy, it presents how bazaars operate quite differently from the neoclassical idea of *homo economicus* and, in some cases, its opposite ideas of reciprocity and redistribution. Bazaars or market exchanges are in-between, an idea that historian Fernand Braudel developed in the twentieth century to emphasize that not every type of economic exchange is monopolistic and that there is a dense middle layer of competitive market exchanges. A bazaar economy is very much in contact with everyday life, or the *longue durée*. Indeed, if we consider these distinct yet interactive layers, we can build an understanding of bazaars in relationship to capitalism on one side and everyday life on the other. I argue that the bazaars display more substantial contact with everyday life than with high finance and the speculation of capitalism. Most critical literature has focused on capitalism as an all-encompassing system, and it is so in many ways. Even a cursory look at the literature about the gaming economy finds that it uses the concept of *playbour* to show the infiltration of capital into all aspects of everyday life, including leisure activities. But what we lose out on by emphasizing the problematics of capitalism as the only critique necessary for our times is to ignore places and practices that are not exploited by capitalism in the exact way of institutional and professional players. Places like bazaars are so misunderstood or ignored that the same criticism that would work for middle-class professionals or peasants losing at some level the distinction between productive and nonproductive time might not exactly work for bazaar actors.

The bazaar strays away from being strictly a capitalism pawn because there is still considerable control that the petty bourgeoisie of bazaar traders and vendors enjoy when it comes to controlling their businesses and not working under someone. They can choose what type of products they bring into the marketplace. Not everything has to go through big capitalist supply chains or follow their price logic. In that way, a vegetable vendor can sell a cucumber from his patch one day and decide to buy from his neighbor another day. The same is the case with the video game traders I studied in Delhi; they do not depend on one distributor network and creditor to sustain the business. Bazaar traders and street vendors control their finances. They are free to circulate money among different actors using a host of networks, some formal like banks but also *hawala* and informal credit. The possibility of being independent businesses puts them in a slightly tricky position compared with someone directly employed by a capitalist enterprise.

Of course, that does not mean bazaars are out of the reach of capitalist power. Bazaar dealers aren't secure in their position in the urban economy, because the argument about ignominy works here, and despite the relative independence of bazaar-level actors, none of them play a crucial role in the public sphere, particularly in deciding the fate of spaces where they operate. They are not the ones celebrated as business innovators, and in the rare case that they are, for instance as frugal innovators, the story becomes an individual narrative of heroism rather than bringing out the struggles they face on an everyday basis. Their economic power isn't strong enough to shape significant economic and urban policies. The position of the bazaar economy, somehow not entirely under the grip of capitalism and still maintaining its independence, does not provide any tangible form of power and agency in the genuine sense.

The actors remain the non-elites of any given situation, and they survive by carving out a resilience relationship with the commons of everyday life. That is, the global bazaar economy finds refuge in the urban commons of sociality, abandoned buildings and goods, streets, and ruins, waste, and recycled products. Each chapter of this book presents facets of an urban bazaar economy. These elements—aesthetics, knowledge, ethics, and change—exist because bazaars are in closer contact with shared resources than with capitalist structures in their day-to-day operations. In other words, unruly everyday life impinges on the bazaar economy far more than state laws, global supply chains of branded products, formal market devices, and algorithms of pricing and advertising. This has allowed bazaars to survive in the crevices of global capitalism without ultimately becoming its shadow.

A good contrast is the digital economy of e-commerce platforms that are now the biggest competition of bazaar-level exchanges, hanging like a bridge over actual transactions with their self-sufficient manner and only distant interactions with the travails of ordinary lives. With ubiquitous internet connections and cheap smartphones, there is a push toward adopting specific centralized structures such as e-commerce for shopping and digital payment for other transactions. This model gets superimposed on everyday life and is about profit maximization for certain groups in control of the digital infrastructure of aggregators, service providers, and third-party mediators.

Unlike the e-commerce economy, another way of life is not superimposed when bazaars navigate the latest products, such as Delhi's traders and vendors dealing with video games. A new product is embedded in the societal fabric of the bazaar and adjusts to the rhythms of human and nonhuman networks rather than destroying existing ties. This symbiotic relationship is why talking of unique characteristics of a bazaar economy makes sense, as the street-level economy worldwide is closest to the rhythm of ordinary life. It absorbs a maximum number of people and practices, keeping alive diversity of exchange by putting client relationships and bargaining at the center. In this way, bazaars adjust to varying demands. They are rooted in the social context rather than introducing something entirely alien that might be convenient from a comfort standpoint but, in the process, also creates isolated existence. The latter has been the experience with elite-level digital economies of platforms and digital credit systems destroying community-level exchanges. Instead, they are capitalist structures that initially dip into the same pool of resources and networks that bazaars do, such as cheap commodities and labor. Once such platforms get a foundation, the model works by wiping out all competition even though it means jeopardizing the societal fabric of interdependent actors and producing isolated actors who have by now gotten used to using their services and are at the mercy of impersonal infrastructure.

Roshan, one of the traders from Delhi's Lajpat Rai Market, notes how difficult it is to have face-to-face conversations with people now. It is almost a dying art, and he says his friends comment on his ability to be a good speaker because he keeps the conversation going with different topics when they meet; otherwise everyone is busy on their cell phones. Roshan felt he had a particular skill to talk and not be forever distracted by the phone. Of course, things are different in the work setting. In the bazaar environment, people speak to attract consumers to the shop, even if it means muttering the names of products sold. Bazaars and street-level economies remain the last economic spaces to accommodate change without destroying community-level interaction and exchanges.

In the next part of the Introduction, I develop a genealogy of the bazaar economy to understand its role through changing times. The early views of the bazaars from medieval, colonial, and postcolonial times give a context to understand the permanent features of a bazaar and its changing political and economic role. Deep into the Introduction, I pick up on the most recent type of bazaar configuration, that is, urban bazaars, and open them up for comparison with capitalist systems via Fernand Braudel's tripartite conceptualizations of economic life. Braudel's work and discussion on the *longue durée* ground the theoretical framework of this book: bazaars' relationship with capitalism and commons, which I keep coming back to in the various chapters. I finish the Introduction by providing details about my ethnography and the trials of studying crowded marketplaces as a woman.

Early Views on the Bazaar Economy

Starting with exchanges on the Persian Royal Road, the Han dynasty was important in making trade between Europe and Asia a regular feature. The market and port towns developed as nodes on trade routes where silk, spices, ceramics, gunpowder, and paper from "The East" got exchanged for silver, gold, horses, and wool from "The West" (Daryaee 2010). Bazaars were the centers of commerce at the time when Europe embarked on its early trajectory of capitalist development. As capitalist commercial exchange established itself as the most significant form of commercial life, bazaars were increasingly represented in relation to this new dominant economic form as pre-capitalist, proto-capitalist, or anti-capitalist.

For much of economic history, the European bazaars of antiquity and the Middle Ages acted as pre-capitalist. When Peter Bang (2011) wrote about the Roman bazaars, he stressed how they shared more similarities with Mughal bazaars than with capitalism. Roman marketplaces resembled Mughal bazaars as both these places sold a range of products and were embedded in a complex web of taxes and networks of mutual favors. Bang's analysis worked backwards to show that certain types of dense market exchanges were as much a part of European antiquity as of modern India. Indeed, in this strand of analysis, bazaars were the central organizing principle of a pre-capitalist world economy (Abu-Lughod 1989) that connected, by way of the Silk Road, India and China in the East via the Middle East to Europe in the North.[4] Peter Frankopan (2015) describes how dense commerce existed between the steppes in Central Asia, China, and Venice before the onset of European modernity. All this work suggests an early world economy organized through bazaar-like exchanges where merchants and traveling tradespeople satisfied the consumer demands of a metropolis like Baghdad that was emerging as a center for learning where scholars, painters, and poets congregated, much like Paris in the early twentieth century.

Toward the fourteenth century, the early world economy was gradually replaced by a system organized around a small number of powerful players, notably the Italian city-states of Venice, Florence, Pisa, and later Genoa. This new "cycle of accumulation," as Giovanni Arrighi (1994) calls it in his book *The Long Twentieth Century,* was structured around a number of novel organizational mechanisms, like letters of credit or double-entry bookkeeping, that were able to formalize economic transactions and increasingly make them subject to calculation. It was also governed by a new, powerful class of merchant capitalists who were able to mobilize and command state power in the form of military might as well as monopolies and other concessions. In the early days of transition from feudalism to capitalism, bazaar-like market exchanges rose in prominence and as a feature of ordinary life, particularly for the increasingly powerful new middle class or the rural English gentry.[5] They created among other things a consumerist spirit. Historians have examined how the vanity fair and charity bazaars helped shape the modern consumer who went shopping for consumer items. The well-endowed shop windows in London contributed to generating a new enthusiasm for consumer goods.[6] New habits, such as "window shopping" and absorbing a shopping experience, were particularly important for women who were responsible for making purchases for the household and became the main agents of consumer culture (Prochaska 1977; Rappaport 2001). Krista Lysack (2005), for instance, puts Christina Rossetti's poem "Goblin Market" into context and develops it as an exploration of desires where women were free to masquerade as different actors, an aspect that was largely unavailable to Victorian middle-class women. At the same time, by participating in "oriental bazaars," women were steeped in stereotypes as these places were not seen as civic and were rather places of degradation of bourgeoisie norms, offering cheap spectacles of dragons, decadence, and magic. The colonial mindset attributed to Victorian bazaars continued as capitalist structures of factories and formal shopping centers began to adorn the high streets of Europe. At this point, bazaars were typecast as insidious places spreading evils and sorcery from the "East," threatening to pollute bourgeois English values. Chinese opium and gaming dens in London raised concerns about racial intermixing in cities. "As Edward W. Said and Rana Kabbani have demonstrated at length, people in Western societies perceive few human realities with more fear, fascination, and overriding hostility than 'the Orient': that ideological construction positing the Islamic, Turkish, and Arab cultures as the opposite of 'us' in 'the Occident.' To associate the Oriental bazaar with Englishwomen—with 'sacred home,' 'happy and innocent virgins'—is to assimilate, to domesticate that foreign presence and all it suggests, making it chaste, respectable, English" (Dyer 1991, 201). Exaggerated images of foreign lands with their strange customs developed at the height of European colonialism.[7]

Bazaars now featured as utterly antithetical to capitalism (Geertz 1978; Lamieri and Bertacchini 2006). In such writings, bazaars got categorized as irrational places with neither adequate organizational structures nor formal communicative channels. In twentieth-century scholarship, bazaars receded to the role of marginal economic systems mainly on account of their seemingly irrational nature when compared to the firm or the capital market (Fanselow 1990). The dual conceptualization of bazaars shows the link that these spaces had with capitalism: how they preceded capitalism and were subsequently marginalized by it as capitalism became the main production logic in industrial Europe, leading to the gradual disappearance of bazaars from mainstream social and economic theory.

It was a classic orientalist framework whereby Europe and the rest of the world worked through binaries and a strategic distortion of everyday commercial practices. As modernity shaped a particular worldview at the cost of others, the alternative systems and forms of knowledge almost disappeared. The disappearance was not so much about their physical invisibility as it was about a lack of mention in mainstream discourses. Indeed, most academic writings in the twentieth century focused on capitalism or the aftermath of capitalist expansion. Not only is this the case with "trickle-down economics" celebrating a laissez-faire approach but also so-called critical approaches were neglecting alternative forms of economic life. For instance, the center-periphery approach, critical in outlining the imperialist tendency of capitalist expansion building on uneven development of geographical regions, failed to highlight other forms of economic life (Amin et al. 1990). Despite their relative absence in official plans and critical discourses, bazaars continued as an important feature of ordinary life. And a particular key role played by urban bazaars has kept this economic system of face-to-face commerce with us as they provide consumer items to a large pool of non-elites globally.

Urban Bazaars

The term "urban bazaar" took shape in the mid-1980s. In England and the United States, this was also a time when there were a lot of welfare cuts, and a large proportion of people were insecure about their socio-economic positions as a result of new crackdowns on collective bargaining in the form of trade unions and less protection of labor rights and dignity. The rise of the urban bazaars is related to the failure of statist plans and, in many cases, a shift from a welfare state to a laissez-faire economy. As the emphasis on propertied classes grew, and the narrative of individual "merit" began to take hold, urban bazaars increasingly became places for displaced groups to engage in everything from dealing drugs to selling knockoffs and counterfeits (Telles 2012). They have become a refuge for many people as non-elites were pushed to the margin to fend for themselves. In such situations, spontaneous and permanent structures of commerce in the inner city incorporated new migrants to the city, agricultural laborers, and petty traders. This mundane reality demands turning the academic glance upside down, focusing not on an Apple of our times but instead on the seedy underbelly of global cities where piracy meets counterfeited products, as has been done in the "globalization from below" literature (Mathews 2011; Mathews, Ribeiro, and Vega 2012; Mathews and Yang 2012). Another example is Alain Tarrius's (2015) "poor to poor networks" of horizontal cheap commodity exchange among a large part of the world population. Tarrius brought the predicament of people pushed by poverty and migration to avail porous boundaries of globalization. Often resorting to illegal and semi-legal channels of goods acquisition, "the ants of globalization," traders and vendors carried "suitcases" filled with electronics from China to Africa and other parts of Asia (see Telles 2012 , 90). This world of globalization is largely invisible to official eyes, sometimes because of just plain apathy, sometimes because of the hidden nature of such transactions, and at other times to obscure the links between legal and illegal networks of favors, of which the office holders are themselves part.

Alongside the "globalization from below" literature, the literature on postcolonial media piracy emphasizes popular economies reclaiming urban spaces for economic purposes. Ravi Sundaram's (2010) and Peter Manuel's (1993) work in India and Brian Larkin's (2004) work in Nigeria among others provide a rich account of everyday technological use. The people at the bottom of the digital pyramid create extra-juridical infrastructure to expand media outreach to the remotest parts of the globe. The pirated cassette culture of the 1990s brought popular Hindu films and folk music to small towns and villages by reproducing original recordings by minor artists. The pirated cassette cultures are just one side of the story. Not just audio files but the popularity of Indian movies in South Asia gave rise to piracy in the video format. For instance, Pakistan became a hub of low-quality copies of movies which then got distributed to households by equally dodgy individual cable TV networks. The same goes for Chinese phones and pirated video games. They are part of making global media available to sections of the population that do not have the money to buy brand-new products. From Chinese phones to arcades, TV consoles, and pirated discs, popular consumers are never entirely outside contemporary processes of globalization (Dent 2012). They experience it in a slightly different fashion—instead of high-definition videos, there are low-quality images and buffering of content. They are experiencing everything; even though pricing and sometimes content are not originally aimed at the masses, they somehow find their way into these circuits and make them their own.

Were it not for piracy, media experiences would still be limited to a select group of urban elites with the economic resources to buy new products and share the latest consumer services. From stolen electricity to low-quality images and pirated CDs/DVDs, such infrastructure keeps globalization from below running. In the same way that Gordon Mathews sees Chungking Mansion as a center of "globalization from below," bazaars are another node that brings pirated, knockoff, secondhand, and stolen goods to various consumers. In most cities today, we can spot small repair shops and carts selling phone covers and battery accessories of different kinds adjacent to a flagship store. This type of street-level trade is a bazaar-style enterprise of flexible prices, selling often unadvertised items and providing an unequal quality of goods. Different types of consumers have come and gone in the bazaars, which have continued to exist since medieval times and before. How have bazaars remained in our midst and yet stayed obscure in their day-to-day workings in urban economies in terms of shaping central decision-making or being in the driver's seat when it comes to designing urban projects? Is there a way to understand the resilience and also relative unimportance of bazaars at the same time? Fernand Braudel, a historian of the French Annales School, shows that it is perhaps the way in which market exchange remains cradled between capitalism and everyday life that explains their relative elusiveness and their tenacity in our contemporary life.

Longue Durée of Everyday Life: Braudel in the Bazaar

Braudel's economic sociology is developed in his three-volume work *Civilization and Capitalism* studying the fifteenth to eighteenth centuries. It was published in France beginning in 1967 and translated into English in 1981–84 (and summarized in the admirably short volume *Afterthoughts on Material Civilization and Capitalism*). *Civilization and Capitalism* (Braudel 1977) offers an empirical corrective to Marxist and neoclassical narratives of the history and emergence of capitalism and an empirically more sophisticated account of the relationship between markets and capitalism. Empirically, Braudel counters the narrative—common to the Marxist and neoclassic tradition— that capitalism emerged from the market competition to later develop, mainly in the twentieth century, into a monopolistic system. On the contrary, Braudel stresses that capitalism has its origins in the regulation of markets on the part of small cliques of powerful interests, like the Venetian and Genoese traders who, in the thirteenth to fifteenth centuries, took control of trading routes and established an inter-European financial market that they controlled and shaped. Capitalism, Braudel suggests, is not about markets. It is about controlled forms of exchange, what he calls anti-markets:[8] prices are not set by demand/supply dynamics but instead are raised from above by powerful economic actors (De Landa 1998).

Braudel uses the metaphor of a three-story house to reveal how activities develop in different zones while being part of the same edifice. First is the *longue durée* of everyday life (Moore 1997), where change is slow and continuities remain over centuries. At this level, things go on outside of the reach of markets and capitalism. Here we can locate things like friendship, family life, much of human interaction, and, perhaps, part of the contemporary sharing economy. It is also the place for what Gibson-Graham (2008) identifies as a plethora of noncapitalist everyday economic practices, or the "everyday communism" that David Graeber (2014, 69) sees as taking up most of everyday life. At the second level are markets and "small exchange": the village market, the farmers' market, and everyday goods where ordinary people interact with slight differences in power between individual actors. Braudel (1983) identifies attributes of the market economy as face-to-face exchanges, an aesthetic of crowds and chaos, and the presence of competitive market actors. Third and finally, we have the level of "great exchange," the merchant networks that controlled long-distance trade in the Middle Ages and the early modern period, or today's financial markets (Arvidsson 2019).

Essentially Braudel provides us with a schema to organize economic activities. For the longest time, particularly in the twentieth century, whether it is in the school of Italian Marxism or a large part of critical theory, it was hard to comprehend any different type of economic systems without it being in some ways subsumed by the capitalist enterprise. The generalization was partially true as it was difficult to see anything as residing outside of capitalist enterprises. Other than altruistic motives or transactions governed by reciprocity and redistribution in modern societies, it isn't easy to think about economic activities and profit in general as noncapitalistic. Markets and bazaars, for example, were thought to be the same as capitalism. Following Braudel's scheme, it is easier to see the interaction between the different spheres without each layer losing its particularities and giving voice to people and nonhuman actors dominant in each layer. The markets and bazaars discussed in this book are in contact with capitalist structures. They are in many ways governed by them, particularly if we look at the circuits of branded products, the formal distribution channels of raw materials and finished products, and the rising presence of e-commerce platforms. But something else is part of market exchanges, something that is prominently represented not through their proximity to capitalist structures but instead through their relationship with everyday life. The exchanges emerge from people's diverse realities that guide them to develop a relationship with shared resources. For instance, many market actors do not have a choice to speculate and amass massive wealth, as they are working with household capital and legally and otherwise marginalized to the extent that they have to develop dense interaction with the bottom layer of everyday life. In fact, this book looks not at just any element of daily life. It focuses on resources that are somehow shared because they have escaped a formal value chain of private property—ruins, friendships, abandoned commodities, waste, and embodied skills—in other words, urban commons.

Structures of Everyday Life and Commons

Ordinary people have always used common resources to procure livelihood sources. The medieval commons were shared pastoral grounds and forest areas that community members accessed large parts of the year. People used common lands for grazing cattle and collecting firewood, among other things. They became a collective resource for peasants and ordinary people to compensate for their limited access to material assets, which supported small-scale "industrious" market participation as commercial life gradually developed in the early modern period.[9] As a successful model of community ownership of land, commons have remained in the academic and critical discourse to imagine an alternative to capitalist private accumulation. We saw this optimism in the writings of Elinor Ostrom (1990), who argued, in direct opposition to the economist Garrett Hardin's notion of the "tragedy of the commons," that communitarian governance is precisely what has safeguarded existing commons from the threat of "free-riding" that Hardin's ([1968] 2009, 243) argument centers on.[10]

As one of the earliest proclamations of collective rights to land by the people, the commons offer a radical alternative to a proprietary regime. In her book *The Caliban and the Witch,* Silvia Federici (2004) shows how enclosure of the commons is intrinsically linked to the question of gender, and in particular to women's role in public life. One such effective construction was of targeting women as witches. Federici argues that the "demonization of the 'witch[,]' the very instrument of these divisions, [was] necessary precisely to justify the ban against individuals who once had been considered and had considered themselves as commoners" (Federici 2018, 21). In fact, Gayatri Spivak's (1988) essay "Can the Subaltern Speak?" relates to a similar situation of land control in India. Instead of "witches," her focus was on widows. Traditionally, in many parts of India, including West Bengal, women jumped into the funeral pyre following their husband's death. While many have pointed out the patriarchal nature of such practices, including the social reformer Raja Ram Mohan Roy, Spivak pointed out the economic nature of such sacrifice. The glorification of *sati* and women forsaking their share of ancestral property are pieces of the same puzzle.

"Commons" hints at alternatives to capitalism by highlighting how the rights of the many to land and other resources were transformed into the property of the few. As a result, ordinary lives had to suffer the most—be it women in Europe, widows in India, or peasants and nomads globally. In his book *The Great Agrarian Conquest*, Neeladri Bhattacharya (2018, 339) shows how during the British rule in Punjab, "colonising the commons" became a mechanism to bring nomads within the taxation system. The British imposed a grazing tax, *tirni*, on the pastureland of West Punjab, emphasizing that even wilderness was under their control and not for free public use. There is no one way of describing attacks on common land that otherwise guaranteed free movement and livelihood to a large section of people. In Amita Baviskar's 2020 book, *Uncivil City: Ecology, Equity and the Commons in Delhi*, she brings such debates to contemporary times. She explores how, under the garb of "bourgeois environmentalism" and the image of a "world-class skyline" (2020,

9), commons such as the Yamuna River, street life, and the tree cover of the Ridge in Delhi are under perpetual threat from elite bodies. She highlights the firm idea among middle-class residents, corporations, and supreme court judges about the management of commons; often those sentiments are about regulating the flow of ordinary life dependent on these resources. The result is a story of continuous strife. As one slum colony gets demolished, others crop up on the banks of rivers and secluded areas in cities.

It is on the contested commons that bazaar economies globally depend to procure a living income. Bazaar economies accomplish this not just by protecting and subsisting, or by using nature's commons such as rivers, lands, and forests, but also increasingly by activating an evolving urban commons of discarded consumer goods, e-waste, ruins, and household objects. The possibilities for people to somehow carve out livelihood prospects around traditional and new commons have not entirely gone unnoticed by scholars and activists working in the area. Most of this attention has been on the digital commons of hackers and ethical designers. Radical commons-based movements highlight the contribution of actors holding sophisticated technological skills, be it the expertise to work with 3D printing, Github, or coding, to produce an alternative society of shared resources and output.[11]

Commons or Undercommons?

How people carve out livelihood prospects around traditional and new commons has started to get some attention from scholars and activists. Most of this attention has been on the digital commons of hackers and ethical designers. Other forms of resistance and re-appropriation go unacknowledged, especially everyday forms of resistance of marginalized groups.[12] To remedy the oversight, scholars like Stefano Harney and Fred Moten (2013) argue for an "undercommons" that represents marginalized groups, in their case the suppressed black, indigenous, and queer voices in the US. Jack Halberstam (2013, 6), in his introduction to the book *Undercommons*, writes,

> The undercommons do not come to pay their debts, to repair what has been broken, to fix what has come undone. If you want to know what the undercommons wants, what Moten and Harney want, what black people, indigenous peoples, queers and poor people want, what we (the "we" who cohabit in the space of the undercommons) want, it

is this—we cannot be satisfied with the recognition and acknowledge-
ment generated by the very system that denies a) that anything was
ever broken and b) that we deserved to be the broken part; so we refuse
to ask for recognition and instead we want to take apart, dismantle,
tear down the structure that, right now, limits our ability to find each
other, to see beyond it and to access the places that we know lie outside
its walls.

Halberstam points out that Harney and Moten evoke a wild space when
they speak about undercommons, a place that because it is unregulated is not
liminal but rather is feral, existing outside of the preordained ways of organizing life and labor. In this respect, the notion of "undercommons" suggests a
radical politics of starting everything anew, to have an entirely new perspective on the world. This rethinking of politics for marginal groups is powerful
because of the possibility of freeing oneself from any subjectivities other than
the ones built on empowering and sustainable relationships with the world.
However, many marginal lives do not necessarily formulate their everyday
lives through a radical political position. They are not given the choice to write
a new chapter from zero. There are always priorities to be met whether it is
paying rent, sending children to school, or obtaining the basics for survival.
The day-to-day lives of ordinary people are about surviving in a competitive
environment, as most represented in cities that act as a pull factor for the
unemployed, migrant workers of all sorts, traveling performers, and social
outcasts. The focus on the immediate survival needs in a competitive environment is urgent for many lives in South Asia, where survival concerns sideline
an organized resistance.[13]
    While some of the imagination and action inherent in a concept such as
"undercommons" is available to Delhi's bazaar traders, other radical stances
are less suitable to their condition and experience. For instance, Delhi's bazaar
actors operate from an undercommons as they carve out economic opportunities outside formal capitalist employment. But they do not conform to
the identity politics that such a concept suggests. Mostly bazaar actors do not
consciously define their grievances as a reflection of a radical and celebratory
political position. This is a critical problem because global non-elites have a lot
to gain from a concept like "undercommons" in breaking from the so-called
shackles of elite domination. But in reality most non-elites in cities are busy
securing survival needs, and whatever emancipatory polities emerge often are

an unintended consequence of such efforts. Rather than a self-consciously political position, bazaar actors' interaction with urban commons operates at a
less visible level of everyday dealings. It does not take a political or ideological stance. Still, the bazaar's resistance appears through everyday practices
of bringing old and unused items into life, a certain openness to accepting
people of different strata into the marketplace as a temporary home, and creating urban experiences outside bourgeois propriety. And as much as undercommons would be a political category for non-elite economic actors, in this
book we witness their more humble ways of bringing available public infrastructure and shared commons to the realm of trade.

Delhi As a Field Site

Delhi is a fascinating site to study because it has witnessed historical shifts
from close quarters. Anthropologists and historians, journalists, bloggers, and
city walkers alike have mused about how there is not just one Delhi but multiple Delhis—one of the streets and monuments, and another of the high-rise
apartments and malls. In the city, monkeys coexist with magicians. Writing
the history of Delhi, Patil and Ray (1997) state that few ancient metropolises
have as remarkable a history. Delhi, a variant of *dhilli* or *dhillika*, appeared in
the Bijouli inscription dated AD 1170 that described the rule during the early
Chahamana dynasty in western India. Tarikh-i-Firishta, compiled in the sev-
enth century, notes that Delhi derived its name from Raja Dilu or Dhilu. As
varied as the city's name so too were the multiple influences shaping its geography. At present, Mughal, British, and postcolonial influences are three main
architectural and aesthetic elements that one notices in the city. The walled
city of Shahjahanabad, popularly known as Old Delhi, bears witness to the
Mughal influences on the city's landscape. The walled city, "built and rebuilt
from the 16th century onwards, was a mosaic of mixed-use practices, where
homes, work-places, shops, places of worship and governance were piled on
top of each other in untidy profusion. To colonial eyes, this apparent anarchy
had to be regulated in order to prevent the spawning of seditious thought and
action" (Baviskar 2020, 38).

    After the 1857 uprising, a large part of Shahjahanabad was destroyed to
lay railway lines, and the British continued the process of rewriting the urban
landscape of Delhi as they moved the country's capital from Calcutta to
Delhi in 1918. Central Delhi with commercial parts like Connaught Place and

Lutyens Delhi, which houses the Rashtrapati Bhawan (President's House), is an example of the British colonial expansion. We see a representation of European modernism with clear lines separating work from commercial zones.

Each of these transformations has interested scholars to analyze changed approaches to governance affecting residents and their ways of being. In particular, colonial governance was a mode of surveillance and disciplining of the population whereas a walled city like Shahjahanabad appeared to be antithetical to the modern logic of hygiene and well-being.[14] For British colonizers, therefore, it was important to segregate spaces as much as possible based on their ideas about ventilation, disease control, and privacy. In a postcolonial context, a significant change has been in the direction of encroachment on agricultural and livestock land—*lal dora*—or the red line delineating different urban villages, which kept shifting through bureaucratic records and interventions by local communities (Pati 2019). A part of this process was to bring communal land under private use. To meet the demand for urban land to build, among other things, modern consumer spaces, parts of urban villages came under real estate extension as former inhabitants sold land to private actors. The South Delhi area and its list of malls are part of the most recent changes made by private real estate firms. Despite strategic plans to make Delhi into a European-style city, it has maintained some of its messiness. The past continues in an altered city through ruins, and diverse lives surviving in the fringes of the city.

The three marketplaces I studied are part of the postcolonial development of a city into a modern metropolis, where they are imposed on the traditional and enduring ties of village and community life.[15] Lajpat Rai Market, which is in the old city, is perhaps the closest to the aesthetic universe of a Mughal Bazaar.[16] Although the marketplace came into being in the 1960s, the surrounding areas are narrow lanes. In these dilapidated buildings, hawkers and shopkeepers sell books, trinkets, spectacles, edibles, and wedding trousseaus in an architecture that is part of the city built by Shah Jahan. Noticeable urban redevelopment projects have widened the narrow streets to cleaner and broader avenues. Time will tell if a continued presence of Mughal bazaars will be part of Old Delhi or if they get incorporated into new urbanism altogether. As it stands, it is still very chaotic. It hosts a range of people from peddlers to beggars and ear cleaners on the street, almost a perfect representation of a bazaar captured in this book: high-decibel social life, an unruly aesthetic, nonstandardized goods, and diverse participants.

Another marketplace covered in this book is Palika Bazaar. This marketplace is adjacent to colonial architecture as Robert Adam inspired the crescent-type architecture, which influenced places like Bath in England and shaped Connaught Place, a building surrounding the marketplace. Today, Connaught Place is home to many offices and shopping places that serve middle- and upper-middle-class consumers. In contrast, Palika Bazaar caters mainly to middle- and lower-class consumers. Built in the 1970s, overlooking a British architectural marvel, Palika Bazaar was meant to represent postcolonial high-modernism as the first underground air-conditioned marketplace in the country with an added aesthetic novelty of being dome-shaped, so that it appeared like a mushroom aboveground with grass growing around it.

Of the three marketplaces, Nehru Place shares the environment of the most recent expansions to the city. South Delhi has witnessed maximum development taking over new swaths of land either to host partition refugees or, in recent times, to boost real estate development in the form of housing, educational institutions, and high-end marketplaces. Nehru Place is not on the poshest side of South Delhi. Rather it was adjacent to enormous slums that have been relocated to make space for offices and recreation. In the middle of the buildings in the central marketplace with Microsoft offices, insurance companies, and legal consultants, the street vendors I studied sell printed software and games on the pavements and corridors of the first floor of the many buildings in Nehru Place.

Historically the three marketplaces represent Mughal, colonial, and postcolonial expansions, sharing space with buildings from those times. However, an element that ties these marketplaces together is how central they have been in promoting media modernity in India since before the internet and the arrival of formal distribution channels of electronic products. Since the 1980s, media markets have played a prominent role in "attracting thousands of customers as well as distributors, head load workers, and booking agents for goods." These markets are connected to "small-scale electronic industries (Lajpat Rai Market), grayware assemblers of computers (Nehru Place) and the demand for video cassettes and CDs (Palika Bazaar) from cable operators and the population at large" (Sundaram 2010, 92). Local traders and street vendors began to sell electronics in these marketplaces, first under stricter trade regulations until early in the 1990s and then much more freely after the trade deregulation policies of 1992. With relaxed trade restrictions, the type of consumers changed in mass marketplaces from a more elite category to ordinary people, who no longer depended on smuggling networks to get global goods. Instead, these marketplaces supported the media and electronics needs of an average household that had information about media goods but did not always have the resources to buy original products (Deka 2016). These marketplaces were at the forefront of media modernity in India when other channels of acquiring imported and local products were negligible. With time, their influence has declined. Now they have a new role in their approach to access points, recycling old media and testing the limits of legal and illegal by making media goods available to a broader section of global non-elites through piracy and selling secondhand, stolen, and knockoff goods. The three marketplaces have become a proletariat media society by attracting a specific type of people, selling goods of uneven quality, and disregarding the legal and illegal divide that bazaars are known for historically. Lajpat Rai, Nehru Place, and Palika Bazaar in Delhi are the empirical voices of this book to portray, primarily through the exchange of video games, how street-level economies operate.

Traders and Tinkers

The first use of the word "tinker" dates back to the fifteenth century, deriving from a tinkering sound. Later usages of the word refer to the verb "tink" meaning to "mend, solder, rivet (rarely to make) pots and pans as a tinker" (Ekwall 2008, 63). As a particular type of activity, tinkering emerged in medieval Europe to absorb groups of people who failed to establish stable employment arrangements; many of these people were travelers and existed on the fringes of society. By definition, the act of tinkering did not need a lot of resources to fix things: Roma travelers for instance went house to house soldering broken pans and pots. About the Irish tinkers, Gréine (1934) notes their capacity to swap carts from one day to the next. Some days tinkers would come with a brand-new cart they had swapped for an old one in the course of earning some extra money through buying and selling different possessions from horses to tent-covers, harnesses, and even boots. Apart from earning some quick money through swapping items, Irish tinkers also used tricks to attract customers. For instance, Gréine points to the presence of the "gladar box," used to simulate money by pouring solder into the box and distracting the bystander by asking for water. The tinker used the time when the bystander wasn't looking to put a coin in the gladar box to give the impression that the box made coins. Often bystanders were impressed with the performance and wanted to invest money in such ventures. The word "tinker" best represents the traders and street vendors of this book because they share the marginal status of their predecessors, who were, in some ways, outcasts of their societies. Further, the electronic tinkers use the same type of simple tools and sleight of hand that Irish and Roma tinkers used in the past.

As Sarah Hill (2011) observes among young repair people in Santiago de Cuba, tinkering is about approaching old objects with a new vision and bringing into life objects that have run their course. "'New' resources for objects of utility emerged only from the careful tending of the shards and tatters of 'old' objects as they disintegrated through use" (4). The capacity to combine objects from different times and stages of wear and tear to eke out a livelihood is what connects tinkers across cultures. Things and practices that aren't conventionally seen as producing an income are opportunities for an itinerant group of peddlers and traders. Many marginal figures, including the traders and street vendors discussed in this book, use rudimentary tools to fix electronics and other consumer products. In fact, in recent years, the word "tinkering" has been employed specifically to refer to the nature of the work of computer repair people. Their task of "soldering" motherboards, heating metal to revive damaged parts, is similar to their medieval precedents' soldering of pots and pans using a similar technique of heating and metal work.

Delhi's small-scale traders and street vendors join this community of inventors and innovators who have found themselves outside of privileged knowledge systems. In the Indian case, advanced technological graduates come from elite institutes such as the Indian Institute of Technology and other top-level engineering colleges. Since the 1990s, multinational corporations based in India and abroad have absorbed a large pool of software programmers trained in elite technological institutes in India. Their technological proficiency and ease with the English language put India on the global export map of software and software-related services. In this high-achieving context, everyday technological use and innovation are not seen as particularly glamorous. The tinkers of the three bazaars in Delhi come from a long tradition of working with the materiality of electronic products existing outside formal knowledge systems. Lajpat Rai Market had traders whose extended family sold "transistors" in the 1980s and VCRs and televisions in subsequent decades. The present-day seller has upgraded the products based on the latest trends, and video games are one of their newest additions. In Palika Bazaar and Lajpat Rai, traders are from small-business families whose members also sell electronics in other marketplaces in the city like Karol Bagh and Sadar Bazaar. Many Jain and Hindu traders in Lajpat Rai Market are from families that were partition refugees and were given a space in the marketplaces to start a new life. In fact, families have been in the electronics trade for generations and shops have been passed down from grandparents to children and grandchildren. Another category of traders is new migrants to the city; many of the shop assistants fall into this category. Shop assistants acquire a place in particular shops by making chance visits to the marketplace or they have acquaintances that refer them to work under particular traders. Many of the street vendors of video games in Nehru Place are from demolished slums in the area and the Kalkaji and Alakanada neighborhoods close to the marketplace. They currently live in the slum rehabilitation JJ colony Madanpur Khadar not very far from the marketplace. Nehru Place was an after-school playground for many of the young street vendors. After dropping out of school, they loitered in the marketplaces and, seeing their friend or neighbor making quick money by selling pirated software and games, got involved in the trade.

This book faces the question of how to see an extended group of small-scale traders and street vendors as a singular category of bazaar actors. There is an obvious economic gap between the two groups: on average, a street vendor earns monthly about ₹ 25,000–30,000 and a trader approximately ₹ 100,000. One way to contextualize the group of petty traders and street vendors in the same bracket is through similar conditions of urban living and experiences of marginalization. In a Marxist framework, a key way to frame noncapitalist pursuits is to see a large number of actors without possession of such valuable assets as land and who have lost control over the means of production, particularly sections of the peasantry that are tenant farmers, landless laborers, and market actors. After all, these categories are part of economic activities and in many cases associated with market exchange without having ownership of distributive networks of lands, capital, labor, and production all put together under one unit (Sanyal 2007). The section of traders and street vendors is outside of private capital networks and mainly employs household capital acquired through traditional and familial networks. In this regard, both groups of people face the brunt of policies and measures that are not designed with their interests at heart. The protest by traders against the 2006 sealing drive run by the Municipal Corporation of Delhi to close unauthorized commercial establishments (Mehra 2012) is one example of how small-scale traders were left feeling vulnerable. Many of them found their shops shut overnight without indication about when they could reopen their businesses.[17] Similarly, the demonetization of 500- and 2000-rupee notes in 2016 pushed informal actors to take stock of their cash-only commerce. Measures by institutions and government impact small-scale traders and show that at various points, the "bazaar or intermediate classes" (Harriss-White 2013) underwent displacement and marginalization more commonly faced by slum dwellers and the city's poor. Despite economic gains through their trade, the fear of persecution and unstable economic opportunities is a burning reality for small-scale bazaar traders and street vendors. There are also actors of the bazaar economy, primarily merchants that are part of speculative trade in agricultural bazaars or huge urban wholesalers, who can mobilize politically quickly enough to exert pressure on government but they are not the focus of this book. Some of those actors have already moved away from the competitive sphere of market exchange to that of almost monopolistic accumulation, making them capitalists.[18]

The economic actors in this book are reeling under tough competition; they are fighting to make ends meet from one day to the next, a genuine survival concern for street-level peddlers, new migrants, and vendors of many global cities. For more rooted small-scale traders in shops, the pressure is psychological, being unable to have a strong foothold in the urban economy and having the permanent fear of persecution for selling a specific type of goods or not maintaining the right kind of contact with state entities for mutual favors of some sort. The body language and verbal complaints about the present state of affairs are fair enough evidence of how traders and street vendors consider themselves outside a power network that is much more secure for other elite groups in an urban context. On numerous occasions, Delhi's electronics traders and street vendors, for instance, praise the Chinese approach to business. Whether their economic pursuits are small or large, everyone gets support and encouragement to continue their enterprises as long as they are profitable without legal and economic sanctions. One trader even mentions that the only interference by the Chinese government with individual business is that it gets 1 percent of the total profit. Otherwise, small and large businesses are left to their own devices. And there is no hierarchy of judgment that just because a business is small and not part of the formal circuits of lending agencies, original products, or international laws and regulations, they are somehow inferior to others. In fact, in the trader's opinion, whether the business is making a profit or not should be what counts, and he feels that if he had the same business in China, his worries would not be the same. His level of respectability would be different as he can run a profitable business. Whether it is actually easy to do business in China is not the point here. Rather such observations indicate the acute sense of marginalization that bazaar traders and street vendors feel in their current situation.

In many ways, to talk quite broadly about electronics traders and street vendors in these three Delhi marketplaces is to represent the fear and anxiety that does not get much focus because of the empirical difficulty of seeing exact similarities in their economic position. Nonetheless, their predicament in the current scenario says a lot about the conditions of urban living. It suggests how sections of people engaged in urban informal labor do not feel at all secure about their current position despite their having forms of engagements with state and private actors on an individual basis. A sense of precarity comes from a perception of their weakened bargaining power in deciding key policies and laws that another group would most likely choose for them. And there is a real sense that bazaar actors are getting less and less of the carrot and more of the stick with a dwindling number of consumers, being pushed toward moving into a taxation bracket and into accepting credit and not just cash. What was in previous years a stable position of attracting a large number of consumers to sample a wide variety of goods is no longer there with the easy availability of global products at doorsteps. Also, it is becoming less comfortable to sell gray products in bazaars. Although they continue to do so, many actors are now taking careful steps to show part of their transaction as legal, as they know the amount of surveillance over individual activity has increased. Many of them now have bank accounts, and some street vendors are filing income tax returns. Mainly, having to use a digital payment mode more often means their transactions aren't hidden, and it is only a matter of time before someone asks them to show receipts. To avoid losing their income, they declare some of it to appear to have everything running according to the rules. The need to be on guard adds another layer of anxiety to bazaar actors as they are not just fighting for their present position but would also lose the privilege they have accrued over their long time in the market. The experience of marginalization makes it possible to compare traders and vendors of different financial brackets and to globally see similarities among noncapitalist exchanges as having a more precarious status than those engaged in more systematic modes of production and monopolistic enterprises.

Methodological Explorations

The empirical material for this book is from a year-long ethnography of Palika Bazaar, Nehru Place, and Lajpat Rai Market. I started my fieldwork in September 2012 and spent twelve months in the field until September 2013. After that, I continued to visit the marketplaces for short periods. The visits to the marketplaces from autumn 2013 to spring 2022 gave me a longitudinal view of trade in these marketplaces. It provided me with a firsthand account of how traders and street vendors in these marketplaces encountered change, among other things. The first thing I realized when I started my fieldwork was that it would be difficult to replicate any of the classical tropes of ethnography. Bazaars are boisterous places with little to nothing that a researcher can offer to better a day's prospects for the traders. My attempt at participant observation appeared to create more hassle than help. Each shop had enough people to deal with incoming consumers. Being a woman and relatively unversed in haggling did not help the traders in closing their deals. I learned quickly to adapt. What I missed out on in participating in the rituals of the face-to-face marketplace, I made up by observing the traders in their day-to-day activities. I had to learn to respect the traders' space and cause minimum trouble in their daily routines. So, I used a range of methods, from semi-structured interviews to conversations and observation. I have conducted 38 interviews among traders in Lajpat Rai Market and Palika Bazaar and 50 semi-structured interviews among street vendors in Nehru Place. All the interviewees are men between the ages of fifteen and sixty-five. The average age of street vendors in Nehru Place is nineteen, whereas traders in Lajpat Rai Market and Nehru Place are older, reaching into middle age. Some interviews were in a single sitting, whereas others took more than one day. There was no strict questionnaire, but the idea was to gather as much information as possible on trade routines, how bazaar actors procured goods for their shops, the distribution network, what they thought about bazaar knowledge, and anything else that preoccupied the traders and vendors on a given day.

Apart from the interviews, the data come from casual conversations and observations in the field. Conversations among traders, distributors, and consumers deepened my analysis of the everyday life of bazaar commerce. I found free-flowing conversations the most helpful method for ethnography in busy marketplaces as it allowed me to include as many actors as possible without disturbing the marketplace setting. As focused interviews meant that the trader or street vendor had to give me time out of their schedule unless trade was slow, tagging along with ongoing conversations and prompting topics became one of the most efficient ways to gather data in the field. Conversations became the most organic way to gather data as the times when traders and vendors were on their own were often when it was most difficult to break their countenance. They were willing to participate in my topics when they were amid a bargain or gossiping with people. When traders and vendors were on their own, they often refused to engage with me, and I left them with their brooding selves. Of course, this was not always the case; there were times when a trader would speak to me when nobody else was there, but it would take longer for him to warm up, and we would take time to reach a topic that would make the conversation come more naturally. I revisited the information gathered through casual conversations in the face-to-face interviews scheduled later in the week. When different interviewees began to echo each other's views, that moment was a point of saturation. At other times, following a string of conversations over time helped me construct a coherent narrative.

Most of the data were recorded in handwritten field notes as recorders and cameras were not always welcome in the marketplaces. All the interviews were in Hindi. On average, I spent five hours a day in these marketplaces. Although several subjects became a part of the ethnography, the focus of the interviews has been on the traders and street vendors of video games. There were a few with whom I had developed a strong rapport, making it easier for me to revisit questions with them and ask for further clarification.

Interpretation of Data

The observation method was helpful, mainly to record the routines of trade. Nonparticipant observation gave me a way to be part of the natural setting and not disturb the trade flow. I recorded who came to the shop, what the traders were doing on particular days, and the rhythms of a market day—shops opening at a particular hour, the busy hours of the day, and the lulls. I observed the body language of the traders from slow business hours to when they were animated in the middle of a bargaining session. Observation was the most useful method to cause minimum intrusion. Whenever conversation and interviews were part of the data collection, there was a concern about interpreting such data. Does one take the speech of traders at face value? What about the performativity of language? Is everything that the traders and street vendors are telling me reliable pieces of information? With time, I developed a few mechanisms to build conversations and interviews as robust methodologies. One such technique was to broach similar questions among different interviewees at different points in time. If the repeated questions prompted similar answers, I took that as a sign of reliable information.

It was convenient to compare notes from the different marketplaces as the bodily demeanor and the speech patterns, including jokes and fables, were part of all three marketplaces. From a theoretical point of view, I found that following de Certeau's principle of being attentive to informal language structures helped me discern traders' worldview. De Certeau's (1986) *Heterologies: Discourse on the Other* provided a framework to envision an alternative to rational and institutional language as a way of understanding the world. He placed importance on the materiality of language—the lived reality of the speaker guaranteeing a privileged position to know dimensions of the world that are otherwise lost when the focus is on established structures and institutions. That is why for de Certeau, discourses (forms of social interaction and practices) are far more interesting to capture the subject's unique understanding of the world. He emphasized a way to think outside history without giving in to the Hegelian dialectic of being in the sphere of religion and theology. De Certeau describes the mystic, the savage body, and utterances; everything comes together as knowledge. Taking inspiration from Michel de Montaigne's essay "Of Cannibals," de Certeau projects how the alternative language based on material life would look: "The body becomes a poem. The song symbolizes the entire social body. The warrior's song transforms his devoured body into the genealogical memory of his group, and into a communion with the ancestors through the mediation of the enemy" (1986, 76).

During my fieldwork, I was careful to not miss the varied utterances. I found it helpful to include jokes, banter, anecdotes, and emotive bodies as alternative knowledge systems. No interview or conversation was formal. Jokes, distractions, and interruptions were part and parcel of conversations. It took me some time to understand why such levity and anger were part of street vendors' and traders' idiom. I had to see the interjections as part of the motion that actors went through in a competitive market environment. As the anger most often came from somewhere and was directed at someone, it wasn't difficult to connect those emotions to everyday concerns. The heterodox forms became invaluable data. For example, I found that traders and street vendors made jokes when trade was slow. It was a way to defuse the tension of an unsuccessful market day. But lingering at the back of tricks and taunts were serious concerns. Traders and street vendors did not end frustrating conversations in a pessimistic tone. I often found that after complaining about the struggles of an unsuccessful business day, they told feel-good stories to each other. These were the times when fables were a way to transcend the travails of face-to-face commerce. I became vigilant when specific topics were viral in the marketplace, like when there was a raid or a protest. The next few days would be about that particular cause or issue. The street vendors' and traders' projects mainly involve their immediate life and surroundings. Although they might be upset with macro subjects, those became a topic of gossip rather than spurring them into action. With time, I learned to connect different forms of speech to particular events or concerns of trade. Being able to use the fluidity of conversations alongside more strategic questionnaires gave me the possibility to construct the social and economic world of bazaar actors.

The Ethnographer's Voice: Between "Male Gaze" and Friendships

I first visited Palika Bazaar as a master's student in 2007. Somebody from the crowd pulled my hand to direct my attention to their shop. The shopkeeper used such force that I turned back and found that he was trying to sell me a red puffer jacket. The incident discouraged me from visiting the marketplace until the time of my PhD research. It was in the back of my mind that such an incident could occur again. On the first day in the marketplace, I did not have any tactics. The only thing that was in the back of my mind was that somehow I had to make people talk to a stranger on a busy market day. That was an uphill task, as I would soon find out. In the first shop, I explained my reasons for me being there and sensed an awkward silence. I thought my motive was not clear enough and went on to provide the trader with all sorts of assurance that the research was for my thesis, and I was not in the media or a government spy. I found that even though they related to me as a research student, what was strange was having a woman researcher in the marketplace. I got various queries: "Why did you choose Palika? Could you not choose some other respectable place?" Or people offered me alternative field sites: "These days you can do all kinds of research on the internet. If you want to work on video games, you can Google it." I listened to the well-meaning advice. I knew it was not going to be easy to talk to people. The first day went by making small talk. I went from shop to shop, and everyone greeted me with coldness. I was a complete outsider. I was back the next day. That day, there was some commotion in the marketplace. I went back to the first shop in the inner circle of the marketplace. I asked the person at the counter what was happening there. He explained to me how after a sting operation by a TV channel, the police came and raided pornographic materials from the shops on the first floor. That day I was happy to get a clear response. The traders did not ignore me. But their enthusiasm to talk to me dwindled quickly. To make matters worse, the trader from the next shop came in and said, "You came back. Did you not see what happened? This market is not the place where women come unchaperoned. You do not look like someone desperate for men." By the look on their faces, I understood everyone agreed.

As days passed, I became part of the environment. I don't think the traders were ever happy to see me. They just weren't outrightly rude to me. I do not think market actors gave a different version of things because I was a woman. They did not appear to hide any information or intentionally censor things just because I was of a different gender. With time, I was not just a silent observer but got dragged into the conversation. Like the time when a couple passed the shop and the girlfriend was wearing shorts, the remarks flowed: "Look how she is showing off her legs (giggles). These people have no sense of dressing. Look how properly you dress up." Such value judgments I found uncomfortable, but I was nervous to start an open debate on sexuality and gender. It seemed a hard bargain—what if I lose their trust? I didn't want to broach a sensitive topic and leave it halfway without developing a safe space for dialogue and interaction; as the only woman in many of these conversations, I felt outnumbered to debate traditional gender roles and sexuality. In fact, I was not even sure how deep bazaar actors' conviction was about these issues. After about five years in the field, I had gone back in jeans and a jacket. Nobody took notice. Yet I was scared to have the conversation. Is this kind of dual ethic allowed in the field? These are difficult questions. I, of course, chose to perform a conventional gendered identity, such as dressing in something that did not disrupt the status quo. At other places, I dressed in a *salwar* suit, which gave some the idea that I was a social worker; this was the case in Nehru Place where Manushi, a non-governmental organization (NGO), was acting as an intermediary between state actors and the roadside vendors to find them a permanent spot. Many of them came and talked to me about their problems. They brought a chair and offered me a place to sit. I got used to being treated in a certain way. I made it clear that I was not part of any NGO, but the age difference made them reverential. Most of the street vendors were young men in their late teens. I forgot I was a woman in a male space. The power dynamic worked in a different way here. The street vendors had experiences of women like me bringing positive change to their lives. It was a privileged position. Appearing to be from a different class position, I created my bubble in this densely crowded marketplace. No matter how busy they were, some still took time out for me and offered me tea.

Some other instances headline the intersectionality of gender politics and how one never wholly moves out of the margin. The following tells of one such incident: There is the desire to record every conversation when one is in the field. Especially when one is in a busy marketplace and finds everyone is more interested in trade than in giving interviews, one cannot resist if someone voluntarily offers to chat. I was happy to find a willing young man who appeared to have time on his hands. I had not seen him before and guessed that he might be another street vendor. After speaking to him, I had a feeling that he was not interested in any of my questions but was more curious about my personal life. He insisted that we go to the nearby McDonalds and chat there. Most street vendors did not have the time to talk to me at length, so I went along. He pestered me for my phone number. After a while, I started getting uncomfortable and came out of the place. He followed me until I hopped on an auto-rickshaw. I dreaded those five minutes when I waited for the auto to arrive in what was turning out to be a deserted place. No matter how much I thought my gender was a non-issue, there would be times I felt different as a woman in a masculine space. I was uncomfortable when conversations shifted to the topic of marriage, which came up more with the traders than the street vendors. The traders were mostly older than me, and these conversations had a paternalistic tone. The queries could be as simple as "so when are you getting married?" They said that I should not postpone fundamental life decisions beyond a point.

There is no clear answer to what it means to be a woman ethnographer in a bazaar. I enjoyed it when my gendered identity did not jut out like a sore thumb and seamlessly flowed into the scheme of things in a society otherwise categorized by class, caste, sex, and religion. Perhaps this came out most beautifully in one of my last visits. I was back in my usual hangouts, and the awkward conversations about my personal life had just begun. I knew the drill and was waiting for everyone to have their say. Then suddenly the elder of the two brothers whose shop I was in pointed out "how in life some people are slower; they like to see life pass by because when it was the time to act, there were many things that needed attention." At that moment, I knew I had not just acquaintances but allies in the bazaars.

What Follows

The chapters in this book outline how bazaars are unique in their approach to economic life; how knowledge, price, and innovation work in the bazaar economy; and how in their day-to-day operation bazaars are quite distinct from capitalist enterprises and share far more with the commons of everyday life than with a destructive accumulative logic. Detailing the world of Delhi's bazaar economy is a way to speculate on the presence of bazaars globally and their capacity to employ non-proprietary knowledge, objects, and tools to facilitate trade. Each chapter explores how everyday noncapitalist economic systems work, how they engage with the basics of any market economy such as knowledge and pricing. But as this book progresses, we see not only the rituals and rhythms of face-to-face exchange but also get glimpses of the ethical life-worlds of traders and street vendors. In many ways, the ethical life acts as the shock absorber of a competitive market economy. Contemplating the trials and tribulations of bazaar commerce through an exalted register of Hindu ethics enables the traders to see failure in one sphere as fulfillment in another. The chapter on the e-commerce platforms shows how traders are engaging with these platforms in their day-to-day business. Examining the various stages of becoming familiar with a new technology, the chapter gives an overview of the struggles that bazaar actors went through to establish an empowered relationship vis-à-vis their latest competitor. Overall, the chapters in this book present the unique characteristics of the bazaar economy and its reliance on urban commons for commerce. It also gives us a sense of what happens when bazaar actors fail to capitalize on available resources. What keeps them going? Developing the chapters from the sensory presence of bazaars to aspects of everyday commerce moving toward management of failure, this book is an elaboration of noncapitalist economic systems operating in contemporary times.

Chapter 1, on aesthetics, features an introduction to the physical experience of the marketplace, showing how aesthetics is a process to record ordinary lives. The chapter goes into the discussion of bazaar actors' use of excesses that would otherwise be wasted: rubbish, ruins, and speech to maintain commerce on a day-to-day basis. This chapter presents the sensory life of the bazaars, and how the quintessential crowded places, noise and din, and "garbage" of such economies exist both in the register of aesthetics and material realities of the people. Through examples from different marketplaces worldwide, the chapter gives an overview of why bazaars globally feature similar chaotic aesthetics.

Chapters 2 and 3 on price and innovation are an exploration of what these bazaars do. How do they trade? Both these chapters show bazaar commerce as intrinsically different from capitalist economic systems. A stabilizing feature of most economic systems—price—is determined differently in bazaars than in formal shopping places. Chapter 2 focuses on a genealogy of price to carefully place bazaar pricing as a unique system merging social and economic metrics. The later part of the chapter investigates bargaining as a common principle that stabilizes the otherwise volatile world of bazaar prices. The chapter ends with a discussion on how bazaar bargaining compares to capitalist fictions and corporate narratives.

Chapter 3 on bazaar innovation gives an idea of how bazaars continue to exist despite tough competition and an absence of state support. Practices of tinkering challenge dominant notions of creativity and intellectual property rights[19] and copyright infringement. The bazaar trader's idea of creativity and ownership is much more communitarian, as it is part of a more extensive network of embodied knowledge and skills rather than emphasizing the Enlightenment figure of the individual genius. The chapter provides a more political way to engage with *jugaad*-style fixes than what is currently available. We see that bazaar innovation is in conversation with activist-led peer-to-peer networks of knowledge production and possible forms of collaboration.

Chapter 4, on ethics, serves as a meta-narrative to show how traders negotiate their everyday struggles. The emphasis on becoming a good market actor mitigates trade-related disappointments. An everyday interpretation of sacred texts, proverbs, and fables assists traders and street vendors in navigating their daily struggles. The chapter argues that, in the absence of an institutionalized support network, subjective interpretation of Hindu texts appears to give the traders a justification for and acceptance of operating in an economy of small profits.

Chapter 5 on platforms outlines how bazaar actors navigate one of their latest competitors, e-commerce platforms. Even with their latest challenge, we see bazaar actors galvanizing age-old tricks of working collectively with

semi-legal arrangements. After much effort, they manage to find an equilib-
rium and arrive at a place where bazaar actors remain independent tradespeople while making use of services provided by e-commerce platforms. The
Conclusion picks up on the loose pieces to look critically at the extent to which
the commons-based resources of a bazaar economy can genuinely develop
into a radical alternative to capitalism. It analyzes issues of communalism and
gender to see the extent to which such systems can develop into a more inclusive social and economic form.

1   Bazaar Aesthetics, Commerce, and Commons

I like jeans that have multiple zippers.
—*Amit, shop assistant, Palika Bazaar*

POPULAR AESTHETICS LIKE THAT of the bazaar economy has had but a marginal presence in academic discourses. This tendency is not just a recent one. Classic writers on mass aesthetics, like the Weimar theorist Siegfried Kracauer (1995), placed the masses in a passive role in relation to the aesthetics of modernity. Their preoccupation with the development of fascism or the advent of the culture industry had them see the masses as spectators or, more dangerously, an object of propaganda politics. From Kracauer to Haug (1986), the discontent with mass aesthetics is widely visible. Kracauer writes, "The masses are forced to see themselves everywhere (mass gatherings, mass pageants, etc.); thus, they are always aware of themselves, often in the aesthetically seductive form of an ornament or an effective image" (1995, 62). His famous reference to the American "tiller girls" was a way to illustrate how the popular classes perfected a bodily disposition in performances, an attention to discipline that was later productive for capitalist and fascist agendas.

A similar reproachful attitude toward mass aesthetics persisted throughout the writings of the members of the influential Frankfurt School, with the possible exception of Walter Benjamin. No doubt Benjamin (1969) saw art losing its aura of authenticity by the process of mechanical reproduction inherent to modern technology such as the printing press and photography. But he was not completely against such processes. In his opinion, popular art and processes of massification of classical art led to the democratization of elite culture, which had previously been exclusive to certain groups. But his contemporaries of the Frankfurt School such as Horkheimer and Adorno (2002, 42) labeled popular art as a product of a "culture industry": standardized and formulaic products that dissuaded ordinary people from having an autonomous and independent point of view. In this overarching perspective, bazaars, informal street markets, and other popular commercial spaces have figured as marginal phenomena, residuals of a premodern commercial world, at the most a business for anthropologists or ethnologists. A similar perspective has remained in most of the more recent literature accompanying the globalization of consumer culture. The focus has been on brands, shopping malls, and other exponents of the new global "ecumene" of modernity (Hannerz 1989). However, bazaars are not merely a residual phenomenon doomed to become extinct. The social form of the bazaar is being revitalized and is growing in importance as the popular masses enter consumer modernity. And bazaars come with a highly particular kind of commodity aesthetics, a particular way of framing the symbolic relations that actors have with the objects surrounding them, and their practices.

To some extent, this new salience of bazaars and popular consumer spaces has been brought forth by the growing literature on piracy, or *shanzhai*, phenomena.[1] The focus of this literature has been on the transgressive nature of piracy. Such literature made visible how unauthorized digital reproduction or knockoff textiles, footwear, and media challenge global capitalism, either legally or symbolically, by embodying alternative forms of agency. For example, William Hennessey (2012) suggests that the Chinese *shanzhai* phenomenon can be understood as a rebellion against the new "sumptuary" laws—similar to the laws regulating consumption in early modern Europe. Similarly, Andrew Chubb (2015) shows how *shanzhai* has been associated with rebellion against American-style consumer culture and with a kind of Chinese, anti-globalist populism. In this chapter, I offer a complementary perspective. I focus on an aesthetic that expresses a collective relation to a kind of popular commons, made up of waste, dilapidated buildings, and commodities withdrawn from circuits of bourgeois consumption.[2] This is a world of old media objects, gadgets of all kinds, and accessories formerly used by upper- and middle-class households. These objects have entered mass marketplaces through a recycling and secondhand economy. Furthermore, the popular aesthetic comes alive through speeches and modes of storytelling integral to the bazaar's particular bodily aesthetic. All of these aspects constitute a shared resource that facilitates bazaar commerce. For instance, the sociality of traders helps them close tricky negotiations and develop new commercial opportunities by making new friends and turning visitors into collaborators. In this chapter, the aesthetic dimension of the bazaars is a physical manifestation of the "commons," whose relationship with the market is probed deeper in subsequent chapters. Bazaar aesthetics brings to light the way everyday commons looks, its primary characteristics, and how to frame such aesthetics as a domain of popular lives.

On Excess

One key attribute of bazaar aesthetics is excess. Many things appear in abundance—cheap goods lying in parts of the shop, rubbish, and loquacious people. Such abundance is in clear contrast to the rational organization of supermarkets and malls. Here, commodities are lined up in an orderly fashion and objects occupy designated spots. Instead, bazaar excess is unruly, ensuring possibilities of employing excess for trade. The use of bazaar excess for trade is spontaneous, and not all excess can be put to productive purposes; parts of it are useless. It is because of the capacity of excess to fall outside of capitalist enterprises that social theorists have analyzed excess as a radical category (Weiss 1989). Sacred rituals of premodern societies and certain contemporary forms of excess, for instance in avant-garde art, are antithetical to the rationalizing tendencies of modernity. Community-level excess is visible in traditional rituals of gift giving, for example, where the spirit *hau* portrays the extra of gifting rituals among the Maori. In fact, societies with a clear separation of sacred and profane activities manage excess quite efficiently. In such arrangements an excess of profane activities seamlessly get spent through rituals and worship (Pawlett 1997). It is in modern societies that such interrelationships get more complicated. The relative absence of customary rituals to navigate excess in modern societies has led theorists like Bataille (1985) to see capitalism fulfilling the role of expunging excess. Losing organic ways to expel excess, modern subjects now participate in perverse forms. To see a way out of the dismal modern condition, Bataille brings up avant-garde art as a way to counter the excesses of capitalism. Such excess—excreta, waste, mourning, underground performances, and spectacles—cannot be directly used by capitalist societies for profit.

However, Gidwani and Maringanti (2016) observe that a little scope is available to modern subjects to participate in "profitless expenditure" (see Pawlett 1997 , 92). Everything from knowledge to nature and money is part of a calculative matrix of ensuring that nothing goes to waste. No matter how many attempts are made to produce things outside of capitalist structures, it is difficult to exist outside them. Even waste is used by capitalist structures to their advantage. Gidwani and Maringanti's research among scrap traders in Bholakpur shows how waste management connects to a global economy of recycling. Here, capital extraction happens with minimum consideration for workers' everyday health hazards and struggles. Indeed, capitalist profit extraction extends to most aspects of modern societies. Even things like electronic waste, metal scrap, and garbage, excesses that fell out of production loops, have an economy of their own. Is that all? In modern times have we lost all spaces that are outside of capitalist control? Despite the intrusive nature of capitalism, there are pockets where economic activities are not operating in their accumulative logic. Bazaars and street-level economies often produce noncapitalist excess.[3] Seemingly useless pursuits become part of productive enterprises without necessarily leading to practices of rent extrapolation and private ownership. Such noncapitalist ways of being form part of life spilling from private quarters onto the street and refuse to follow the strict separation between productive and useless pursuits. An image that comes to mind is clothing racks on the road or children playing cricket on the road. There is a confounding use of space: Is the street a space for traffic or business, or is it a playground or yard? Here, the notion of private property innate to capitalist extraction does not apply. In the same vein, commercial activities from the street enter the home, as when people in the Global South sell snacks and knickknacks from doorsteps. Such lifestyles are antithetical to "the bourgeois self's desire for plenitude and freedom, anchored in private property and secured by the state" (Gidwani and Maringanti 2016, 118).

The area between the home and the street is not anybody's personal property. It blurs the idea of private property by using spaces and objects that are for the public. Moreover, ordinary encroachment on public spaces is often temporary and less intrusive. Ad hoc arrangements of a clothing rack or a table on the street are difficult to pin down as lasting encroachments, as they can disappear overnight. Simple objects like tarpaulin covers and structures of bamboo can create makeshift shops. In her study of bazaar calendar art, Kajri Jain (2007) shows how ordinary people's use of objects and space challenges a bourgeois understanding of the private and public sphere. In her study, the motifs of gods on calendars sit uncomfortably in contrast to a bourgeois attitude of understanding religion as a personal affair not to be put on wide display. Bazaar art using religious motifs presents a different way of looking at religiosity: not just as a personal belief system but also as a way of life. The aesthetic of calendar art is a testimony to an approach to life that does not see an intimate sphere as separate from the rest of the society. Such a tendency is also present in other aspects of bazaar life, not just in the aesthetic configuration of products. Popular aesthetic presence is often against the established bourgeois ideas of form and beauty acquired through modern architecture and planning, deciding the optimal use of space. Gossip and rumor, congregations, and commerce are excesses of ordinary life that are "out of place" when imagined from the controlled and orderly lives of bourgeois homes.[4] But from within, they are the nuts and bolts of ordinary life.[5] All manner of excess forms part of the bazaar environment—crowds of people, "grotesque" bodies, salacious speech, stolen objects, garbage, and ordinary and e-waste.

Site of Contestation

The emphasis is usually on the pheriwala [hawker], who is the focal point of the stall, and as well on a small range of products and services: for example, a public telephone and coconut milk, cigarettes and chewing tobacco. The arrangements are usually minimal—a sackcloth on a wooden platform, a matchbox-like structure with shelves, a handcart with a wooden or aluminium top. Decorations are functional where they exist, perhaps consisting of gaily colored sachet strips of betel nut, chewing tobacco, or shampoo suspended from a string running horizontally across a shelf, or of plates of artfully cut fruit. If food is being made, the smell of the oil, the condition of the utensils, the quality of the foodstuffs, and the personal hygiene of the cook are all on display. (Rajagopal 2001, 98)

Contraband also provided work for tens of thousands of people. Many worked at the port, ferrying arriving shipments from ship to shore or unloading small boats at the dock. On the streets of Forcella, they sold contraband on small lightweight tables and overturned cardboard boxes. The widespread and visible participation of residents and the tolerance of state authority contributed to local public feelings that such work, and the presence of powerful crime clans, was quite ordinary. (Pine 2012, 48)

The above descriptions are from two different cities: Mumbai and Naples. The language of disarray and chaos is the same. Yet there is also something else. The sensory overload connects to non-elites' use of urban commons.[6] In *The Southern Question*, Gramsci probes how the Italian south got relegated to a subordinate position compared to the industrial north as the unification of the country was based on the fervor and strengths of the center and the northern parts without much consideration for the particular requirements of its southern regions. Subsequently, the absorption of cheap labor from the south in factories of the northern region continued the process of marginalization of certain parts of the country. In his book *The Art of Making Do in Naples,* anthropologist Jason Pine (2012) develops the popular aesthetics of Naples in great detail, connecting it to the national and local question of inequality. Pine analyzes the links between political structures and organized crime and the complex ways in which ordinary people create their own means of survival by accessing informal arrangements, whether it is roadside vending or the *neomelodico* music scene. The same is the case for street markets in India, which bring together lives and a diverse range of commodities. Often such admixture results from postcolonial developments of modern cities with the zoning of spaces and people into residential, commercial, and industrial complexes. In such top-down arrangements, elite lives flourish in prime properties and areas, and a much bigger group of people are left to their own devices. This group of people find opportunities in the street-level economy and informal work as construction laborers, bazaar traders, and domestic workers. In different contexts, non-elites slip from recent developmental projects. State politics that should have provided security for disadvantaged sections instead often orchestrated projects there to benefit private capital. No doubt accumulation of wealth by a few has been justified by the prism of trickle-down economics, but the actual trickling of resources to the bottom has been highly limited. In such a scenario, ordinary people establish their own infrastructure within formal structures not by building things from scratch but by using available resources to their benefit. Detailing the process of marginalization of ordinary lives in Ghana where information communication technologies (ICTs) focused heavily on urban areas, Lu (2021, 310) writes, "Due to the external orientation and urban bias, both the state and large transnational companies have generally ignored the ICT demands of Ghana's rural population, leaving them to pirated or secondhand technologies. The main distributors of such technologies are usually informal traders traveling with their suitcases and buying in small quantities."

Contemporary cities share the aspect of uneven development where certain regions and groups of people face the brunt of a singular model of development. While exclusive plans at times are the result of a lack of a political will, at other times researchers have noted more insidious motives to work in the interest of private capital. Lisa Barthelmes (2012) writes about how street vendors in Hanoi faced marginalization with Vietnam's modernization from 1986 onwards introducing new economic reforms. After 2007, when the country joined the World Trade Organization, there were further changes to the urban plan. Supermarkets, boutiques, and malls quickly appeared in Hanoi. "In the context of these modernization efforts, mobile street vendors in Hanoi are regarded as visible manifestations of backwardness and do not fit into the government's vision of a wealthy state and rational economic development. Mobile street vendors are considered residual, non-productive and obstacles to traffic, representing a backward Vietnam as 'remnants of an undesirable past'" (Barthelmes 2012, 5). Such absence of imagination about the needs of ordinary people is a reality of many places. As possible evidence of elite planned marginalization, Hasan Karrar (2020) analyzes crackdowns on informal places of business such as the Almaty bazaar in Central Asia, where goods from shipping containers are bought and sold. After recent fires in the area, malls and multistory constructions replaced older inhabitants, hinting at an intentional destruction of communal infrastructure. The same is the case with Indonesian street vendors and street marketplaces (Yatmo 2008). Many of them were removed from prime locations, appearing "out of place" as the country took off on its path to modernization.

Gertrud Hüwelmeier (2018) uses the terms "ghost markets" and "moving bazaars" to show the process of displacement of bazaar actors from one day to the next. In Hanoi, where she conducted her fieldwork in Chợ Mơ (Mơ-market), the market was demolished to establish a commercial center. Different vendors and traders were relocated to temporary sites without a clear idea whether they would ever return to their original site, where they had attracted a stable income. Instead, what the traders got to hear were the usual round of words used to propel redevelopment projects, such as building a "civilized and modern" city and a "clean and green city." The steps taken by urban planners are precisely what disturbs the rhythm of ordinary life. Displaced women traders told Hüwelmeier how they lost their regular clients and are finding it increasingly difficult to establish enduring ties in temporary marketplaces. Even customers mentioned that new malls did not support their mobile shopping habits of buying from their motorbikes as they now had to park their vehicles before they made any purchases. Most of the time redevelopment projects leave a long trail of destruction for ordinary people to pick up the pieces (Chattaraj, Choudhury, and Joshi 2017).

Bazaar Excess

Bazaar speech is unregulated, coarse, and at times offensive, as opposed to the more refined speech pattern of the bourgeoisie. In Delhi's bazaars, for instance, traders did not hesitate to call each other by nicknames that wouldn't be seen as particularly civil in any context that does not have the same air of familiarity and shared sense of humor (Deka 2020). There was also a lack of propriety in openly discussing the flaws of a person. No matter how awkward or cringe-worthy the name calling may appear to an outsider, in the bazaar leg pulling is common. The same absence of inhibition and formality guides most conversations. Establishing a certain rapport is part of bazaar sociality.[7] Anyone can be a joke's target, mainly in an inane fashion. Although a trader sometimes is seriously offended by jokes directed at him and he either leaves the shop or retaliates, most of the time the topic and words chosen are so mundane that the joke appears gimmicky. For instance, many traders in Palika Bazaar would talk about a person's superstitious nature to make fun of him or to portray him as unreasonable. They would say someone would do *panni ghumana* (rotate black plastic bags) to ward off evils. Such a reference would bring a smile to everyone's face as they thought it was ridiculous to think a black plastic bag would stop an evil spell in trade. But there was a thin line between joking about it and someone doing it in their shops. One day I saw a shop assistant literally dragging a black polyethylene packet in the air to catch the evil spirit as he had not done *bahni* (first sale of the day). Everyone else, including me, was amused. A grown man trying to catch air in a packet and leave it later in the dustbin was not something one sees regularly. Others were making fun of the naive shop assistant, but he continued unfazed by the taunts and jokes.

Comparable to the uninhibited bazaar sociality, working-class language codes studied by sociologists differ from standards set by the formal education system and are disadvantaged as a result (Bernstein 1964; Willis 1977). Even before Bourdieu and others showed how working languages were seen to carry low cultural capital, comparisons between elite and popular lives developed in the context of the European Reformation. In *Rabelais and His World,* Bakhtin talks about the unique sociality of marketplaces when compared to Renaissance elite spaces such as Church, palace, and courts, which were marked by civic virtues:

> The marketplace of the Middle Ages and the Renaissance was a world in itself, a world which was one; all "performances" in this area, from loud cursing to the organized show, had something in common and were imbued with the same atmosphere of freedom, frankness, and familiarity. Such elements of everyday speech as profanities, oaths, and curses were fully legalized in the marketplace and were quickly adopted by all the festive genres, even by Church drama. The marketplace was the center of all that is unofficial; it enjoyed certain extraterritoriality in a world of official order and official ideology, it always remained "with the people." (Bakhtin 1968, 153–54)

Bakhtin emphasizes that popular marketplaces were fecund with "speech patterns" and gestures otherwise prohibited or frowned upon by aristocrats. Only during carnivals do the "grotesque body" of the jester and clown take center stage.[8] The rest of the time in the Middle Ages, elite life valued functionality. Bakhtin outlines Rabelais as an antithetical figure to the rational man, someone whose bodily movements and gestures did not conform to the elite's norms of that time. There were repercussions to being on the fringe. While figures like Rabelais were at the center of carnivals, which were a less significant element of social life, there was more scrutiny around their actions. For instance, English historians Stallybrass and White (1986) connect the decreasing importance of fairs and carnivals to an increased presence of "capitalist rationality" of the Renaissance. As Stallybrass and White write, "The history of the fair has been written as a story of long decline. And the suppression of the fairs has been thought in two opposing, but mutually reinforcing, ways: either as the necessary triumph of the civilizing process or as the brutal stamping out of popular culture by the Church and the bureaucratic, centralizing State" (32). The growth of factories made certain practices less attractive. Upholding moral standards of the church benefited the state and bureaucratic structures in implementing the discipline and order of modern factories. The aesthetic and moral discomfort that fairs created in the European public milieu, from the Middle Ages onwards, persist in the contemporary bazaar economy. In medieval times, officers and learned aristocrats tried to change the face of such "disgusting places." In fact, a lot of the writings on the contemporary bazaar economy in South Asia have focused on the impact of "bourgeoisie environmentalism" in changing its aesthetics. Bourgeois lives are a "common denominator" for the rest of society to meet a particular standard of living. As often happens, it is the bourgeois definition of security and a good life that popular classes adopt as a desirable framework. Such adoption of bourgeois values cannot be merely seen as mimicry (Bhabha 1984) because actual benefits are attached to a bourgeois way of life—landlord rights, less fear of eviction, and status to name a few. But for many non-elites to reach a certain standard of living is a long shot. Much of their life is spent in chaotic assemblages. In the back of their mind, there may be an aspiration for an orderly life, but their present is nothing like the conditions prevailing in bourgeois life, nor could they have simply brought such a lifestyle to fruition. There is less order and more disarray and transgressions.

In-depth accounts of what this disarray, chaos, and excess mean to the practitioners themselves have figured in the works of anthropologists. Hoek and Gandhi (2016) see bazaar interaction as non-sociological sociality, "forms of entanglement that do not necessarily map onto prevailing analytical categories such as religion, ethnicity, gender, age or class. These are non-normative sites of sociality where familiar vectors of social relationships are often attenuated" (68). One specific example is mass gathering and the discomfort associated with it. That a group of people turn into a mob acting out of sectarian identity is not unheard of. Nor are the images of crowds being part of propaganda politics. But there are also banal reasons for people to congregate in certain places, like being bored with one's own company and seeking relief in the company of friends and strangers. Such meeting points dot South Asia under banyan trees, near tea shops, parking lots, street corners, and parks. Not all congregations are big, but sometimes their size can swell. After a major incident, political and personal, what is otherwise a group of a few people can expand to include neighborhood women and children. Through his ethnography on the Meena Bazaar in Delhi, Gandhi (2016a) describes the crowd through a series of linguistic categories: *dhakka mukki, bheed, khalbali.* The prevailing crowd can cause *khalbali* or excitement breaking the monotony of a routined life. On a hot day, it can be experienced as congestion and *bheed*. At times, the crowd is a sort of external force on the body, pushing and shoving people in the marketplace, known in Hindi as *dhakka mukki*. The "hermeneutics of the bazaar" (Gandhi 2016b) is an exciting starting point to record meanings that insiders attach to varied practices and experiences. Words used to describe the swelling crowd show the subtleties that a sensory experience means from the inside. What is otherwise just a body of people takes on new meaning based on why and when such crowds occur in marketplaces.

Crowd and Customers

On an everyday basis, people crowd the narrow alleys of Lajpat Rai Market, the corridors of Palika Bazaar, and the squares of Nehru Place. Making your way through the busy bazaars, you rub shoulders with consumers, bystanders, laborers carrying cartons on their shoulders, distributors, and delivery personnel. The diverse group of people is a crowd best avoided on a hot summer day. But for the *bazaaris*, the crowd is people who do not come to purchase things and are there in the marketplace to do *timepass*.[9] Pointing to a group of young men huddled together in the inner courtyard of Palika, Rajesh remarks, "These people are not here to buy anything. Some of them have come inside just to get some cool air. After finishing their cold drinks and snacks, they are out of the marketplace." Other times, people referred to a large group of people as "tourists" and "loiterers." They are there to wander, window shop, and spend time with family and friends. Arvind from Palika remembers a time when there used to be a queue outside the shops early in the morning. During those days, very few people came to do *timepass* in the marketplace. In the 1980s bazaars fulfilled a crucial role in the media economy by linking semi-legal networks of smuggled and imported goods directly to consumers. People queued up for imported products they would not find in other places. Arvind laments the change of times in the bazaars, from being one of the most important electronic hubs, to being denigrated, to attracting very few serious customers really in the marketplace to buy something. And like Arvind, others feel that there is a rise in a useless crowd in the marketplace. Other unwelcome people are young lovers who, in the eyes of the traders, are wasting their lives away when they could spend their time doing something more meaningful like being at school. The aimless wanderers in the marketplace do not add any economic value to the traders, and they often become a source of annoyance. The traders do not see the link between people wandering in the marketplace and the possibility of accidental purchases. In their view, wanderers can be spotted at a distance by their bodily demeanor, hands in their pockets and a lazy gait. The way that their eyes wander from shop to shop indicates to the traders that these are not people looking for anything specific to buy. A trader observes, "One can only buy something when they know what they have to buy." There is a certain level of sympathy for loiterers who might spend money if they had some in their pocket. But such generosity is not extended to suspicious-looking people who aimlessly roam the marketplace. In past decades, Delhi was part of several "terrorist" attacks in busy marketplaces. Such incidents led traders to see abrupt congregation as dangerous. Especially when business is slow, the propensity to see crowds as dangerous increases. Traders and street vendors will murmur about how nobody can say why so many people gather in the marketplace—if everybody is there to pass time or they are up to something. In such moments, I felt hostility from bazaar actors toward the rush of people in the marketplace. Most likely their fears are misplaced, and their anger is based on the crowds not seeming to bring any business to them.

There was a distinct type of hostility toward young couples, whose presence in the marketplace during the day put them in a suspicious position, dressed in a particular way and moving arm in arm when they should be in school or accompanied by elders. The choicest phrase would be reserved for such couples. "Look how they think themselves to be some Bollywood hero. Soon they will run out of steam and turn from hero to zero." Often such uttering put others in a jovial mood, and they went on for a while commenting on their clothes and lack of style. No doubt a large number of young people visit a marketplace like Palika, but unlike traders' observations, not everyone is out on a date. Many get tattoos, a business that has risen significantly in the last few years. Many shops now sublet their space to tattoo parlors. Usually hidden away either in the shop's rear or adjacent rooms and attics, they were popular with young people who got tattoos made by novices at a reasonable price.

Outside the irritating elements are the people whom the traders meet for business. No matter how many people are inside the shop, it is not considered a crowd. The rush of people in the shop is welcome. Suppliers come to the shop with new items fresh from local manufacturers of games and accessories. At times, official distributors of Sony and Microsoft are in the marketplace to see if shops need restocking of company products. Delivery personnel inquire if the shopkeepers want an extra hand to deliver goods from the shops to consumers' doorsteps. While not all the people who gather at the shop enter into a market exchange, the shop's occupancy indicates that there is potential for a business deal. In fact, many complaints of the traders are about loiterers in the corridors of the marketplace and not in the shops.[10]

Delhi's bazaars thrive on diverse sets of people, some more welcome than others. They contribute to the sociality of these places. It is only a matter of a few steps before an annoying bystander enters a particular shop and becomes a desirable consumer. A less preferable situation is when one of the wanderers enters the shop asking for job opportunities. Most of the time traders reject such requests. Occasionally they put a new person on a trial run for a week. If they like the work of a new hire, they will give him a job with a regular salary. There are also instances of people entering the shop to have a chat. Conversations start with a stranger entering the shop asking about the whereabouts of another trader or inquiring about a recent incident in the marketplace. Such queries can spark long chats. And this stranger might spend more time in the shop observing what is going on, intervening in the ongoing exchange between a buyer and the seller, and continuing his interaction with the trader after customers leave the shop. Topics in such conversation are open-ended— politics, weather, products—and appeared more an attempt at filling time with some punchy stories along the way.

The aesthetics of the crowd in the bazaars oscillates between desirable consumers, useless wanderers, and good company. Bazaars attract diverse urban lives from the periphery, people who don't belong to formal consumer spaces and are left intimidated by them. They may have been in the city for a short time and bazaars appear to be one of the first welcoming places where there are more people of their kind sharing similar economic, geographical, and linguistic ties. While shopping complexes and plush malls are the "temples" of modern consumerism, bazaars are the temples of proletarian consumerism. A marker of proletarian consumerism is when the urge to shop must confront the constraints of money, information, and access. There is never a shortage of desire and aspiration. In fact, ordinary consumers want far more variety in goods than is available to affluent consumers. The choice of colors and design is one aspect and the experience of a product. Take the example of video games. Often, buyers are not content with a particular franchise's gameplay—its plot and how players interact with the game—and they would just not go with it; gamers are vocal about their complaints and changes they want to see. Most underclass gamers would wish the gameplay to reflect their state of existence.

They would like to see characters like them in a franchise like *Grand Theft Auto*, and they would make their preferences known. This is where the bazaars step in. Traders and street vendors listen to ordinary gamers' demands and try to bring the desired changes to their customers. Sometimes, bazaars come up with cheats and fixes of their own. Instead of a Western protagonist on the cover of a game, they would put a local character in a familiar setting; this slight change in the aesthetic would put gamers at ease at the outset. They would feel that the storyline is close to their reality and not necessarily alien to their existence. In Delhi's bazaars, *Grand Theft Auto* had a turbaned Sikh on a tractor in Punjab on the cover, one of the many aesthetic discretions bazaars took to meet the demand of their consumers.

Congestion

While the crowd creates congestion, an aspect that Gandhi (2016a) observes in his ethnography of Meena Bazaar in Delhi through the notion of *bheed* (cramped public spaces), there are other elements of an aesthetic of congestion that characterize bazaar-like places. Analyzing the paintings of Jhabvala, Mohammed Sayeed points out that a "starting point to understand the architectures of congestion is to start counting the number of layers—of walls, buildings, floors, objects, motifs, stairs and so on. Spatially, what hides what? And temporally, what might have been built before and what might have been added later?" (Sayeed 2017). Where better to understand the multiple layers of congestion than in the urban bazaars? In fact, Jhabvala's painting describes a scene of a marketplace in Old Delhi similar to Lajpat Rai and its surroundings. At first glance, the heightened aesthetic shocks and awes people who are not from Old Delhi. For the residents themselves, the density of activities reveals the presence of traditional lifestyles and modern elements of state and private infrastructure, local and foreign tourists, and electoral politics.

The challenge is to continue to exist in a changing city and yet maintain an old way of life. That is why the dealings with state actors are complex. Inhabitants of the area have to negotiate with democratic institutions while being part of religious and nonreligious traditional affiliations. One such field of constant negotiation is the use of public places. Business activities extend from the shop to passages and walls outside the main establishment. One can peel back the different layers of Delhi's bazaars. The main street is for vehicles, rickshaw pullers, and pedestrians. Street vendors, ear cleaners, and local ice-cream sellers use pavements adjacent to the marketplace. Then one reaches the entrances to the bazaar, meandering into small passages of tarpaulin-covered makeshift shops and permanent spots. The bazaars have many alleys, corners, and turns to accommodate different trade (see Figure 1.1). Many vendors use the corridors of inner buildings for business. Using every spot in the marketplace, corridors, verandahs, and passages, traders and street vendors employ public spaces for commercial purposes.[11] The tussle continues; sometimes these extra-juridical arrangements appear as eyesores, especially when a minister or dignitaries visit this part of town. Cleaning up informal encroachments is prompt. Delhi is not alone in this. There were stories about walls going up overnight when Brazil hosted the Rio Olympics in 2016. On the other hand, a long time would pass without any disturbance. Extensions would be added to businesses without raising alarm. Authorities looked the other way. In most cases, it is a matter of timing. If official actors feel undue pressure from the top or their usual monetary arrangement isn't optimal, the traders and vendors know of such discontentment because the issue is directly brought up with them or there are official raids.

Lajpat Rai Market, Palika Bazaar, and Nehru Place are part of modernist state plans to include particular groups of people who faced economic hardships and political persecution as a result of specific historical events such as the partition of India and Pakistan in 1947. The sites of India's high modernism absorbed a large section of people who, until a historical crisis, survived in cities through odd jobs. There was an understanding that at a certain moment, the diverse group of petty traders would learn to live up to the standard of these spaces as model citizens. But things did not pan out as planned. "All three media markets of the 'long' 1980s grew out of planned developments; Palika Bazaar had careful zoning in the initial phase, and Nehru Place had a large public plaza. At their best, they were expressions of the DDA's [Delhi Development Authority's] blank urbanism, planning's own generic city, a form of bureaucratic escape from the memory of the old city and partition. The infrastructure of the planned markets began crumbling soon after their inception, coterminous with the crisis of the planned city. Nehru Place's public plaza became a bazaar; Palika's zoning system collapsed, and Lajpat Rai market expanded into sidewalks and backyards" (Sundaram 2010, 100–101). The frustration with these places not living up to certain standards is most visible in the active measures taken by legal officials to curtail untoward behavior. Raids and relocation of people are frequent. Street vendors positioned in the front of a marketplace can be moved to another site, losing

Figure 1.1. View from the main entrance staircase of Palika Bazaar into the inner circle (author's image).

a strategic business spot. Constant negotiations around rent, air-vent repair, and leakage are headaches.

The story of regulation of street life is not a story unique to Delhi. As Anjaria (2016) notes in the case of Mumbai, street vendors faced forced removal as their spot came under the radar of real estate speculation and the Bombay Municipal Corporation's eye for optimal use of public space. These measures were the start of a surveillance regime and of linking people's position to property ownership. If people owned private property, they became ingrained in a civil society with ordained rights and privileges and protection of one's assets. Those who did not gather enough material assets lost touch with the rationale of city life and its emphasis on safety and discipline. It became easier to persecute vendors and laborers in the street under the new civic plans of maintaining order and aesthetics of elite groups. "Road infrastructure in particular offered the most compelling logic for evictions and removal of settlements considered dangerous to the city. To open the city was to make it healthy and clean; the sense that disease was spread through a theory of miasma spatialized the problem of sanitation" (Anjaria 2016, 50).

The rationale behind cleaning up Delhi's streets was similar. While cleanup operations under British colonialism were legitimized through an emphasis on health and the well-being of the population, most recent plans were pushed to attain a feeling of a world-class city. In order to fulfill the vision of a developed metropolis, most construction has been driven by private capital. Many saw the Commonwealth Games of 2010 as a threshold year when Delhi resolutely developed into a city for the country's rich and the middle class. In particular, the redevelopment of South Delhi was administered through private capital and catered to the demands of elite consumerism.[12] As of now, the popular classes are hanging on to places they occupied before the current corporate-driven allocation of capital and resources. They make maximum use of public spaces, the state-built modernist buildings and their immediate surroundings. Here, the road is not just a "machine for traffic." The chaotic street life "can dissolve hegemonic preconceptions and disrupt notions of smooth passage, unhindered gazing, detached self-containment, convenience and antiseptic sterility so entrenched in Western regimes of urban spatialisation" (Naik 2015, 21). There is a true democratization of streets in the Global South particularly in and around popular marketplaces.

Here, the streets offer refuge to the homeless, the itinerant beggars, and those seeking a chance to start something new. It is not unheard of in the marketplaces that a specific individual had nothing upon beginning to sell odd items in the marketplace, later fortified a hold in the business, and achieved better circumstances. These are not stories about individual resilience so much as about how few resources many of them had when they started frequenting busy marketplaces.

For the street vendors in Nehru Place, for instance, some who were bullied in school felt they had a much better time being in the marketplace than in school. One thing led to another, and they could support families, some of whom included a parent who was ailing or worked in other precarious jobs; the easy and stable money that young street vendors brought in by selling pirated wares improved their situation tremendously. With time, they could build family houses thanks to this extra earning hand. Without the marketplace, the absence of formal education could have pushed the young vendors further down the hierarchy. The proximity that young street vendors had to Nehru Place came out quite well in some of the anecdotes. They remembered coming to the marketplace as children and climbing the mango trees. It was a playground for them. No doubt for young minds, a marketplace like Nehru Place must have provided many stimuli, few of them alienating. They made countless trips to the marketplace before they got shifted to Madanpur Khadar colony after eviction from slums in the area. But they never got out of the habit of visiting Nehru Place even though now they lived a few kilometers away from where they were before, closer to the marketplace. Many stories went on to tell of a certain sense of disappointment with school and then how the playground became their place of work. In some way, their work is still quite childlike, calling out to strangers and weaving different stories to get their attention—playtime pursuits. Money made many of these teenagers an adult as they shared family responsibilities, but the marketplace continued to be a place where they met with friends and spent the day sharing foods, snacks, and conversations. Many would not miss a single day; they liked how time went quickly, between talking with customers and with friends, and did not know how to fill their day sitting at home with their families.

The ease that varied actors felt in busy marketplaces is remarkably different from the unease they felt going to middle-class consumer spaces. They find it challenging to fit into private capital–driven consumer spaces which, for the lack of a better word, can also be understood as a western regime of urban spatialization. After all, London comes up among city planners and elite citizens when they think of the route that Delhi should be taking for its future development (Liang and Sundaram 2011). Street vendors in Nehru Place perceive a place like Select City Walk, a mall located not far from the marketplace, as intimidating. Saurav, a street vendor in Nehru Place, is uncomfortable with the guards that stand outside the mall. He feels that they are scanning people like him as if they have no business being there. A question that others don't have to face but people like him do is, "What are you doing here?" Saurav says that people at the mall think that *bazaaris* have no business in an upscale marketplace.

The uneasiness is on both sides. Saurav does not feel like he belongs in a mall, particularly the ones in wealthy neighborhoods. His life and friendships are often limited to his neighborhood and bazaars; upscale malls are a world in themselves. They are places that emerged in conversation as a mythical other that, in some discussions, were made fun of because of their closed and snooty nature and, in other fora, brought out a more profound side of a bazaar actor's life: that they were an outsider in the cityscape. Contrary to the image of the fortified malls, Saurav agrees that there is a certain openness to the bazaar: "Rarely is someone stopped entering the bazaar. There can be security checks in some places, but nobody is judged based on their attire." In fact, there is no typecasting of people entering the marketplace; as this book discusses, bazaars ultimately want more and more people to increase the chance of a random visit turning into a lucrative trade opportunity. The aggregation of a diverse set of people has defined the physical geography of bazaars. The keen awareness that the aesthetics of congestion—moving commercial activities onto public land—has created a unique temporality and sociality for the bazaars. The same congestion that can appear unruly and chaotic from the outside becomes a survival strategy from the inside. The possibility of turning free space into business opportunities has brought new meanings to the use of space and density of activities.

What is the legal status of a wall or a pillar in the immediate exteriority of a shop? If a vendor starts displaying his products on boundary walls, should he pay rent for it and to whom? Or imagine a scene when a trader puts a box outside his shop and decorates the top of it with different things. Some days, it may be a few mobile phone cases, and on other days some used DVDs. As the evening comes, the box disappears into the shop and might appear some other day. The flexible nature of such business spots makes an understanding of private property and public space quite tricky. While a lot of the encroachment is tolerated or ignored on most days, there are times when the indiscriminate use of public spaces is an eyesore. These are the times when a kiosk or a table is seen as a threat by state authorities. In situations like these, often the owners find the makeshift arrangements destroyed within an hour by a raid. Of course, the traders and street vendors are annoyed with these interventions. They regroup since the overhead costs are low (a tarpaulin cover works as a roof, a desk and bench are office furniture, and sometimes a plastic sheet on the ground is enough to carry out trade).

The stress of escaping the official gaze and the lack of security has led street vendors, especially in a marketplace like Nehru Place, to seek help from non-governmental organizations to secure a permanent spot. To an extent, they are successful as many garment vendors have a permanent spot in the marketplace. But the messiness does not disappear with new sets of regulations. The number of vendors swells. What started with a few vendors selling games and clothes becomes hundreds. Such competition is not naturally welcome and there are tensions between different groups. But bazaars have this almost magical quality to layer different activities. Formerly unused pillars become prime selling points. Or areas that were previously ignored because they are at an extended wing of the marketplace are occupied by new settlers. Such elasticity of bazaar space goes well with walkers and bystanders. It continues a sense of curiosity and novelty to even the most mundane of places. On almost every visit, the chances of the marketplace looking different are good. I ran into police checks in Palika Bazaar that were not there the day before. A simple step can change the flow of the marketplace. All these small changes add to the sensory experience of urban bazaars. One day, inside Palika, I notice a shop owner is gone. And a new shopkeeper is there. Further down the marketplace, I am introduced to a trader's relative who is learning the tricks of the trade. He will soon open his shop in some other marketplace or even find a corner in the same shop if the trader is happy with his progress. In a way, it is possible to assess several people by seeing the space of a single shop used for multiple purposes. The more avenues of business that a shop space can accommodate, the better the chance for new people to be part of bazaar commerce. Every inch of the shop is used for trade. If the main trader has extra space, he rents that part out to another trader that sells complementary items. For example, a trader selling watches rents out part of his shop to an accessory trader and repair person of watches.

Lajpat Rai is perpetually changing. New entrances are carved between buildings, as new shops open in unused alley. There are times when old paths get blocked, and the construction of a religious site or a metro track requires rerouting people in alternative pathways. The main street outside the marketplace acts as a loose boundary, and objects, people, and different types of trade get accommodated in the space. Entrances and courtyards absorb new street vendors and traders. Previously quieter parts are busy with activities. In Nehru Place, old businesses disappear, and new shops take their place. Over the years, the entrance to the marketplace from the Delhi metro exit has become busier. To attract daily commuters and visitors, a lot of eateries have opened on the front side of the marketplace. Also, the southern wing has expanded. Earlier this site had mainly garbage bins, but now, alongside a few textile shops, street vendors have begun to use the space more frequently. Urban bazaars are ephemeral, but the change is more within the geography of the marketplace than completely expanding into new terrain. Even when the main trade of the marketplace expands into adjacent streets, traders do not colonize new territories as they face the possibility of eviction. This is the privilege of state and private capital that bulldozes trees to build new malls and business parks. Bazaars continue to evolve with the times, adding new actors and new products within the radius of the physical marketplace. Change is brought, more than anything, by new people and the experimental use of old infrastructure to produce new outcomes. This is the reason why rather than being capital intensive, changes come from an assemblage of human and existing resources.

Certain agreements are behind the novel use of spaces. When traders and street vendors employ the front of someone's shop to hang their products, it is understood that there is some kind of prior agreement between them. If there is no rivalry between the parties, deliberations often resolve smoothly. At times they are of a transactional nature. For instance, a trader allows a street vendor to use the space outside his shop if the vendor is willing to point new customers to his shop. Usually, having complementary commodities helps establish partnerships. For instance, a trader with an antivirus solution for computers is more likely to allow a group of electronics street vendors to use the space outside his shop. The chances that a customer of software and games who owns a personal computer can be persuaded to buy antivirus software are high. The same exact transaction would not emerge between electronics and garment vendors. But trade dealings do not define all relationships. Traders tolerate each other's business out of goodwill and trust. For instance, even in the marketplace for electronics, bazaar inhabitants include ear cleaners, lamination specialists, fruit sellers, clothes vendors, and scrap dealers. One way of looking at the heterogeneous mix of people is to see how people are a resource in the bazaars and assist each other on a day-to-day basis. "Every vendor possesses a keen awareness of the various uses and users of the street. The vendor depends on the bus traveller, the pedestrian, the office goer, the lounger" (Naik 2015, 41). From an outside perspective, exchanges appear chaotic, predating the modern world. But from the inside, these practices are precisely about ordinary people holding onto their way of being modern—incorporating people, and spaces, including the lived city.[13]

Everyday Objects and Tools

Fanselow's (1990) article on the bazaar economy in India cites Fox's (1969) work, *From Zamindar to Ballot Box*, to talk about the bizarre list of wares in the marketplace. Geertz, Geertz, and Rosen's 1979 account of Suqs in Morocco gives a more detailed description of what these odd retail items look like: pharmaceuticals, grains and edibles, and sex workers. Even contemporary bazaars have many objects and tools that in the first instance appear useless and bizarre. Nonetheless, they do play a role in commerce. Many odd articles on the shop desks are there because they are tools for industrious repair (see Figure 1.2). Repair is a kind of work that does not have a clear trajectory. Customers can come with any type of problem on any machine—new or old—and it is up to the trader to find what is wrong with it and eventually fix it. It may be a matter of cracking a recent console or fixing parts of old consoles. As a result, not much gets thrown out of the shop—who knows what may prove handy in the future? This is why what looks like trash at the surface is not be instantly thrown away from the shop. A piece from an old machine can be the missing part needed for a future repair. Not just old machine parts but toothbrushes, lighters, hammers, scissors, screwdrivers, safety pins, glues, cotton balls, and erasers cram shop desks. These household items are tools.

During a typical repair, Harish takes the hammer from his desk and hits an Xbox One gaming console at strategic spots to open the machine. Rather than spend time unscrewing individual bolts, Harish saves time by opening the console with a few strokes of the hammer. Once the motherboard is on the shop desk, Harish brushes it with a toothbrush to get rid of dust and other impurities. He moves on to do a deep clean of the motherboard with cotton balls damp with a solvent.

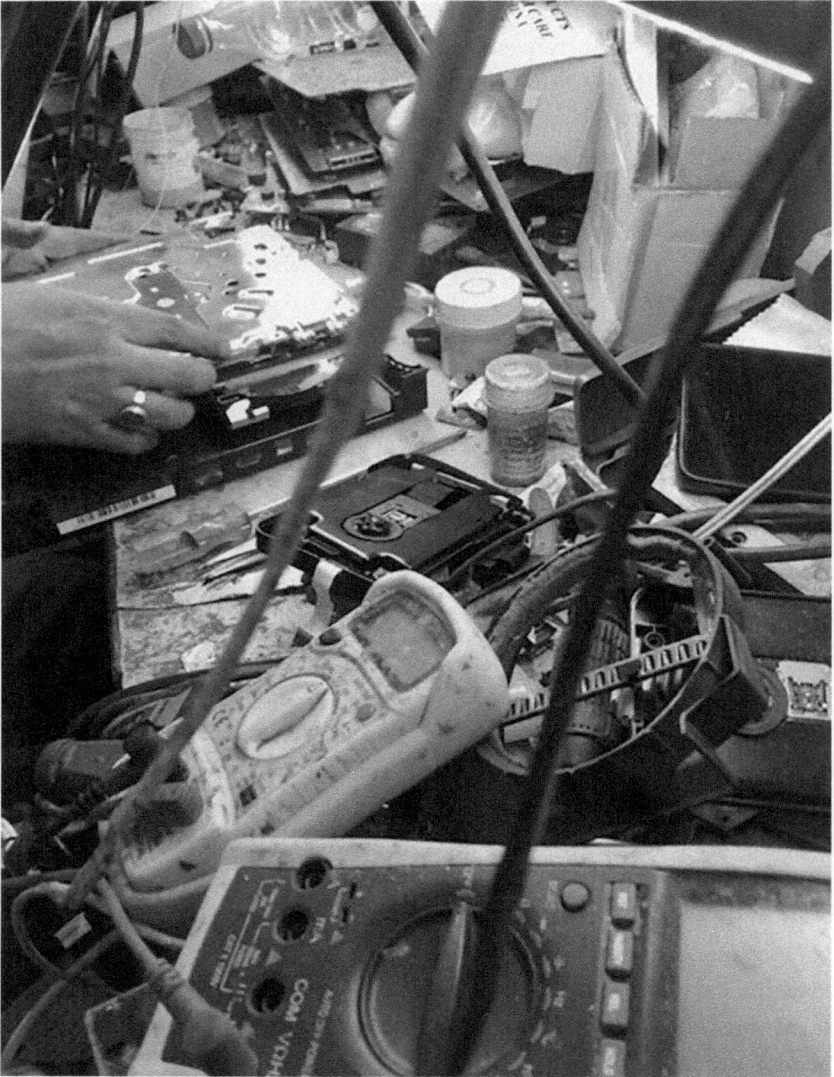

Figure 1.2. A repair person's desk at Palika Bazaar (author's image).

First, Harish tries a few simple tricks to see if the machine can be fixed without much effort. One of the tricks is to use a lighter and emit heat at different parts of the motherboard. If the console starts to work with an initial cleaning and heating, Harish does not perform an exhaustive process of repair. The initial fixes do work in some cases. With the hope that simple techniques are enough, it has become almost a routine for Harish to repeat the process of cleaning and heating for new repair work. In the same manner that cotton balls, hammers, and toothbrushes are handy, there are times when a scissor, safety pin, and screwdriver assist in removing small parts from the motherboard and fixing nuts and bolts of consoles. Repair work creates a unique aesthetic where essential tools sit side by side with advanced technological products.

> Two teenage boys huddled under the anemic light of a 7-watt compact fluorescent bulb with the tiny guts of a Sony PlayStation 2 spread in front of them. One of them used a broken screwdriver to pry open the toy's hard shell and separate its defunct screen from a delicate nest of circuitry. The other boy, Ruben, showed me its replacement: a screen scavenged from another instrument—"just the same," he stated confidently. (Hill 2011, 1)

The above is the description that anthropologist Sarah Hill uses to introduce us to the repair scene in Santiago in Cuba. But this could be a scene anywhere from Delhi to Dhaka (Jackson, Ahmed, and Rifat 2014). Backyard innovation is integral to bazaar aesthetics. The push to solve problems opens up the possibilities of imagining any available resource as carrying endless possibilities. As with the gameplay of video games, where gamers use cheats and tricks to get by challenging situations, repair work is about identifying strategic points to turn a difficult repair project into a success. Street practitioners try different permutations and combinations. Opening and closing consoles, powering the machine on and off, and removing the motherboard and connecting to a new screen—there is a range of tactics available to repair people. As a result of this attitude, they collect parts from different machines to find a solution. Delhi's tinkers use portable TV handsets to play new games. Such appropriation creates a retro aesthetic, things that belonged to another era yet are used to play video games like Super Mario and Street Fighter. In Lajpat Rai Market, a small TV plugged into a hanging electricity board is on top of the table in one of the corridors of the main building. Two repair people sit on a bench in front of the TV. No matter what the original game display is, on the portable TV set it is neon blue. In one sense, the lo-fi aesthetic can be seen as a reduction of the variegated experience of brand-new products, but on the other hand, such an aesthetic is democratizing. Certain images appear a certain way in the bazaar played with portable TV sets. And the gaming experience adjusts to this peculiar aesthetics—the neon color is not necessarily an omission of different stimuli but a proletarian way of making technology familiar. In a way, the drab media images remove distraction, and tinkers move quickly from the surface to see and undo what lies beneath. Often young men manage the repair table, and sometimes two people sit on a single chair spending hours before the screen trying different options. Perhaps the time-consuming nature of experimentation is why such work is more for young aficionados. In Lajpat Rai Market, traders employ young repair persons to work on the basic repair. Even if the repair work does not go as planned, the trader does not lose much as his expenditure in gaining extra hands is low. The young men spend days working in front of old monitors on simple furniture and with stolen electricity, not even taking their eyes off when bystanders pass.

As Sarah Hill (2011, 1) notes, scavenging is the main element here, the possibility to rescue parts of abandoned consumer items. She observes that "present-day Cuba functions like this everywhere. Economy and society hum along to the din of remaking—take Cuba's world-famous fleet of half-century-old American luxury vehicles. The original brand names tell merely the origins of Frankenstein inventions that continually morph through remaking into cars that bear but superficial resemblance to their original selves." Scavenging has its aesthetic. The mismatch of objects creates completely novel aesthetic experiences, like the neon blue screen and other times when such experimentation gives rise to blurred lines and shaky images. Speaking about repair work in Rundu, an open-air marketplace in Namibia, Jackson, Pompe, and Krieshok (2012, 109) point toward its "bazaar-like arrangements. While nominally a trading center, the open market functions as a defining social institution of the Kavango in general. It serves as a daily stop for many of Rundu's residents, whether to eat food, buy fabric, sell a chicken, or watch a soccer match. Over ten individual shops/stalls in the market deal in technology (both computer and cell phone); no fewer than five of these are dedicated to repair." Such density of activities is suitable for scavenging things that can be picked up from anywhere and used somewhere else. It is in the excess of stimulus that an unconventional combination of objects and practices come into fruition. Take for example the habit of Delhi's repair people to use the cover of old consoles to fix broken parts of new ones. The possibility to juxtapose technology arises because in the bazaars different objects congregate without any particular product taking center stage. There is a relaxed attitude toward the materiality of technology that makes the constant assembling and disassembling a routine affair. One is not searching to rise above the chaos to a certain world of order. Rather, in the chaos exists an indifference to individual products that make different combinations possible as one is not committed to any one way of doing things or, in this case, assembling parts. In bazaars, objects are not entities but are attached to something else as accessories, tools, and modified versions. The interconnected network of things and people are immediately visible. This sensory aesthetic is starkly opposite to branded commodities of supermarkets and malls whose presence is demarcated from waste, and rough work is frowned upon and pushed to the rear of the facility.

Bazaar Commodity Aesthetic

Still relevant is Karl Marx's discussion on commodities taking on exchange value, losing their social character, and appearing as an objective relationship between things. The popularity of brands is one such area that brings to the fore commodity fetishism as the immaterial values of logos and insignia claim higher value than human relationships of production. Bazaars are not outside the world of brands. Even when branded goods are not the most popular items for sale, bazaar traders often repair a Sony or a Microsoft product. Most shops carry all kinds of commodities produced locally or imported from China, which the traders refer to as "Made in China" or "use and throw" material. The combination of an exciting mix of commodities creates a unique commodity aesthetics. In his ethnographic work among street garment markets in Tamil Nadu, anthropologist Constantine Nakassis (2012) highlights the multifaceted world of counterfeits and knockoffs through his concept of *brandedness*—or to be a brand *like*. He points to the addition of the letter "n" to sportswear resembling that of the company Columbia: the result, Columbian, becomes an example of such brandedness. Nakassis's (2016) work shows how the world of brandedness is frothy and points toward an ambivalent zone where there is neither a direct reproduction nor a complete ignorance of the semiotic universe of corporate brands.

Some items in the bazaars do not exist in the semiotic universe of global brands. Or rather the similarity is so vague that it is difficult to plainly spot the source of aesthetic inspiration. No doubt, "Made in China" handheld games such as PVPs are knockoffs of Sony's PlayStation Portables. But PVPs have so many different colors and styles of packaging and design that it is difficult to see each piece as a mere copy. It is of course much easier to label bazaar-like places as not creative enough to come with original ideas—a sentiment that is shared both by traders and consumers in the bazaar. The very fact that one uses the term "Made in China" is a derogatory way to speak about products that lack innovation. Their main attribute is to be cheap copies and inferior in quality to the original branded objects from US and European companies. But if we look at objects, apart from a few where the inspiration of brands is clearly visible, there were many with their own semiotic universes of words and images. Svetlana Boym (1994) is right when she says the problem arises when we look for external explanations and sources of inspiration for popular aesthetics rather than framing it in the world of practitioners. In her historical work *Common Places: Mythologies of Everyday Life in Russia*, she pieces together Soviet everyday life through a palimpsest of objects, from painting to the communal apartment, to envision a popular aesthetic of products. However unreasonable and awkward a combination of banality, kitsch, and symbols might be to an external observer, the choices of people who hoard knick-knacks can only be understood through specific experiences of subjects. "The objects in the personal display cases of the communal apartments are neither bare essentials nor mere objects of status or conspicuous consumption. If they represent a need, it is an aesthetic need, a desire for beauty met with minimal available means, or the aesthetic 'domestication' of the hostile outside world. They are not about defamiliarization, but rather about inhabiting estranged ideological symbols" (Boym 1994, 159).

Similarly, Delhi's bazaar aesthetic is shaped by several factors—state policies, desires, scarcity, and "style." That bazaars today look a certain way did not develop in a vacuum. The physical appearance of objects and the revelry in the bazaar manifest ordinary struggles and celebrations. Much like the Soviet communal apartment, objects and bodies in the bazaar are a "domestication" of the sphere of elite control. In a way, bazaars' minimal influence on the civic society has pushed actors in the informal economy to experiment with resources within their reach. The scarcity of material resources motivates people to hoard random objects. An absence of material security pushes bazaar actors to accumulate things that they can access without needing to procure new resources. Such excess is about aggregating all manner of things with an understanding that the overbearing abundance of random objects will counter the shortage of security and capital. Sometimes more is just more in the bazaars as long it points toward the capacity to compensate scarcity of different sorts.

Postcolonial Consumerism

Bazaar consumerism has had a marginal presence compared to elite consumer practices. From just a cursory look at the consumption history of modern India, we see that the movements that gained ground did not come from ordinary people but from elite sections who subsequently shaped consumer spaces. In the Indian case, modern consumer history is marked by two important events. The first landmark moment was the country's independence struggle including the boycott of products that weren't *swadeshi* (indigenous). Leela Fernandes (2006) observes that consumerism carried a specific meaning for freedom fighters, which set them apart from subsequent groups of Indian consumers:

> In the '60s and '70s, this whole bit of accumulation of wealth was still suffering from a Gandhian hangover. Even though there were many families who were wealthy all over India in the north and south, if you notice, all their lifestyles were very low-key. They were not exhibitionists or they were not into the whole consumer culture. Now I see that changed completely. . . . You want to spend on your lifestyle. You want your cell phone. You want your second holiday home, and earlier, as I said, people would feel a sense of guilt—that in a nation like this, a kind of vulgar exhibition of wealth is contradictory to Indian values. I think now consumerism has become an Indian value. (Fernandes 2006, 29)

In the post-independence era, after trade liberalization policies in the 1990s, the country welcomed global products in a big way. The "new middle class" of urban white-collar professionals were the main consumers of branded products. This demand prompted the arrival of the global consumerism of shopping malls, luxury automobiles, and gated communities. In Fernandes's (2009) work, she shows how the state took a back seat in urban areas and focused its energy on towns and villages instead. She attaches to the urban middle class a sense of agency that was unavailable to rural places as a result of resource constraints and other problems that made the state take the paternalistic position of the service provider to a greater degree. In such an analysis, the consumer patterns of rural areas are a by-product of state-led plans rather than having an autonomous existence.[14] Of course the question arises, within this bipartite separation, do we get an accurate picture of the urban non-elites? Do they not consume? Or do they consume global products in a completely different fashion? Although not the target group for most urban projects, popular classes are key consumer groups of cities. Especially with smartphone use, a new set of app-based desires is gaining ground in small towns and cities globally. In his research among popular consumers in Delhi, Srivastava (2014) describes how couples from less affluent neighborhoods went on dates in malls. One of the highlights of family gatherings is the experience of dining out with family and friends. In Srivastava's analysis, popular consumers today form part of new consumer spaces, particularly malls and shopping complexes in their neighborhood, even though they might not venture out for luxury. Or they might incorporate symbols of posh consumerism in suitable ways. For instance, an expensive meal might be out of reach for many people but not the experiences of going out, posing for photos and hanging out with friends. More and more, popular classes are complex urban consumers who maximize the use of digital media and resourcefulness to compensate for scarcity of one kind with an addition of something else. There is no one way of pointing out how this gets done, but going to the bazaars is an integral part of framing their subjective desires in a way that is closest to what their economic position and social awareness allow.

People buy things in the bazaars after seeing the latest trend on their Vigo videos and TikTok. They will be at shops showing images and videos to the traders and inquiring if any of the shops carry the T-shirt worn by such and such an actor. Of course, they aren't looking for the exact T-shirt but something along that line or a faint resemblance. In fact, most consumers would like it if the particular garment had a duplicate version in the marketplace. After all, these places are known to enhance a product, adding multiple features to an existing prototype and making it more attractive from the point of view of accumulating various visual stimuli. There is a crucial difference between how the elite and the popular classes consume that brings us back to the brands and brandedness debate. For the elites, brands are markers of "authenticity" and exclusivity for the super-rich. In contrast, for non-elites the world of brandedness is about owning nearly anything that resembles a brand and carries its vestiges. The flexibility of consumer choice brings a host of symbols, fabrics, and styles within the gambit of consumerism and hybridizes familiar characters with the idiosyncratic preferences of local consumers. A T-shirt in the bazaar can carry a Nike swoosh alongside the TikTok logo. The arbitrary placing of brands with anything trending at a given moment showcases a popular aesthetic of consumption, marked by a distinct mode of symbolic appropriation. Brandedness is as much about resembling official brands as creating a pastiche of different symbols that are relevant for the present. This is why garment brands combine social media logos and Ferrari symbols on the same garment. There is an overcompensation for material constraints by flooding the marketplace with "cheap and cheerful" garments and an overload of powerful symbols (Deka and Arvidsson 2021, 498). The rationale is, if a particular sign or sticker (as logos are known in Delhi's bazaars) is trending, there is no harm in putting a ton of them on a single garment. From the production point of view, it does not make much difference whether traders use Adobe Photoshop to edit a single logo or to put quite a few on a T-shirt. The backyard manufacturing units in the vicinity of many bazaars enable the production of small batches of garments with different aesthetic configurations. If anything, the commodity aesthetics of the bazaars rely on an excess of stimulus with minimal production cost. Just like the fast-moving videos on phones and memes of all kinds, bazaar consumerism churns out quick batches of eye-grabbing electronics and garments. In fact, a quick look at the journalistic pieces in the area show how TikTok was an aggregator of popular desires and sentiments (until it was banned in India in 2020). From couples dancing in the rain to makeup tutorials for everyday women, the gags and performances indicate what popular consumers find enticing. This space is not just about popular desires and explorations. It also increasingly finds itself antithetical to what middle-class aesthetics and politics see as acceptable, their presumption about morality and limits of civility. Instead, the unassumingness of working-class videos and their use of laboring bodies is a novel sight that is otherwise not taking center stage because of their invisibility in public space or not being sensitive to the bourgeois definition of privacy and taste (Nayanjyoti 2020).

With the ban on TikTok, Instagram's Reels is an alternative, and it is trying to occupy that space but not with the same degree of success (Y. Sharma 2021). The aesthetic of Instagram is already a world removed from popular lives. Its emphasis on high-quality videos alienates large sections of rural and urban poor people who do not record videos on a fast internet connection and expensive phones. Even after the TikTok ban, new types of trendsetters have found platforms. Local apps and Facebook videos are still favorite ways for popular consumers to appropriate trends. And bazaars mediate to produce usable versions of virtual trends to keep popular aesthetics a pulsating sphere in contemporary urbanism.

Bazaar Excess and Commons

> Nowadays, "every traveler knows that airports, highway systems,
> downtown skyscraper centers, and suburban sprawl look the same
> the world around."
> —*Mbembe 2004, 393*

By analyzing bazaar aesthetics as a representation of the lived experiences of the popular classes, one observes how the experiences in a city like Delhi are similar to other cities of the world, particularly in a postcolonial context. The above quote from Achille Mbembe describes Johannesburg through the orderliness of elite lives and the contrasting excess of ordinary living. Mbembe brings the everyday black experiences in the same city space alive through the notion of the "apartheid city." Also, Delhi has two kinds of excesses: one marked by newness, money, entitlements, gated neighborhoods, and residential associations, and another featuring a ton of waste, knockoffs, ruins, decadence, and street life. Mbembe describes how both types of excesses have a relationship with objects, although in different ways: "In an age when desire is inculcated even in those who have nothing to buy, the metropolis becomes the place where the superfluity of objects is converted into a value in and of itself" (Mbembe 2004, 405). Both kinds of excess share their relationship with exchange value, in an urge to accumulate goods and a desire to be a modern consumer. However, what crucially distinguishes capitalist surplus from ordinary excess is the relationship each has with public spaces, communal areas, and waste. Most middle-class and elite consumption in cities has destroyed old architecture to build a prototype of a neoliberal city. On the other side are lives that draw on the past by existing in places that are part of mid-century state projects. Delhi's bazaar actors take refuge in the modernist buildings and marketplaces, which have become too dated for elites in the new millennium. In place of cleanliness and order, there is now a more relaxed attitude.

These are the places that bazaars inhabit—the twentieth-century state architecture, and the street—where the excess is created not by the new but by the
expressive use of available public spaces. Akshaya Kumar (2014) brings out the
ease and dalliance of popular lives in a Bhojpuri cinema hall:

> While the slums are resettled outside the cities and public land is
> handed over for private enterprise, particularly big malls, the recon-
> figured Indian cities have left little space for lower-class inhabitants
> to find—not buy—leisure. Here, they could stretch themselves out,
> put their legs on the seat in front, eat gutkha (crushed betel-nut-based
> savoury substance) and spit everywhere, fiddle with their mobile
> phones at will and shout at the top of their voice, "Chalu karo!" ["Get
> on with it!"]. (Kumar 2014, 188)

With an irreverence and unawareness of the pulse of a new city, urban underclasses continue at their own rhythm and pace. It is like two different
frames of mind living in the same city. Elites rise above the street to create
their model places, following patterns of often homogenized global urbanism,
clean lines, and vertical living. The ground below is where diversity prevails.
On the road, there is a mixing of lifestyles, old and new architecture, and
bodily and commodity forms that are a bricolage of urbanism and not maps of
a particular dimension. The relative absence of hurdles in marketplaces such
as Palika Bazaar, Nehru Place, and Lajpat Rai allows vendors and traders to
expand their trade onto the street. This laxity is seen more in the use of public
spaces of popular use, which do not face the same expectation of cleanliness
and orderly inspection as would be the case in elite neighborhoods. There is
an understanding between state officials and ordinary people that this or that
trespassing would be tolerated based on an agreed understanding dependent
on mutual favors. The attitude toward product use is like the subversive use
of public spaces. No one particular style or form dominates, nor is there one
definition of newness. "One person's trash is another person's reality" rings
true in the bazaar. And the presence of products from brand-new to those in
various states of wear and tear does not necessarily indicate impoverishment
per se. There is a lot of agency attached to products of different types, although
they might be lacking in elite standards of beauty and use. To give a simple example, stolen or secondhand iPhones in the bazaars end up serving the varied
needs of buyers. For an elite consumer, that would never be a choice for moral

and quality reasons as it is expected that such a device would not provide the best experience. But the same phone for a bazaar buyer is quite useful. They can get past different checks and use the phone relatively free of other security locks. The same is the case with buying counterfeit goods instead of originals. A buyer might feel more at ease if not bogged down by the cost and care that an original product demands. And it can also be a matter of simple choice where the original aesthetic of a product is not attractive for some buyers, the visuals are not captivating enough, nor does the color scheme stand out to the buyer. In bazaars, such personal preferences get easily fixed. If a particular type of product is not suitable, then another set comes out. And what if the alternative is not at the moment in the shop? Even such a predicament is not a problem. Someone can get it from the next shop with an agreement to settle the financial gains at a later time.

The bazaar excess has a strong commons component by existing in places and among objects not defined by proprietary regimes, neither private nor legal. This is not to say that bazaar actors do not have a sense of personal property, but their general overview of the use of spaces and goods is not limited to just personal use of space. In other words, the stranger and the outsider, the ruins and the decadence, do not become an alarmist concern until such times as they become a pressing concern for survival. The lack of pressure to maintain a perfectly harmonious aesthetic and clean interiors creates a relaxed use of public spaces. And unrehearsed lives and livelihoods can be accommodated within a marketplace. A view of bazaar commons as an aesthetic project highlights ways of bringing into commerce non-proprietary urban resources: discarded and neglected modernist state architecture, the ruins and waste of elite consumption, marginal and diverse people that make cities their home.

2

Bazaar Pricing and Bargaining

Nobody wants to buy goods at the posted price.
—*Saurav, street vendor, Nehru Place*

A CONCERN FOR MOHIT, a trader in Lajpat Rai Market, is the rising number of consumers who despise spending money. According to him, they are the typical *ek ke sath ek free* type (buy one get one free), always looking for discounts and sales. Mohit almost gets the impression that consumers think all bazaar commodities are stolen. And the price that a trader charges is an indication of avarice and chicanery and not based on any rational calculation. A challenging task for Mohit is to make consumers realize that bazaar pricing is complex, and it goes through a whole set of negotiations.

A critical look at the trajectory of price makes apparent several variables, not all of which have to do with individual utility; social principles such as justice, sympathy, and a search for the "common good" are also factors (Hénaff 2002). For Aristotle, the social attributes of market actors and the utility of an object together form a just price.[1] And only at a certain point in history does the social aspect of the price get sidelined to almost entirely disappear in favor of the idea of individual utility maximization. The political changes in Europe during the Age of Enlightenment were a crucial juncture that disrupted interpersonal economic relationships and replaced them with an isolated calculative market actor. Markets for goods and labor markets were now increasingly

71

positioned as autonomous areas outside of social control.[2] Part of this process is a utilitarian understanding of value and price.

Karl Polanyi's (1944) seminal work *The Great Transformation* presented an alternative to this point of view, where price is embedded in a cultural and social context. His intervention brought back the notion that price has a subjective dimension. What started as a critical inquiry by the likes of Polanyi found further elaboration in the mid-century scholarship of economic sociology and later by the attempt of the new field of economic sociology to reinstate the social into the economic sphere.[3] This literature has been forceful in maintaining that price is part of other regimes of value or "worth" (Beckert and Aspers 2011). Rather than a superficial understanding of value, one can decipher the "worth of goods" through a thorough analysis of the lived worlds of the subjects that attach differential value to goods. It is now an accepted idea that price as monetary value is one element of the value regime of a product. Studies have shown for instance how the art market depends on galleries, the individual reputation of artists, and auction houses to determine the price of a painting. Similarly, in the oil market, environmental controls and international politics affect global prices. In informal marketplaces like bazaars, prices are equally contingent on many factors. Depending on the type of goods sold, and on distribution channels, prices differ. The following sections develop different aspects of bazaar price and how negotiations occur between buyer, seller, distributors, and importers.

The World of Bazaar Price

How is price organized in the bazaar economy? At first glance, the bazaar price is similar to that of other retail places. Despite that, buyers often take the posted price as a starting point to bargain and not as an indication of the final price. The general impression is that the posted price is only a talking point and has little to no connection with the selling price. One of the reasons why bazaar buyers hold this opinion is because they feel outside of the information loop. They have a sense that sellers are trying to cheat them and that to pay the posted price is to surrender to their whims. Indeed, even buyers in formal retail marketplaces do not have perfect information about products, but they can use tools that mitigate the risks of buying low-quality products. They can find advertising information, compare prices in retail brochures, and read reviews. In the bazaar economy, however, few of these mechanisms are available to the buyer. In the absence of strict adherence to posted prices, other considerations are relevant. Goods of a heterogeneous nature and consumers' lower reliance on posted price are reasons why the price-making mechanism in a bazaar economy has been called "irrational" and "bizarre." Information searches and processing are far more chaotic in the absence of formal channels of knowledge exchange. This can have to do with formal quality controls and recognized channels of goods acquisition, aspects that are not always present in the bazaars.

"In the bazaar, information is poor, scarce, maldistributed, inefficiently communicated, and intensely valued" (Geertz 1978, 29). Information asymmetry works more in favor of the seller than the buyer. Another fact creating uncertainty is the perception of bazaars as full of "cheats." "Chicanery" is an age-old stereotype about bazaar traders. Practices of selling adulterated products perpetuate a sense of distrust between buyers and sellers about the just price. Fanselow (1990) points out the inability of a bazaar economy to get over these uncertainties, and the reputation of cheating means that bazaar prices exist in muddy terrain. Even when both buyer and seller are operating in an economy of nonstandardized goods, the seller still has information about the quality of the product that the buyer is not privy to. In ways similar to what Akerlof (1970) described in the market for secondhand cars, the seller has an intimate understanding of the product, including production costs, raw materials, and supply chains. But such asymmetries cannot be so extreme as to prevent any rational exchange. "Akerlof showed that markets might not emerge if it is difficult to determine the underlying quality of the items traded while only one side of the market (typically the seller) has information about the items" (Aspers 2009, 111).

Geertz (1978) observed that in bazaars clientalization—the development of a persistent tie between a buyer and a seller—and bargaining practices create a level playing field. Here, relationships created by shared codes is crucial. A visible demonstration of consensus often occurs at the end of the market exchange. Out of lengthy bargaining emerges a price that both parties agree on. In their study of Javanese peasant markets, Alexander and Alexander (1987) point out that the dangers of flexible price setting are exaggerated. In their opinion, there are mechanisms, like shared cultural codes between buyers and sellers, that prevent bazaar price from being anarchistic. Traders are "linked by shared, common-sense, taken for granted understandings about how trade should be conducted and how it is conducted" (498–99). Bazaar economies feature an apparently flexible price-setting mechanism that sits atop more enduring ties of shared culture. Both the buyer and seller are aware of each other's restrictions. In Delhi's bazaars, buyers and sellers can assess to a large extent the financial constraints that other actors have in their everyday life. Each actor belonging to a specific economic class understands what the other sees as a necessity and a luxury. In the case of electronic products like video games, they are not a necessity at the same level as other household purchases such as food items. So, the seller in Delhi's bazaars is careful not to outrightly ask for very high prices for video games because at no point will the buyer see possession of them as an utmost necessity. Access to this type of knowledge establishes a price consensus by relating to each other's preferences and limitations of belonging to a similar cultural and economic universe (Beunza, Hardie, and Mackenzie 2006).

Bazaar Price and Cash Economies

One aspect that has to be taken into account while talking about bazaar prices is that most transactions are made in cash. Most traders and street vendors start their businesses with household capital, and one sees minimum intervention of formalized credit institutions either to invest in ongoing trade or to start businesses from the ground. Instead, pulling cash from savings and borrowing from family and kin networks is a way for bazaar actors to make up for their lack of financial assets. Another reason for dependence on cash is that it is mostly anonymous and untraceable once the transaction is over. Selling products without receipts keeps transactions discreet. Were bazaar traders to provide documentation of their business dealings, this would often mean revealing information about tax evasion, black market dealings, and semi-legal transactions (Fanselow 1990, 259). Mediation by formalized third parties like banks being minimal, the traders have to keep credit records by themselves. To keep track of every transaction, the traders scribble their daily or weekly acquisition of products on pages of notebooks. This calculation is often rudimentary. There are no double bookkeeping registers. A piece of paper torn from the back of a notebook is where day-to-day accounting happens. Pen-smudged handwriting, illegible at times, is how one records different financial transactions. "The absence of complex bookkeeping and long-run cost or budgetary accounting makes it difficult for either the buyer or the seller to calculate very exactly what, in any particular case, a 'reasonable price' is" (Geertz 1963, 32–33).

A method that bazaar traders use to not get overwhelmed with different calculations is to have immediate cash exchange for many deals and delayed credit arrangements in other contexts (Guyer 2004). It is the reliance on cash that enables bazaars to procure goods from different sources and also keep open registers of credit at least with a few market actors. "Cash circulates in the market in particular ways and through particular routes, taking on different context and meaning as well as changing in moral and physical texture as it rolls through different spheres of social connectivity" (Heslop 2016, 542). The period offered for payment does not work in the same fashion between different intermediaries and traders. In my experience, the wholesalers are lenient about extending credit to individual traders. Based on their previous experiences and ease of doing business, the wholesalers do not chase the trader on a day-to-day basis. The scene is different with a distributor who procures goods from big wholesalers and importers and sells them to individual traders. The credit arrangement between trader and distributor involves a small amount of money. He prefers to get his commission at the end of a day's business. The constant scrutiny puts pressure on traders, and they detest the evening hours when distributors do their daily rounds. Most of the time distributors accept the excuses traders give for why they are not able to make a payment that day. But there are days when distributors are impatient and make threats about giving the trader an extra day to pay these debts.

Such is the nature of cash dealings that it is not just about the exchange of money but also about managing a set of precarious relationships. In his ethnography in Sri Lanka, Heslop (2016) notices similar complexities of cash transactions in a busy vegetable marketplace in Dambulla where not only does cash circulate between different groups of people, but particular rituals follow such exchanges. Friendships developing under such situations cannot be at the risk of losing money. Heslop describes the predicament of the buyer Suranga in the Dambulla marketplace who has to be careful about not sending any wrong signal to any of his creditors. "Suranga, like other buyers I observed, visited many stalls and his exchanges within them were often jovial, but always short, perhaps to avoid the risk of cultivating a prolonged social contract which may facilitate the burden of future obligation" (542). It is like watching a dance to see traders and their creditors in action. Each one is trying to avoid sending the wrong signal to the other person that would jeopardize his business prospects. Sometimes the interactions were kept prompt, and on other days, the conversation moved quickly from commerce to personal matters; it was as if both actors knew the other's temperament for the day and behaved accordingly to not overcommit to anything.

Informal credit systems are not without their fair share of problems. The prolonged postponement of payment puts the trader's business at risk. During my fieldwork, one trader at Palika Bazaar lost his business because he was unable to pay back money even after an extended period of credit. The "*hawala* network," which is used to cover loose ends of trade—for instance, repayment of loans to creditors by third parties—further complicates the traders' dealings.[4,5] Borrowing and lending between a number of actors means that traders and street vendors were in a difficult situation if any of the arrangements did not go as planned. It is easy for traders to lose track of the money they borrowed from different people. More than confusion, one can also see such forgetting as intentional. The traders don't like to always remember how much money they owe to different people. There is an emphasis on keeping day-to-day trade afloat and worrying about big things later. When a particular trader at Palika Bazaar faced difficulties, comments were made that he was borrowing too much. The warnings did not dissuade the trader from carrying on his business as usual. He kept acquiring goods from local distributors. Moreover, to stay a competitive trader, he borrowed heavily from his overseas *hawala* agent to pay taxes for some imported products. Hence when the time came to pay back his lenders, he had to give up his shop as he had already overextended his whole network of credit. It was disheartening to see his friends in the marketplace worried that this particular trader would have to give up his spot, until someone passed along the news that he was okay and was doing home delivery now.

Notable among cash transactions is *hafta*, protection money. Some of these payments are made to local gangs, which was seen as extortion by many traders in Palika Bazaar. Yet as the evening sets in, traders passed a five hundred rupee note to the gang member who came to collect daily payments. Some other cash payments were made to secure a position in the marketplace. An example is the *hafta* paid to the constable in Nehru Place to protect them from frequent raids and removals. Of course, with the regular constable, things are settled quickly and the daily payments are just one more expense that the leader pays apart from *dehadi* (daily wages) to the vendors. Things become complicated when a familiar constable gets transferred to another place. How does one establish initial contact? By no means can the leader just approach a new constable and offer him a bribe. This can cause more trouble rather than help. What if the new constable plays by the book and the group leader gets a penalty for bribing a state agent? In one case, in the initial days that a new constable was posted, the body language of the street vendors was more tense than usual. They were alert to see where the new constable was located to avoid unnecessary contact with him. Things moved slowly. The leader tried to establish first contact with new officials through familiar channels. It was a fortunate moment when the leader found out that the new constable is from the same village as a vendor that sells clothes in Nehru Place. Instead of calling the constable on his own, he asked his friend to talk on his behalf. After the leader got the green light, only then did they exchange numbers and payment negotiations began. And once both parties settled on an amount, business went on as usual.

The Entry Price for Company Products

There is often more going on behind the scenes than is immediately visible when it comes to dissecting the universe of bazaar price. Goffman's (1959) metaphors "front stage" and "backstage" are one way to describe the pricing universe of bazaars. Price negotiation occurs behind the counter before the product goes on display. The front stage of the bargaining ritual between a buyer and seller happens only after negotiations between the seller, intermediaries, and the manufacturer. Despite the lack of familiar "market devices" (Callon, Millo, and Muniesa 2007; Cochoy 2007) such as reliable posted prices and institutional mechanisms to standardize information, bazaars have developed tools to cope with uncertainties and create a stable price system. Beneath the calculation is the underlying logic of the minimum price; the trader is unwilling to compromise on that. In other words, the minimum selling price of the product becomes the center against which further price negotiations occur. One important consideration is the price at which a product enters the marketplace. This set of calculations depends on the place of origin and how the product has reached the marketplace. Did the product come from a local manufacturer, a franchise, or is it imported? A further set of calculations depends on the human and nonhuman actors involved to get the manufactured product to the marketplace. The cost of transporting items from one marketplace to another is another expense that determines the price of a product.

In most shops in Delhi's electronic bazaars, a few unopened video game consoles are strategically placed in the shop. Usually, these items are inside glass cabinets at the eye level of buyers. Sometimes unopened consoles are at the front of the counter where they have maximum visibility. Branded products such as Sony PlayStation, Microsoft Xbox, and Nintendo Game Boy are not the most popular products in Delhi's bazaars. If it were up to the traders, they would like to sell many more of these original products. They face stiff competition from malls and franchises centrally located to attract middle-class consumers and the city's elite. A few original consoles target the unusual moneyed buyer who visits the marketplace to buy original games. Companies provide a 10 percent discount to the traders on branded products. The expectation is that if a consumer is buying an original product, they will pay the posted price. But this is not the case. Even with branded products, bazaar buyers like to get a good deal that they would probably not expect if they were buying in a shopping mall or a formal franchise shop. After all, the reputation of bazaars is such that no price is final until both parties have had their say. With a 10 percent margin, traders do not mind settling on a price a little lower than the posted price. The difficult part is to find that unique buyer who is ready to spend at least ₹ 5000 or more to buy a brand-new gaming console. The pricing calculus otherwise for company products is simple. With a reasonable profit margin, both parties settle on a price amicably, and not much energy is spent to establish the going price or to bargain to the last penny.

Price Setting for Secondhand Products

One type of goods that find a place in bazaars worldwide is secondhand products. Something old and unusable manages to secure a spot among desirable goods. Used electronics and household items are part of the product range in mass marketplaces. Selling secondhand connects bazaars to a unique consumer group that might not be welcome in elite consumer places as these places are hardly likely to have items in their shop windows and other areas of the shop in various stages of wear and tear. In bazaars, though, the scene is different. Secondhand DVDs, consoles, and games will be in the same cabinet as brand-new items. Beverly Lemire (1988, 23) writes about how the popular classes took to secondhand clothes and household products as early as pre-industrial England and among laboring classes in 1700. A motley bunch of "working people, from coal heavers to office clerks, from shopkeepers' wives to servants" started buying consumer products not as brand-new items but as something that had already had their run in affluent homes. Lemire makes an astute observation about how the purchase of secondhand products is intimately connected with the far-reaching impact of consumer goods in modern societies. Not everyone has the money to buy new products, but the desire for consumer goods runs across all social classes. The monetary gap is the reason why popular classes globally prefer secondhand products. Thrift shops and vintage goods have become attractive to middle-class consumers. But the quality and style that upscale vintage shops curate differs from the secondhand products sold in mass marketplaces. Lemire focused on the sale of shoddy goods and rags in eighteenth-century England. In twenty-first-century mass marketplaces, secondhand goods have a similar reputation of being of an inferior quality. The push to buy secondhand games, for instance, comes from the possibility of striking a good bargain and not having to spend a huge amount of money. In Delhi, buyers come to the bazaars to buy second-hand gaming consoles and DVDs of used games. The traders and street vendors use various tactics to make the secondhand products appear brand-new, whether by repackaging a game or putting new price tags on the games' cover. These measures do not necessarily lead the buyer to guess the original price of the product wrongly. The buyers of secondhand games are aware of the selling price of a brand-new DVD. The packaging does not fool an experienced buyer into thinking of a used game as brand-new. Such tricks can at most fool an inexperienced buyer.

Traders go to great lengths to create a web of "deceits" to target occasional buyers who do not have an estimation of the price of secondhand goods. In such situations what deceives the buyer is the new packaging with cellophane. There have been cases when an inexperienced buyer bought a secondhand DVD at the original price. The situation is different for experienced buyers. They have information about the release date of the new version of a game and its maximum retail price. With the DVDs as well, there is a clear idea among the regular buyers about the popularity of a specific franchise and how much time it will take to reach the marketplace. For instance, what impacts the price of a secondhand product is the possibility of having it in the first weeks of its release. The traders can ask for a heftier price for fresh secondhand products. The short time lapse advantages the trader as they know that most avid gamers do not have enough money to buy brand-new DVDs, but they definitely have an appetite for new games. In a week or two of a game's release, avid gamers reach bazaars like Palika to inquire about the prices of used DVDs. And in most cases, sellers cut a good deal and secondhand games quickly disappear from the shelf. The general assumption is that secondhand items would not sell for more than the price at which the product was sold brand-new. Therefore, the margin of price negotiation is between the amount that the trader spent to buy it from the first consumer and the amount at which he sold it to the second consumer. Depending on the results of the backstage negotiation to acquire a used console or DVD, the trader can offer a lucrative asking price to the next buyer. Even regarding secondhand goods, the ultimate price rests with the bargaining process. The trader would not go below the buying price of a secondhand DVD. He would try to make a profit of at least 5 to 10 percent. This is why it is essential to keep the buying price in mind, as no matter how much both parties are willing to bargain, the trader would not sell a product at a loss. There have been numerous instances where the trader has withdrawn from the bargaining process as the price offered by the buyer did not cover his expenses of getting the product.

Lara TV Game and Entry Price for Local Consoles

Another product that navigates a complex register of backstage pricing is locally manufactured games. The local versions of *Lara Croft* are a good example to investigate the backstage price of locally produced games. *Lara Croft* enjoys a cult status as one of the most popular franchises with a female protagonist in gaming history. The popularity has meant that a handful of knockoffs are available in the mass marketplaces. The counterfeited versions came in many forms: some tinkered with the gameplay, and others with packaging. A local manufacturer, Soroo, made copies that were doing a good business in Delhi's electronic bazaars. Primarily geared toward consumers in small towns and villages, TV games were a desirable alternative to console games.[6] The *Lara* TV game assembled by local manufacturers used imported parts from China. As one of the traders in the Lajpat Rai Market observed, it is only to save customs duty that Soroo does the final assembling in Delhi. Otherwise, the hardware is for the most part manufactured in China.

Nonetheless, locally manufactured products abide by a different price-making mechanism. Intermediaries such as distributors have a significant role in setting the asking price of a product. It is the distributors who come with new stocks of locally manufactured games. They visit different video game shops in the marketplaces and make a list of future orders. When the distributor comes to the shop, the traders often cannot resist the temptation of ordering a new product. They think that if they don't stock new products, they will lose a prospective consumer to the neighboring shop. In the end, the bazaar traders have comparable items. Even if new products enter the market-place, the novelty soon wears off as it does not take long for every other shop to display their newest items on the shelf.

During my fieldwork, I saw a few shops in Lajpat Rai Market featuring LED bulbs at the front of shelves formerly used to display game cartridges. The traders were confident that this was the item that would take the market by storm. Indeed, in a couple of weeks, most shops in the marketplace had at least one counter dedicated to various shapes and sizes of LED bulbs. The result was a price war of sorts. The trader has to compete with other shops to maintain a competitive price. The possibility of increasing the price is low as the chance of another trader selling the product at a nominal price is high.

On top of that, the profit margin for the locally manufactured game is low. This has to do with the fact that locally manufactured games do not carry the same reputation as the originals. Consumers are not willing to spend a considerable sum of money to buy counterfeited games. Most traders settle for a profit as low as 2 percent between their dealings with distributors and consumers. The rationale for settling for a small margin is to clear the stock in a short amount of time. Selling out the entire quantity is an ideal situation. In reality, the trader is often stuck with unsold inventory. At this point, the trader tries his best to return the unsold stock. As this arrangement is not beneficial for the distributor, he allows the trader some extra time to sell the leftover items. The negotiations continue until it reaches some resolution. Either the distributor agrees to take back the unsold items, or the trader moves the stock by passing it down to other distributors catering to neighborhood market-places. In the latter case, the trader is likely to go with an even lower profit margin. It is rare, but it can happen that the seller just manages to remove items without making any significant profit.

Imported Products and Intermediaries

Many video gaming products, including cartridge games, handheld con-soles, and accessories, come from China. Usually, there are two channels for acquiring imported goods. One is the direct import of stock from a trusted vendor in China. Another option is that a local trader travels to places such as Guangzhou in China and gets new supplies. In this instance, the trader could test new products and order relevant items for his shop. In both these transactions, custom duties form a central part in determining the cost of the product. Usually, when Chinese wholesalers courier items for specific traders in Delhi, the trader has to think about the parcel's size to avoid a high customs duty. There are measures that traders take to avoid paying customs duties in full. Lying about the product type or sending imported goods in different batches are some steps taken by bazaar traders.[7] Excluding the money spent on purchasing and delivering Chinese imports, the traders have a good profit margin to sell products to a direct consumer. The profit margin has become particularly lucrative for accessories of video games. Big companies do not invest as much money and research to make different accessories to suit the specific needs of individual gamers. The bazaars are a hot spot of unique accessories. Gamers come to the bazaars looking for personalized joysticks, adaptors for games, and also mouses. In theory, traders can quote any market price for these items knowing that not many other places will be selling them. However, an exorbitant price is not very likely because Chinese products have a reputation of having a "use and throw" quality to them. Indian consumers will spend only a certain amount to acquire a "Made in China" gaming accessory from the local marketplace (Corwin 2018).

In the case of individual importers bringing products to the marketplace, the traders depend on the specific importer to offer an initial price. Here, a crucial factor is the reputation of the importer—no importer can survive long in the marketplace by quoting an outrageous price. The traders also do their homework. They compare prices between different importers before agreeing to acquire goods from a particular dealer. They speak to their contacts in China to know more about the product that the importer is selling to them. Almost all traders have a reliable contact in China who gives them a realistic estimate of the selling price of a new product. The profit margins for goods acquired from importers are small, and the trader's strategy for these products is to sell a large amount at a low price. These are the products that become popular in the marketplace for a brief time primarily for their novelty and an affordable price tag. As in the case of locally manufactured consoles, the profit margin rests between ₹ 2 and ₹ 1 profit. Despite the stiff competition for imported goods, the traders gamble on the newness of the product to sell a large number of products in a short period of time to distributors for other retail outlets and to direct consumers.

Intermediaries such as distributors and importers are central to the price-setting mechanisms in urban bazaars. In his analysis of the grain market in Naya Bazaar in Delhi, Denis Vidal (2000) observes that it is the intermediaries that compare prices between different wholesalers and deliver grain to other distributors and shops in the region. Describing the daily scene of negotiations unfurling in Naya Bazaar, Vidal writes,

> Every morning, dozens of intermediaries will visit each trader in Naya Bazaar to enquire if they have some load of grain to be sold. After assessing the quality of the samples, they will enter discussion with the traders to sort out what can be reasonably expected from a given load of grain. Having made their first round of the traders, they will have a certain amount of grain samples and will renew contact with certain traders, either by telephoning them or by meeting them directly. This time their aim will be not only to assess the offer of the day but also to find in the market a demand which corresponds to it. (Vidal 2000, 136)

For Vidal, the intermediaries are the ones that navigate the marketplace, circulating supplies between different actors. These people loiter in the main marketplace to mediate price with buyers situated in other marketplaces in Delhi and also outside the city. Similarly, Mekhala Krishnamurthy (2012) argues that in the state wheat market in Madhya Pradesh, the intermediaries' role was significant in determining which farmer gets to use the weighing scales without showing receipts, the issuing of which took extra time. These prior "settings" advantage certain actors and cause delays and disappointments for many who did not get to use the weighing scale earlier. In a wholesale market, the role of intermediaries is crucial—they act as prime channels for the acquisition of goods and information. Also, much is left in the hands of the intermediaries to determine who gets to sell a new product first. If an importer does not have a good relationship with a particular trader, he can postpone supplying new products, making the trader lose out on peak periods of business. Delhi's Lajpat Rai Market, Palika Bazaar, and Nehru Place all function partially as wholesale markets although they engage with face-to-face customers daily. Each marketplace caters to distributors supplying other retail outlets in the city and also to other regions of the country and small towns. In this regard, they periodically act as wholesale marketplaces. This feature is not surprising—as Vidal (2000) also noticed with the grain market in Naya Bazaar, the hybrid quality has to do with the location of these marketplaces. Delhi being the capital city and an important node of commerce, it is unsurprising that many of its marketplaces have the capacity to satisfy different networks because manufacturing and import connections move through these marketplaces.

Bargaining and Market Price

The previous paragraphs have shown that backstage is where negotiations occur between sellers and other actors before the product reaches the final customer (Caliskan 2007). These negotiations provide traders with a fair idea of the margin of bargaining. As far as the lowest price is concerned, information asymmetry plays out in the trader's favor. Ultimately, he has reliable information about the money that changed hands to get the product into the marketplace. The knowledge about backstage negotiations gives the trader a sort of surety to call off the bargain at a particular point when he knows that it makes no sense for him to continue any further. Amid a heightened bargaining session, there have been instances when a trader calls off a deal at the very last minute. As a bystander, one expects that a product gets sold even though for a small margin. But often, the trader is not ready to negotiate for his lowest margin of profit. That is something always in the back of their minds, how low can they go, and often it can show a resilient side of bazaar actors as they appear to have confidence that the product can be sold at a more profitable margin some other day.

What about the maximum profit from a transaction? This is where bargaining is evident as a social system. In theory, the maximum market price can go as high as the ignorance level of a particular customer. Here rests the perennial paradox of bazaar commerce: information asymmetry and the difficulty of attaining a rational exchange. But that is only part of the story; bargaining is not a one-way street. The customer is part of the same social and cultural universe as that of the traders. The similarity of the economic and cultural background of bazaar traders and customers means that many of the tropes used for bargaining are familiar to both parties. What appears to be the turf of the traders is actually a social field and both parties are aware of the rules. About a peasant marketplace in Indonesia, Alexander and Alexander (1991) write, "The Javanese material suggests that these disadvantages [referring to delays in trade agreements] are not inherent in the bargaining process: where both participants have equal power to negotiate and are equally well informed, bargaining is quick, efficient and equitable means of agreeing on a price. Where one party is more powerful or better informed, the conventions of bargaining are maintained, but one party sets the price— which is very similar to a system of posted price" (507). The momentary advantage that one party enjoys (possessing privileged knowledge) can be reversed during the bargaining process.

The sociality of bargaining is what connects bazaar commerce worldwide. In fact, ethnographic accounts have shown that there are some stylistic similarities in bargaining codes across cultures. Bazaar bargaining opens with icebreakers (Orr 2007). Such niceties include sharing greetings with strangers and long chats with regular customers. With a regular customer, the seller does not immediately move to trade matters. "Participants, before even initiating the bargaining exchange, enter this bartering relationship with a mutual presupposition and expectation of social solidarity" (Chakrani 2007, 45). Regular customers are welcomed to the shops by their names. Traders and customers exchange pleasantries, inquire about each other's health and well-being. After a fair amount of time has passed, the traders initiate trade. In the Grand Bazaar in Istanbul, carpet sellers' "customary welcoming gesture" includes "a glass of tea" (Scalco 2019, 7). In Morocco, traders in peasant markets' exercise an "instinct of sociability" (Geertz, Geertz, and Rosen 1979, 222), most represented in the speech pattern of familiar greetings. Similarly, in the Middle East, bargaining is "initially open with a standardized expression of respect, affection, and common interest or concern. The seller welcomes the buyer into his shop, addressing him by kinship terms as a mark of respect or appreciation" (Khuri 1968, 701).

> Uncle Ji, you have not come to our shop for a very long time. I hope everything is well at home. How are your daughter and son? Oh, they have grown up so much [comment made in response to a photo on the screensaver of the customer's phone when he shows it to the trader]. Next time bring them along with you. (From field notes in Palika Bazaar)

Bargaining rituals have an inherently social character attached to them. Breaking down a particular bargaining exchange, one observes the intensity of communication is maximum at the beginning of the verbal exchange. Sometime later, the thematic price negotiations take place. After the final transaction, there is a more subdued social exchange of pleasantries before parting ways. In most anthropological accounts, while bargaining is a social act, the most enduring form of social interaction is still reserved for clients rather than strangers (Geertz 1978). The relationship with regular customers gets a specific word, such as *prateek* relationships in Haitian peasant markets (Belshaw 1965; Mintz 1960) and *suki* in the Philippines (Davis 1973). The endurance of these ties is a testament to the importance of these networks in market exchanges. When one establishes a cliental relationship, then the possibility to extend credit is higher. The seller has less fear that the buyer won't turn up at a later date. Bonds of trust develop. For the buyer's part, he feels more confident about the quality of a product bought from a well-acquainted vendor. None of these certainties is present when the exchange takes place between two strangers. As a result, the bargaining rituals are representative of fragile social bonds. Ahmed, a carpet seller in Istanbul Grand Bazaar, tells how on an adverse market day he might attempt to "trick" a foreign tourist:

> That carpet, for instance, is probably from Pakistan, but they are now doing it in similar patterns to look like it was made here [Ahmed had told the customer that the carpet was Kurdish in origin]. They have cheaper wool there and they do business with other places, such as India, for weave and dyes . . . not very good quality of course. But if I said this, the customer loses interest. That is why I prefer to tell certain customers that the carpet is of Kurdish origin, for example. If I don't say this to particular customers [especially Germans in Ahmed's opinion] they drop all interest. Other carpet sellers do the same. Even if the carpet comes from China, they will say it is Kurdish, just to close a deal. I have no other choice than to play the game, for I must make a sale for the sake of my family. My son, I believe, might have some of his health difficulties as Allah's punishment for the lies that I tell in this business. But I cannot do otherwise. (Scalco 2019, 7)

Time and again, bazaars have faced the reputation of being deceptive particularly in their dealings with foreign tourists. Information asymmetry is heightened in such instances and traders do their best to use the gaps in knowledge to their advantage. In a social exchange where each participant is interested in getting the other party excited about the prospect of a good deal, the social ties of bargaining often get shrouded in a "performance" of "lies." However, even when Ahmed employs "tricks" and "lies" to sell his carpet, he is aware of his role as a moral actor. A decision to take unfair advantage of a particular bargain is not an easy one. Later, traders contemplate their action. For them, it is important to strike a balance between the profit motive and saving social face. Somehow, profit for profit's sake does not sit well with traders and vendors. In Delhi's bazaars, the art of bargaining is not limited to getting the consumer interested in the product but also to have a just market exchange. The shared value system guides traders to minimize the profit margin of their products if they know their product is not of a superior quality. As such, bargaining with strangers, as with a client, is a complex process rather than a mere act of chicanery. In Ahmed's narrative, it is clear how much a bazaar trader thinks about his conduct. A deal is never just a deal. It is about making the exchange as fair as possible. The inability to do so may provide momentary material gains, but bazaar actors often feel such unfair deals lead to failings in other areas. Just like Ahmed, Delhi traders and street vendors connected their failings in transactions to incurring a moral loss at a later time. Such crisscrossing registers of ideal market behavior guide the bargaining process. The commons of shared codes of conduct and scarcity of money create a price order in an otherwise unruly environment.

Serial Number: Price and Reputation

Chintu, who sells pirated software and video games on the *patri* (pavements) in Nehru Place has a tough time keeping all his customers satisfied. He gets a bundle of DVDs/CDs every other morning from a supplier in Old Delhi. The supplier reaches his usual spot in the marketplace and different groups of street vendors collect their products based on their orders made the night before. Most DVDs are acquired for ₹ 10 and sold as high as ₹ 50. Selling it for ₹ 50 allows the vendors to pocket a ₹ 20 profit after deducting their cost for the DVD and other expenses. But there are a few hurdles along the way. Pirated DVDs are not easily installed on personal computers. Often, one needs a key to unlock a pirated DVD. It is the responsibility of the street vendor to assign keys to the customer. After the purchase, Chintu writes down the 25-digit key on paper and passes it to the customer. The chances of the key not working when the customer tries it at home are high. Even with the best of intentions, the key that Chintu provides can be corrupt. If that happens, a disgruntled customer will be back at Chintu's shop with his complaints: "What type of product have you sold me? You promised all sorts of things when you wanted the money. And then what happened, I tried the password so many times and yet it did not work. Give my money back."

Getting such complaints is one of the worst nightmares for Chintu. He tries different tactics for the blame to not directly fall on him. Chintu asks the person to show the password, and after seeing it, he feigns ignorance. He says he does not know how this number got to the customer as it was out of use for the last five years. All these excuses were made to somehow reduce the blow of being called a cheat. In reality, nobody in the marketplace can give a guarantee for a pirated product. Copies are made with inexpensive machines and quality is known to suffer from power shortages and slow internet connections. It is not that buyers who come to shop at the electronic bazaars are oblivious to pirated products' quality (Bandyopadhyay 2012). Yet, having bought a particular item, they expect it to run well at least for a certain period. For Chintu, the best situation is when the key works and the customer can download his game and software without trouble. If the key does not work, the next best alternative is that the customer does not bother to come back to the marketplace. The worst situation of all is when the customer is back in the bazaar and confronts Chintu for selling damaged products. When such accusations come up, he feels terrible about it. The possibility of humiliation on a later day is what prompts Chintu not to ask an exorbitant price for a pirated CD/DVD. At least by not having paid much money, the customer does not feel completely cheated. And, if Chintu has to provide a refund, he can do so without much difficulty.

Trust and reputation have a role in the bargaining process mainly by capping the price limit vendors quote on their products. This aspect comes out in conversation, particularly when they talk about foreign tourists with whom some of these moral restrictions are eased. The probability of running into the same foreign tourist twice is low. In Chintu's words, "I am not hesitant to quote ₹ 500 for an Adobe CD to a foreigner which I will sell for ₹ 100 to a local customer. I do not feel guilty; they pay in foreign currency. I think they have enough money to spend if they are tourists in other countries." The different standards used for bargaining with the foreign consumer and the local one is not unique to Delhi's bazaars. Touts at tourist destinations such as historical monuments are a well-documented source of profiteering (Chaudhary 2000). In recent years, cheating allegations have been reduced as has the opportunity to cheat. From previous experiences and word of mouth, tourists have become more astute. Chintu does not like when foreign tourists are accompanied by local guides. He knows that the chances of obtaining an unrealistic profit in the presence of a local guide is slim. Also, the guide does not hesitate to intervene in the bargaining process, putting the vendor in an awkward position. Not only does he call out the exorbitant price set by the vendor, he also says it is because of the behavior of people like him that the country gets a bad name, as if to make the vendor feel double remorse. As it stands, the discs of pirated games and software are priced reasonably unless vendors are selling certain DVDs used in architecture and other engineering courses whose market price is high. In that situation, even the buyer is willing to spend about ₹ 500 knowing the originals can go as high as ₹ 25,000.

A bazaar price for a pirated product rests on several considerations, the principal one being winning the customer's trust. As the pirated product can be damaged, the burden of the exchange rests on the trust between the seller and buyer. Even though the buyer knows that the product is not of superior quality, the knowledge that the seller won't give him the worst-quality product seals the deal. These considerations are relaxed when it has to do with an infrequent customer as the stress of dealing with that disgruntled customer is less. Even then it is not an uncomplicated matter as there are elements in the marketplace that make traders and street vendors feel evaluated as moral agents after any deal. This can be their peers, other people visiting the marketplace like the tourist guide, or the bazaar actors' own moral compass that puts sanctions on excessive price and profit.

"Indians Are by Nature Misers"

In many conversations, a definitive feature of Indian customers is seen to be their miserly nature. By "Indians," the traders are talking about the average buyer in the marketplace. Such a customer is engaged in the informal economy like them and lives in popular neighborhoods. They are from small towns and the suburbs with similar cultural beliefs and aspirations. This type of "Indian" is different from middle- and upper-class consumers. In the traders' perspective, an elite consumer does not have to worry about money while making a purchase.

Vinay, a street vendor in Nehru Place, visualizes an elite consumer as someone who does not hesitate to buy a smartphone case for ₹1000 from an upscale marketplace like Khan Market in Delhi. To spend so much money on something as trivial as a phone case baffles him because people in the bazaar cannot afford to obtain accessories at such a high price. They have other expenses to worry about. Further, what confounds Vinay is the lack of bargaining in affluent spaces. According to him, this is another indication of the abundance of money as bargaining is all about economizing. Not having anxieties about money is an opposite picture to the bazaar customer whose prime concern is money. Vinay sees being miserly as a by-product of having money concerns regularly. His logic is that if the chances of money flow getting interrupted are high, people are extra careful with expenditure.

To show the love for money, or the lack of it, Lalit from Palika Bazaar gives the example of a father who marries all three children on the same day.[8] In the context of India, where a wedding is one of the most expensive life events, when someone is trying to save money, the ways of doing so are quite visible. In a similar vein, to show the frugalness of an Indian consumer, Lalit talks about why repair work is so popular. People bring for repair handsets from "baba Adam ke jamane ka" (biblical time). If the back cover is missing from their handset and the dials are illegible, still, Lalit says, customers are not ready to invest a few thousand to get a new mobile handset. Instead, they keep visiting the marketplace for short-term fixes. The image of the *kanjus* or the stingy Indian is at the back of the traders' minds when they are entering into bargaining. The assumption that the Indian buyer is miserly prompts traders to be cautious not to quote a high price, as meeting such a standard is unrealistic. The traders know that the people who come to the marketplace want to buy a product at the lowest possible price. The collective knowledge of characteristic Indian buyers is an order-setting mechanism for bazaar price.

"Our Customers Are from the Slums and Popular Neighborhoods. They Do Not Have ₹ 5000 to Spend on Games"

Behind the assumption that Indian buyers are misers is a far more profound realization that the customers who come to these marketplaces are not the country's elites. According to the 2011–2012 India Human Development Survey (IHDS) jointly conducted by the National Council of Applied Economic Research (NCAER) and the University of Maryland, elites are the people who are likely to have five consumer durables in their household: a motor vehicle, a computer or laptop, a TV set, a cooler or an air conditioner, and a refrigerator. Ninety percent of the population is likely to have only one consumer item, in most cases a television set (Deka 2017). On being asked why there were so many cartridge games in the shop, Mohit from Lajpat Rai replied, "Our buyers live in small towns and don't own consoles. Many of them play TV games when the electricity is there and if not, they are active on battery-run hand-held games." Describing the average bazaar consumer, Rakesh, a video game shopkeeper in Lajpat Rai Market, remarks, "Bichaar ache hain par jeb me paise nahi" (Well-meaning people but with no money in their pockets). As popular consumers face a cash crunch in their everyday life, even simple things such as buying the first game for a child prompt discussion. A couple from Meerut, a town in Uttar Pradesh, visit Palika to buy their child his first game.

Father: Can you show us a good and sturdy game that will last at least a year? We want to give our 5-year-old son his first video game.

Ramesh: What exactly are you looking for? Sony PSP is a good model.

Father: I played arcade games at his age with a one-rupee coin. I do not want anything expensive—he will break it anyway.

Ramesh: If you do not want to spend much, I suggest you look at the PVP console. They are cheaper than PSPs. We have not been getting many complaints about the quality of the product.

Father: Okay, how much are they? (The father is examining the Made in China games Ramesh just laid out on the shop desk.)

Ramesh: ₹ 1000

Father: You said it is cheap—₹ 1000 is too much. Please give us a realistic price.

Ramesh: Only for you I am giving a considerable discount. I see that you have come from Meerut to shop here. And I want your son to enjoy his first video game. 700 is my last price.

Father: Okay, let's settle at 650. We have both had our say.

After becoming familiariz with strangers, the margin of profit is cut even lower. The traders are aware that the customer is not lying when they say they are short on money and that their budget for non-essential products such as video games is small. For self-employed individuals and those engaged in the informal economy, the household funds allocated to buy leisure products are less than the money allocated to essentials.

Just like the buyers, traders and street vendors make similar calculations on a daily basis. I have been part of conversations when particular traders did not want to spend money to buy a new computer at home. After understanding the trade-related benefits of having a computer at home, the trader loses some of his anxieties. Still, he does not buy a new computer; he settles for a cheap secondhand computer. To find the cheapest bargain comes from a spendthrift nature, but this is just half of the story—the real sense of precarity forces a lot of informal actors to be frugal with money. The fear that their situation may worsen from one day to the next encourages bazaar actors to reduce expenditure whenever possible. Many of them have faced a severe money crunch at some point in their life and, whatever it was, they don't want to return to that place even if it means they are unnecessarily cautious with expenditure. A street vendor spoke about when he did not have enough to eat, and the family was moving from place to place looking for work. Without any contacts and savings, it took a while for them to settle in the city after his mother got employment as a domestic worker with a South Delhi business family. Not having any state and other institutional actors helping them in their worst times makes bazaar actors more observant of their spending habits. They know if they face the worst, very few people will come to their aid. In such a situation, it is a good tactic to keep track of expenditures even if they can afford only occasional indulgences.

In fact, the traders and street vendors themselves realize how comical this aversion to spending can sometimes be. The jokes about the stingy consumer are also a commentary on bazaar actors' thrifty nature. Yet they hardly laugh at their own miserly nature, just that of consumers, whose spending habits directly affect traders' and street vendors' income. There is not an ideal bargaining logic to resolve different monetary considerations. The comparable economic position of the buyer and seller puts both actors in a realistic position to understand the place of video games in a list of household expenditures. Even if traders and street vendors get annoyed at the adamant nature of the consumers, they know where that urgency is coming from. Their consumers are in a situation similar to their own, as precarious actors who have to constantly consider today's income in light of tomorrow's struggles. And in all these calculations, often the immediate market transactions suffer unless there is a shrewd trader who knows how to earn a profit despite the odds piled against him.

"Half of the People Who Come Here Are Mad and the Other Half Foolish": Bazaar Bargain and Profit
Field notes: Palika Bazaar, May 28, 2013

It is a slow business day at Govind's shop at Palika Bazaar. I realize sales have not gone well for anybody at the store (for the trader selling toys and phone covers, and for Govind, who sells video games and ordinarily has a boisterous energy about him). We are making half-hearted conversations—sentences are left unfinished. Traders' eyes are on the entrance waiting for people to enter the shop. A thin man dressed in a worn-out shirt and a pair of trousers enters the shop. He asks Govind if he has a DVD of *Tomb Raider*. Govind takes the particular DVD out of the cabinet and quotes ₹ 500 for it. The exhausted-looking man is unhappy with the price. Govind does not attempt to persuade the buyer. He focuses on other things. After idling for some time, the man leaves the shop. On an average day, Govind will not let a consumer leave without engaging in a bargain. To have someone leave the shop on a slow business day is unusual. On the other hand, Govind has a game plan. His tactic changes when he learns that the man works at a gaming parlor. He guesses that this particular customer is desperate for the DVD to keep his regular clients happy. From his experience, Govind knows that gamers do not hesitate to change parlors if they do not find desirable games to play. Further, Govind has adequate knowledge of the stock of other traders in the marketplace. He knows the possibility of finding the same DVD in another shop is slim. Govind's copy of the DVD is a secondhand one and he acquired it from a gamer for ₹ 250 only a couple of days ago. The chance of the customer returning to the shop is good. The plan works accordingly. After approximately twenty minutes, he is back at the shop with a dejected look on his face. He pays ₹ 500 for the DVD. Govind smiles at me and says, "If I had offered to bargain when he first came in, he would pester me to bring the price down. After finding out on his own that only I had the DVD, he agreed on my price. It was an experience similar to throwing a boomerang—I threw it and it came back to me."

Geertz (1963, 33) describes the typical bazaar trader as having an "instinctive shrewdness in evaluating men and material on the basis of very little evidence." While in most anthropological accounts, the bazaar trader is but a figure of "quick wit" and "deceit," the shrewdness of the bazaar trader is dominant in certain encounters more than others. Such meetings display the commercial aspect of bazaar transactions. Nobody in the marketplace is there for charity. Market actors want to make a profit. The less energy spent in that direction, the better. Manoj from Lajpat Rai Market compared the bargaining ritual to a love affair—"You do not say I love you. You wait for the other person to say it." The logic is not very different from Govind's emphasis on the "boomerang" effect. The traders have a better chance of a good bargain if the customers voluntarily surrender to the offered price. Sometimes by withholding certain information or, in Govind's case, by creating a controlled environment, the trader tips the bargaining scale to his side. "Psychological warfare" is about assessing who submits first to the deal, and with years of experience traders have a few tricks to influence a buyer's decision.

At times, the advantage is the trader's extensive information about the marketplace. Through the everyday sociality of the bazaars, news travels fast. Without much effort, individual traders know when a new product reaches a rival's shop and at what price. Amid regular conversations, trade information slips. The shop assistant visiting another shop shares details of his owner's purchases. Or consumers who have visited other shops inadvertently pass information to the next shop. Govind likens the process of information absorption to a doctor knowing his medicines. On occasion he found himself processing information that he gathered from multiple sources. For instance, when Govind learns that one particular consumer is looking for a cricket game, previous transactions related to the same product flash before his eyes. During the bargaining, he remembers prior calculations—the original price of the DVD and at what price he bought it from a consumer and what will be a good selling price. A photographic memory of the transaction trail prevents the traders from making mistakes. It also keeps the trader one step ahead of the customer.

Bazaar price setting is complex. Despite the general assumption that bazaar is a "den of lies and rumour" (Chakrabarty 1991), to employ deceit is only one side of the equation. There are complicated negotiations that happen before the product leaves the shop. Further, there is a shared world of beliefs and common economic resources that guide price-related judgment. The lack of sophisticated market devices creates the impression that bazaars are irrational and unstable economic systems. But the calculus that bazaar traders follow is far from being irrational. The calculus responds to an economy of small profits and cash transactions. Both the trader and customer come from a universe where money is dear to both parties.

After taking into account the economic constraints and insecurities of the buyer, there is still room for sellers to find a nominal to a hefty profit. This is where the storytelling capacity of the bazaar vendor helps. Sometimes the conversations at the shop are so enticing that a chance visitor gets interested in a random product and decides to buy it. At other times, the jokes and tales about the idiosyncratic bazaar buyer also help traders to manage their expectations. They know where they can stretch the bargaining margin and where they should let go, putting their energy to good use. Narrating the charm of video games to the average buyer can shift the intention of even the most disinterested buyer to take an interest in a new product. Simultaneously, the chatter about buyers' annoying habits keeps the energy of the bazaars afloat.

Commerce and Storytelling

Stories are part of the bazaar economy as well of financial capitalism. To manage uncertainty, fiction and storytelling have long been used to articulate incalculable uncertainties into calculable risks. In Frank Knight's (1921) analysis, profits emerge from the ability to manage uncertainty. Writing at a time of entrepreneurial capitalism, Knight described how a considerable part of trade calculation took place at the level of individual actors. "Knight explained the firm on the basis of differential risk aversion between entrepreneur and worker. This interpretation rests on Knight's characterization of the firm as the system under which the confident and venture-some 'assume the risk' or 'insure' the doubtful and timid by guaranteeing the latter a specified income in return for an assignment of the actual results" (Langlois and Cosgel 1993, 457). This was when the "magical" quality of financial capitalists was central to the management of uncertainties, and opportunities followed the risk-takers in the business.

Today the possibility to transform uncertainty depends to a large extent on processing complex data. A lot of these calculations have moved from the control of charismatic financial players into the sphere of algorithms. In many ways, the world of algorithmic governance is one of storytelling. Capitalism operates through language (Marazzi 2008), and the process of making things calculable also happens through the maintenance of what Jens Beckert (2013) has defined as market "fictions." "Stories influence the confidence of investors that markets will develop in a certain direction and thereby influence investment decisions" (228). Briefly put, economic action (like all social action) unfolds in conditions of insecurity. Actors have no reliable means to know the future and cannot orient their actions to any goal. The dilemma is solved by narrating possible scenarios: fictional accounts such as corporate strategies or

expert predictions of stock market developments postulate a fictional future—
developed without a "serious" commitment to empirical facts. To the extent
that it is shared, this imagined future allows for a common definition of goals
and obstacles and makes possible the kinds of calculation that enable rational
action. Beckert thus shares Michel Callon's perspective on economic rationality as constructed by actors and their activities, not as a given fact. In his case,
it is built narratively through fictions.

The comprehensive perspective on fictions and fictional expectations
makes such fiction a feature of all kinds of economic activities. At a very abstract level, the same can be said for any social activity. Any investment of trust
in a business or a relationship is fictional in the sense that one cannot know,
as an empirical fact, what tomorrow will bring. In this sense, all social action
is fictitious, enacted through imagination, and socially constructed through
a collective vision of some kind (Berger and Luckmann 1966). However, there
is reason to believe that creating shared and "stable" fiction about the future,
particularly about the future of markets, has become a more critical ingredi-
ent to (successful) capitalist accumulation in the information economy. This is
because fictions allow for the coordination and calculation of economic activity outside of the boundaries of organizations. The most important example of
such capitalist fiction is brands. Brands are important because they are market
fictions that reach outside of organizations and contractual networks to incorporate actors who have no contractual relations to firms directly. There
are other ways in which collective stories help manage uncertainties. Such
possibilities include imagined narratives about health and progress to promote pharmaceuticals and stable political narratives to boost the stock and
derivatives market (Beckert 2013).

Bazaar Bargaining, Commons, and a Precarious Present

Both bazaar bargaining and capitalist fictions rely on "collective sentiment"
as a communicative tool to manage uncertainties. But where bazaar bargaining differs from capitalist calculus is the time frame within which economic
decisions get made. In the world of finance capitalism, most decisions about
profit accumulation are projections of the future. Financial capitalism works
with algorithms and sophisticated market devices to map the future onto possible investments, to take something social and use it in a fashion to profit a
handful. Instead, bazaar bargaining and storytelling are a common repertoire

of different actors. It is geared toward meeting day-to-day survival needs. Of course, bazaar traders are not fixated on the present as a sort of political radicalism. To the contrary, they have less choice in this matter. Because they are engrossed in a "precarious" (Standing 2011) present and absorbed in an economy of small profits, little capital and disposable assets are available to divert them to other lucrative investments. Most of the bazaar actors' energy is spent in securing the present.

Bhuvan from Nehru Place observes, "I want to earn as much every month that I can pay the rent for my shop. I also do not want to run into any trouble paying my children's tuition fees. My priority is to meet the requirements of the family." He estimates ₹ 30,000 to cover basic monthly expenses. Bhuvan makes monthly more than that through his business, but that did not give him the confidence to take it easy and not worry so much about money all the time.

Describing similar situations of precarity in the bazaars of Kazakhstan, Kyrgyzstan, and northern Pakistan, Hasan Karrar (2017) writes about how a simple question to the traders like how they were doing could not get an answer. They were at a loss of words as "the challenge is compounded by the fact that the sellers did not see themselves as being responsible for their inability to run a successful business. Their decline in fortune, or inability to run a business as effectively as they might have hoped, was never described as being a shortcoming on their part. Rather, the market had failed" (5).

There is a strong feeling that not much support is available for bazaars. And indeed, market actors are left to their devices. The failure is a systematic one as, in an ideal world, small-scale traders and vendors should have enough cushioning to try out new things and not feel insecure about the money they are bringing home. Instead, market actors are constantly worried about drying up income sources, scrolling on phones trying to identify this or another way in which, as marketers, they have been unable to optimize their reach. It is constantly getting worse. So the question is not about money exactly. It is about security. And no place does one feel the critical distinction between the two more than in an economy of small profits. If we count money alone, almost everybody is taking home a livable income, some even a pretty decent one that puts them in an economically affluent bracket. But money does not translate into stability. The liquidity these traders and vendors work with gives them the feeling that everything might disappear from one day to the next. This sensation is not, however, plain paranoia. It is invariably the result of working in a highly competitive place from the inside and extreme pressures of market change and policies from the outside. And not to forget, the market devices that capitalists have at their disposal to turn liquid assets into financial products are unavailable or, say, not available to the same degree as for bankers and investors. In fact, the closest that many bazaar actors come to turning money into capital is investment in a house, but that is still an old-style investment, and a lot of them see it as a minimum of decent living and not in any way making them an economic elite like successful entreprenuers.

One outcome of such a situation is the development of a risk-averse nature. Somewhere in between feeling hapless and stressed about money making, knowing that not everything is in the control of market actors, there develops a cautious self. Such tendencies are prevalent not just in contemporary marketplaces but have also been part of agrarian economies. In his book *The Moral Economy of Peasant: Rebellion and Subsistence in Southeast Asia,* James Scott connects peasants' small landholdings to a risk-averse nature. "Living close to the subsistence margin and subject to the vagaries of nature and the claims of the outsiders, the peasant household has little scope for profit maximization calculus of traditional neoclassical economics. Typically, the peasant cultivators seek to avoid the failure that will ruin him rather than attempting a big, but risky, killing" (Scott 1976, 4).

The bargaining rituals in the bazaar are symptomatic of a survival tendency where price calculus coincides with risk aversiveness. The financial emergencies of peasant subsistence economies and bazaar economies are not the same; resource constraints in the former took the shape of acute crises such as famines. However, both these types of economics use shared resources to improve their life chances. The way to confront structural inequalities can come from the communities themselves. There is of course no way to attribute the reliance on immediate networks to an altruistic nature. It is again more about aligning available resources to fill the gaps. In this regard, the people they meet, the conversations they have, and the relationships they build over the years are what precarious actors often seem to gravitate toward to get themselves out of slippery situations. Certain peasant economies, for instance, rely on specific communal resources that guarantee a survival income. Even at their worst crisis, the community comes to their aid. In the case of peasant economies, assistance was available through periodic distribution of communal lands based on who needs it more at a particular instance. The common land provided pre-capitalist agrarian economies with the much-needed leverage to face difficult situations.

On the other hand, bazaar actors employ common values and norms to their advantage. There are actually quite a lot of things available to market actors, as this chapter shows, things that market actors lean on to stabilize day-to-today market turmoil. For instance they rectify information asymmetry by heavily relying on gossip and storytelling. One way or another market actors manage to acquire the information they need; they activate their networks of kin, friends, and strangers to lay their hands on extra information that is valuable for price setting and striking a bargain. Similarly, traders and street vendors depend on the sociality of bazaar life to keep their trade innovative and cutting-edge for the contemporary buyer. The storytelling can never get so fantastical as to be entirely removed from everyday material concerns. After all, unlike capitalist fictions that depend on the datafication of desires to extract returns in the future, bazaars deal with real people and their emotions. Once in a while, one can take that flight of imagination and invest in an ambitious financial scheme, but largely the energy is concentrated on the present and the commons of storytelling guide everyday economic calculus.

3

Bazaar Tinkering, *Jugaad*, and Popular Knowledge

We are all mechanics here.
—*Sujit, street vendor, Nehru Place*

ON A HOT AUGUST afternoon in Nehru Place, Sujit, exhausted by the increasing heat and queries of passersby, tells me buyers expect not only to acquire products from the bazaars but also to gather information about them. "It seldom happens that when you buy a book, you also expect to get tuition on the book from the bookseller. But this is precisely what we do in the bazaar. Not only do we sell things but also we have to educate our buyers." Sujit points to an important side of bazaar knowledge, how it is not just about pricing and keen awareness of market behavior but also essentially about in-depth knowledge about the product. The allegory of the bookseller giving tuition is particularly striking in the Indian context as "tuition" colloquially refers to individual attention given to the student by private tutors and coaching centers above and beyond schooling hours. Tuition is not just generic lessons but can be tailor-made to suit specific requirements. This is what a street vendor like Sujit has to do. He may have to teach a buyer how to operate a computer one day and discuss gameplay with them another day. To different degrees, the knowledge that makes all markets work is not only about pricing (Preda 2009). Instead, information, knowledge, and skill sets are in the backdrop of the actual trans-action. This information relates to the basic knowledge or know-how about the product and the extent to which a product is amenable to repair and upgrades.

The possibility to experiment is how innovation—modification and up-grades of a product—creates unique sales opportunities in marketplaces. A considerable amount of literature has looked at innovation systems in market-places, including the management literature from the 1970s onwards that has explored how tacit knowledge in actors can be made explicit for the company's benefit. Gestalt psychology, team building, and brainstorming exercises are well-known methods of producing homegrown innovation centers within a firm and a corporation.[1,2] Outside the organized channels of innovation, local cultures of innovation in the bazaar economy have remained mostly invisible to mainstream economic life. Whenever there is an attempt to understand popular innovation systems, discourses have idealized such cultures to the extent that actual practices get decontextualized to produce a palatable ver-sion of social change and innovation.

For instance, in the Indian case, *jugaad*, meaning frugal innovation, has been a catchword that represents an alternative to large-scale capitalist pro-duction systems (Radjou, Prabhu, and Ahuja 2012). In such narratives the con-cept of "frugal innovation" is disassociated from the struggles of ordinary life. Instead, we are presented with an exotic version where innovative practices are presented as almost miraculous ways of using everyday objects, and there is an overemphasis on the ingenuity of individual innovators, rather than a focus on the social contexts where such frugal innovation takes place. As Manu Joseph (2018) points out, "The existence of 'jugaad' is evidence that the circumstances of a society are so bad that its smart people are doing, what smart people in other civilisations do not have to do." Despite the undeniable connection be-tween structural inequalities and the growth of quick fixes, one cannot com-pletely condemn the sphere of frugal innovation. It is undoubtedly one of the most industrious sources of income for many people, and the absence of such arrangements would push ordinary lives into further marginalization. Per-haps such quick fixes are more visible in electronic bazaars than in any other places. It is this connection that led Dertouzos (1997) to romanticize the pros-pect of bazaars turning into electronics paradises where hackers coexist with other creators experimenting with digital technologies. He saw the future of computers as resembling an Athenian flea market and rather than deal in or-dinary goods, traders would offer sophisticated information products.

The presence of divergent possibilities is what makes the field of bazaar tinkering complex. Whereas bazaars indeed carry a no-holds-barred experimental attitude, the practitioners also are from the marginalized section who are pushed to street-level improvising and in some cases risky enterprises of e-waste handling. This chapter contextualizes and discusses some of the optimistic narratives behind "frugal innovation" by investigating the style and methods that are deployed to create such "household fixes." It also questions the need for popular classes to fall back on familiar objects to create livelihood chances. At least in the Indian context, the spread of frugal innovation systems cannot be contextualized without alluding to institutional knowledge and infrastructure that tend to benefit certain sections of people more than others. The tussle between popular knowledge and formal knowledge is not just prominent in today's environment of the privatization of education; India has had a long tradition of elite knowledge that has excluded groups of people based mainly on divisions of the caste system. Perhaps a radical alternative to today's emphasis on formalized knowledge systems could be to envision broader forms of collaboration between popular knowledge systems and activist movements. Before we discuss that possibility, however, we look first at the empirical unfolding of street-level innovation through the practice of bazaar tinkering.

Bazaar-Style Tinkering

Like other commercial places, bazaars are innovative places. The thing that stands out with bazaar-level innovation is the informal infrastructure used to build innovative practices. In this regard, bazaar-level innovation is similar to innovation practices of street-level electronics marketplaces in Shenzhen and other informal marketplaces worldwide that have a distinct way of juxtaposing the useful with the unexpected. The fast fixes, often with easily replaceable parts, are what bazaar innovation is all about; this way tinkering practices evolve with consumer demands and, at the same time, with an eye on global trends.

Saif and his brother-in-law were known as *mistriis* or artisans. Throughout the day they engaged in "grooming," fixing and adjusting all types of handsets for people off the street. The transaction was fairly straightforward. Saif and his partner sat behind the counter and interacted with their customers, who stood on the pavement, sometimes inspecting the devices on display in their very mini showroom. The customers explained the fault and asked for a quick evaluation of the problem. The most common faults, Saif said, included water damage, connectivity problems, and screen or recharging faults, often caused by moisture. The moisture problem was usually solved by prying open the phone and dipping the motherboard in a bucket of chemicals which emitted an unpleasant odor that Saif kept next to his bare feet. A toothbrush was used to clean and dry the board before reassembly. (Doron 2012, 575–76)

The above description is of a street-level mobile repair shop in Lucknow. Popular innovation cultures represent a mix of community knowledge with everyday tools. The possibility of quick and cheap fixes is what has made bazaar-style tinkering unique in its approach to methods and tools. Mostly, street-level repair does not follow a textbook-style method to solve a problem. Rather, repair people learn from the problem in front of them, making use of easily available household objects such as toothbrushes, tweezers, and scissors.

In recent decades, a single word represents Shenzhen-style small factory setups and the techniques of popular innovation: *shanzhai*. The popularity of *shanzhai* innovation has to do with its origin in China, often known as the manufacturing hub of the world. As China provides ready-made parts and finished goods to retailers globally, it is also uniquely positioned to create an alternative economy of cheap copies inspired by the original prototype. The *shanzhai* phenomenon is comparable to bazaar tinkering, where a relative absence of proprietary rules frees the product from the limits of what is otherwise seen as doable and permissible. The Obama phone designed in the look of a classic Blackberry phone during 2008 elections, or the Chinese equivalent of the iPhone, the Hi-phone, were part of street-level innovation paradigms that depended on churning out eye-catching alternatives to expensive originals (Gao 2011; Lindtner 2014).

In recent years, quite a lot has been written about why China is drawn to a "copycat culture." Some have connected the growth of Chinese *shanzhai* cultures to traditional ideas, as the name itself suggests "mountain foothold" and refers to Robin Hood–style guerrilla tactics that challenge elite control (Keith et al. 2013). In fact, traditional Chinese ideas about intellectual property differ widely from Western ideas. In the West, morality tends to be transcendent in relation to the actors and their context. In China, as Jullien (2004) suggests, morality tends to be more embedded in the concrete situation, allowing actors to take decisions on a case-by-case basis. Julien suggests that this is visible in traditional military techniques and in the writings of Chinese philosophers like Laozi and Mengzi. Such moral traditions are, however, not the only factor behind the *shanzhai* phenomenon. Scholars like Bai Gao and Miao Lu have also emphasized the role of distributive networks and the ability to connect the urban market to rural consumers.

The ingenuity of Chinese traders to discover new trade networks is something even local traders notice. Govind, a trader in Palika Bazaar, alludes to the capacity of Chinese goods to address the demands of different consumers. If there is a problem, according to Govind, Chinese traders will know how to solve it. He gives the example of the *Samurai* video games that arrived in the 1980s for approximately 100 USD. It was at that time a luxury product, and only a section of Indian consumers could afford it. Come 2000, Govind says, *Samurai* TV games are everywhere in the market. A *Samurai* game that sold for 100 USD is now available for 5 USD. Govind says China immediately grasped the pulse of the Indian market. What they saw in the Indian mass market was the demand for cheap video games. Accordingly, they tweaked the product to create cheap versions of it. An inexpensive model substituted the sturdy consoles of earlier *Samurai* games. *Halka* (flimsy) chips replaced the quality chips of earlier machines. In fact, Govind is quick to point out that the Chinese economy can satisfy consumers of varying demands because of the possibility of producing different grades of products. High-quality goods would go to a specific type of consumer, and the cheap products get sent to bazaars globally.

Similar forms of adaptability are also prevalent in the case of Chinese phone producers who adopt a rural market–oriented distribution and marketing approach in their domestic and overseas expansion. As a latecomer to the global information communication technology (ICT) industry, China has already developed a unique approach to meet the requirements of the home country and other third world importing countries by relying on informal traders such as bazaar vendors to bring raw materials and finished products from one context to another. The term *shanzhai* also gives homage to the Chinese tradition that helped the country develop into a manufacturing giant meeting the demands of different market niches. As previously mentioned, there is an understanding of a different sense of morality that does not make copies such a dilemma in China, as there is a collective logic to creative pursuits (Thomas 2012). Whether or not it's a moralistic concern, the push toward collective creativity is a part of needs-based economic systems. So engrossed are actors in meeting survival requirements that they do not want to be embroiled in interpersonal litigation arising from property disputes. They would instead use the collective skill set to provide income sources. The situation is a bit different in India, where traditional morality may not push it to become more communitarian or altruistic when organizing labour. Still, economic circumstances might make it more viable to work together with people than isolate oneself.

While street-level innovation systems share many similarities, there is a crucial difference between, say, bazaar-level innovation and the Chinese *shanzhai* model. Most innovations in Delhi's bazaars are about acts of tinkering— repairing broken parts, modifying electronic systems to perform extra functions, and recycling old consoles. Bazaars do not entirely invent a new object from scratch. Analyzing the repair world in Namibia, Jackson, Pompe, and Krieshok (2012) note that tinkering has mostly to do with reuse and recycling and less to do with the purchase of new replacement components. Another attribute is that tinkers often work solo with the help of a few apprentices and the costs are minimal to make it more viable than buying it from somewhere else.[3]

As a result of what is considered a lack of training and sophistication, popular innovation faces marginalization. Areas of concern are whether products are mere copies or instead show signs of originality. Judged on quality and sophistication, street-level innovations often fall short of these standards. But tinkering in popular settings is much more complex and exists in multiple ways. Even though innovations in the bazaars do not always go from concept to execution and are more about working with the hardware of finished products, bazaar tinkering is a vibrant and creative process.

Depending on the product sold, each marketplace has its way of building and sustaining tinkering practices that attract specific consumer types. To give an example from my ethnography, each marketplace has its niche. Street vendors in Nehru Place not only sell software and games but also tinker with the installation of pirated CDs and DVDs on customers' computers. Street vendors there deal with DVDs/CDs more than with consoles; that's where the maximum repair and tinkering happens. Of course, sometimes people also come to Nehru Place with damaged consoles, and vendors are likely to bring them to experienced traders in the marketplace or refer them to traders in Palika Bazaar, for instance. In Palika Bazaar, tinkering with consoles and accessories happens at the level of cracking old consoles and of reimagining a product for an emerging consumer base. In terms of repair and recycling, Palika is at the forefront of working with old consoles and reviving them, fixing the wear and tear of gadgets, and often modifying old consoles to play pirated games. Among the three marketplaces, the Lajpat Rai Market has come up with the maximum innovation, especially reimagining an old product (see Figure 3.1). Traders have successfully brought out new products with small changes undertaken in the shops like adding a feature to an old game to make it more attractive for a present buyer. Such innovation occurs mostly with TV games. Lajpat Rai has been good at bringing together available resources to create different assemblages of TV games that cater to arcades and households in popular neighborhoods. First it was attaching TV games to a console made from wood with a joystick added, bringing the experience of playing arcade games at home. Now traders have even started plugging PlayStation into a bigger TV monitor, and there is a demand for such gadgets for individual homes.

Cracked DVDs and Software

Street vendors at Nehru Place sell pirated DVDs/CDs of software and computer games. When consumers make specific demands, the vendors also install programs on personal computers. The installation can be a complicated affair. The pirated DVDs come with a separate folder, which the customer has to download onto their computer opened by a serial number. The street vendors write the serial number, or *keygen*, on a small piece of paper that they pass to the consumer. Most of the time, the vendors know the 25-digit password by heart, and their job is to pass that information to the consumer buying a pirated item. This is the scene with college students who have a basic knowledge of computers but do not have the money to buy brand-new games and software of different kinds. In fact, some of them are proficient with technology and they give street vendors important information about new software that is in demand. But some consumers do not have any experience of working with a computer. These consumers buy assembled laptops from one of the shops in the marketplace. Their next move is to visit various counters in the marketplace looking for accessories that they can install on their laptops. These types of consumers are the ones with whom street vendors have to spend maximum time and energy. After all, the street vendors are not looking to make a sale only with experienced buyers but also with the more challenging ones. Novice consumers test the street vendors in different ways. Sometimes they may not even know how to switch on a computer. For consumers who don't know the English language, the street vendors have to teach them how to operate

Figure 3.1. A locally assembled wooden PlayStation console in Lajpat Rai Market (author's image).

a laptop by using signs and icons. Often these inexperienced users also come back to the street vendors when they face problems operating the system at home. It takes a lot of patience for street vendors to entertain the different types of customers without appearing irritated and annoyed.

If the method of installing applications is relatively simple, complications can arise from the fact the pirated products require different installation procedures on Windows and iOS operating systems. Such processes become more challenging as most street vendors do not have any technical background. Before joining the marketplace, many of them had not seen a computer in their life. Deciding to work on a machine means that the vendor has to learn how to operate it first. Even when they are not completely ready for the job, street vendors do not like to turn away any customer. They accept any repair work even if they do not have much clue about it. It has happened that street vendors have agreed to work on an expensive computer they have not seen before. Then begins a desperate attempt at solving a puzzle by first using the tried and tested methods and, if the familiar methods fail, taking it to a senior repair person. A street vendor in Nehru Place, Jay, points out, "It is not easy to install pirated software and games. It depends on the computer, its configuration, and the security system. Based on that, the installation process can run into many problems. Sometimes, even the disc can be corrupt and as a result, a bug can get transferred into the customer's laptop. If that happens, we have a unique problem at hand. We not only failed to repair the computer but made it worse by spreading a virus." When malware enters a client's computer, and the street vendor does not know how to fix it, he brings it to a more experienced technician. The street vendors try to learn how the senior repair person fixes the problem. The senior repair person knows that the young street vendors want to pick up his trade secrets and is reluctant to share all his secrets from the start. He makes the process of understanding the nitty-gritty of repair difficult—experienced traders place their hands at a particular angle to hide what they are doing. Or they work very quickly, making it difficult for the street vendors to follow each stage of repair.

The street vendors are looking for an arrangement where they do not share profit with anybody else. If the installation is uncomplicated, they proceed independently and get the entire sum from the consumer. If it is complicated, they approach an experienced person in the marketplace and share the profit. However, the aim of most novices is to develop a skill set allowing them to fix most problems on their own. With this objective, the street vendors are observant about the repair skills of a senior technician. Whatever knowledge they don't get that way, they acquire by watching YouTube videos on similar repair work. With cheap smartphones, in their free time they can look up videos and read comments to understand where they made mistakes before. Usually, after some effort, the street vendors gain a good understanding of basic technical issues and develop into skilled repair persons. They remember the names of the different software and games and what type of security they have to bypass to install a pirated version of games. They learn how to fix broken computers and undertake minor repairs. On top of technical knowledge is a keen awareness of gameplay. Street vendors know the changes in graphics and plot of a particular franchise, and what local cheats have been introduced by hackers. They build an ecosystem of tinkering by familiarizing themselves with unknown technology through available channels of the human and technological assemblage.

Modding and Reballing of Consoles

Both Lajpat Rai Market and Palika Bazaar have repair persons who "mod" old consoles to play new games. Parts of such modding require software hacks that not many repair persons at the marketplace are good at, but there are experienced technicians in the marketplace who know how to hack the security systems of different consoles. Most of the tinkering is with the motherboard of a console. The desks of repair people have at least one disassembled motherboard of a gaming console that they fix during the day. Some of these repairs can be simple like replacing the damaged lens of a console or changing a damaged part. Or it can be more industrious repair where one uses a reballing machine to solder individual units on the motherboard.[4] Behind any repair work is knowledge about the gaming economy. Such knowledge includes the release dates of new consoles and the latest version of popular games. During my fieldwork in 2013, Sony released PlayStation 4. Ongoing conversations among traders, repair persons, and consumers are about the new system's upgrades. Lalit from Palika Bazaar is particularly concerned about whether Sony will have stricter security controls to prohibit the jailbreaking, or removal of software restrictions, of PlayStation 4. "I think hackers would have no chance to meddle with the software of the new console." His assessment came at a time when earlier devices, and Sony devices in particular, were relatively easy to crack as they used a hard drive that lent itself to being hacked, unlike the Xbox console that instead relied on a CD-ROM. Lalit thinks with their latest release, the strategy of the company will be to tighten the security system to such an extent that only Sony can profit from the console. Another trader at the shop has a different view. He is of the opinion that rather than tightening security, in the long run, a company like Sony also benefits from jailbreaks. "It's also to the benefit of the company to keep the security system a little lax so that indirectly it piques diverse consumers' interest in the product. If only Sony-operated systems were available, games will be only part of select households. It is only because of cracked consoles that many more people know about PlayStation and Xbox." Lalit agrees with his friend's analysis that the wide circulation of products to new sets of consumers benefits big companies even if it is through unauthorized channels.

As the release date of the console draws close, the conversation around PlayStation 4 becomes more animated. Traders do not want to lose out on sales because for some reason they are unable to understand the details of a new console. About two weeks after the release of the console, Lalit tells me, "I have seen reviews and read about the changes made to the system. As I predicted, it does not look hackable." There is a fear of losing out on an entire cohort of gamers who, until PlayStation 3, stuck with the marketplace. Cracked consoles provide a unique lifeline to the electronic bazaars as nowhere else will it be easier to modify consoles at an affordable price. With PlayStation 4, the bazaars face the eventuality of losing out on customers who want to upgrade their old consoles. As days go by, the conversation around the new console gets more specific; Lalit discusses with a consumer, an engineering student, the BIOS (basic input/output system) of the new console. Both have already looked at hacking websites like deviwiki.com to understand possible ways to hack the new console. They speak about a certain Russian hacker who provided a link, only to promptly remove it from the website. At least that is a sign that a fix exists, and it is only a matter of time before the information reaches the marketplace. Not having advanced machines, Lalit thinks the hacks that work best in the bazaars are the ones that require less effort. That is why it takes time for a hack to arrive in the local marketplace: it has to be in a form for traders and vendors to easily access the new technology. Meanwhile, traders activate their networks to gain as much information about the new console as possible. Their ears are to the ground, to pick up any bits of information from consumers and intermittently check their phones for updates on the latest console. Some of them also reach out to their allies in other marketplaces to see if they have any new information. In the case of PlayStation 4, all these exchanges do not bear much fruit. In the end, the solution that works for the marketplace comes from China. Chinese manufacturers find a way to install the hack on a pen drive that is on its way to Delhi's marketplaces. Many traders placed orders for pen drives. I find Lalit, for instance, intermittently checking his phone to see when the consignment gets delivered to the marketplace. With such a ready-made solution, PlayStation 4 soon falls out of the conversation. It gets replaced by something else. Some traders now showed interest in a "reballing" machine to capture the market of damaged motherboards.

The modding console scene in Delhi is similar to the scene in other parts of the Global South. There is an emphasis on working on the hardware of consoles. Even when software-related changes are made, they are easy fixes and small changes to the gameplay that makes a particular franchise more suited to the local context. For instance, personal computer (PC) game repair in Brazil does not involve coding. Instead, graphical user interface (GUI) software like in-game editors or other tools get used for customization. Such repairs are tweaks that can make a substantial change to the gaming experience like the addition of one feature or another rather than changing the sound or video graphic in total. "Thus, it is safe to say this type of modding is more inclusive and has the potential to reach broader audiences with no previous contact with the inner workings of computers, algorithms or any kind of procedural logic" (Messias 2020). In the case of Brazilian game repair, tweaks are about making games more familiar by including nonplayer characters in *World of Warfare* and changing the gameplay from English to Portuguese. Sometimes the gameplay might not even change but just a small change to the packaging makes the game more relatable. Indeed, it is the bazaars and similar places that add a local flavor to the globally successful games that come from North America, Europe, and Japan. Street vendors and traders will advertise the local tweaks that they have added to new games, for instance, the inclusion of more thrills and cheats that gamers can use to surpass difficult stages of a video game. Bazaar-level tinkering reveals "current ways of getting access and recovering what Negri and Hardt called the common (shared) aspect of the world," Messias (2020) observes, "not as a line of division between workers and the poor nationally or globally but as hierarchies within the common condition of poverty." There is no doubt that tinkering has a class and geographical angle to it. Especially with video games, the original consoles, gameplay, and design are from the Global North (Dyer-Witheford and de Peuter 2009) and what is left for the Global South is mostly to modify games to make them relatable to a unique consumer. Such tinkering cannot be just a sign of a "common condition of poverty"; it also indicates the possibility of the multitude to be virtuoso (Virno 2004), of course under restrictions but not without imagination. Tinkering with video games is a testament to the spirit of local innovation, showing that despite sophisticated technology and foreign languages, none of these are permanent barriers to modifying media products to suit the needs of individual users.

Recycling and Reuse

A predominant way in which Delhi's bazaars have managed to remain competitive is by reinventing each new product. Once a product reaches the marketplace, it is not only part of retail trade but becomes a sort of raw material for future repair work. The possibility to recycle the hardware of a console provides an advantage to Delhi's bazaars in meeting specific consumer demands. Recycling has to do with refurbishing old consoles and selling secondhand items on the marketplace.[5] In order to refurbish old consoles, traders keep an eye out for customers who want to sell their old consoles at a reasonable price. They keep abreast of the purchasing patterns of the other electronic marketplaces to see what new and old items these marketplaces are hoarding in their shops. Old and used parts help traders replace missing parts during a repair, bringing the so-called zombie-media into circulation. Traders and street vendors have many ways to identify a useful object. One such possibility is through the shop assistants who go from one marketplace to another running errands. Through the information gathered by shop assistants, traders get to know the products of other marketplaces. Sometimes, shop assistants also bring information about machines and parts that are useful for repair purposes. When this happens, the shop assistant goes back to the marketplace to barter for the required parts in exchange for something else. Conversations on the phone between the two traders help each party to find something mutually beneficial. Even if one cannot immediately find exact parts to offer in barter, there is an understanding that in the future when the occasion arises, the trader can redeem his favor. Once an agreement is reached, the shop assistant brings with him a console or parts of a machine from the other trader to the main marketplace. An interconnected network of traders and media objects assist tinkering. In the absence of ready-made parts, the possibility to find tools and parts from a wide net of new and used objects keeps bazaars afloat.

The other major recycling enterprise in the marketplaces has to do with secondhand games. Playing brand new games is uncommon among lower-middle-class consumers and urban poor. Outside of a few hardcore and elite gamers who have money and resources to spend on each game, most consumers are looking for cheap alternatives. The income disparity between urban groups creates a unique opportunity for the bazaars to rope in a wide range of gamers who want to play the latest games with a minimum delay since their release date. The traders in the Lajpat Rai Market and Palika Bazaar know a range of fixes to increase the demand for secondhand games. Some of these tactics involve cosmetic tinkering. Changing how the product looks or feels is one way the traders keep the customers guessing whether what is being sold is secondhand or brand-new as the traders are claiming. A regular client is aware that bazaars will have secondhand games within weeks of their release. It is difficult to fool a regular customer with these tricks of presenting them as new. He knows that even if only a few weeks have passed since the game was released, bazaar networks are strong enough to have secondhand games in their stock. But not all customers are as experienced. They may buy into the bazaar shenanigans. To disguise a used game as new, the traders wrap it with cellophane and tape the edges carefully to hide any wear and tear. Sometimes traders put new price tags on secondhand games. In such cases, traders regularly say, "yeh item toh piche se hi aise aaya hain" (this product came to us in the exact state). Such tactics work as inexperienced consumers cannot know exactly how a particular DVD reaches the marketplace. Traders also do not do much to help consumers with any extra information. In fact, they try to be as obscure as possible about where a game came from.

As far as cosmetic tinkering is concerned, it is not limited to games alone; it also includes the repair of gaming consoles. When consumers drop off their damaged consoles, the traders know that if they can show that it has been a complicated repair, the possibility of earning a high sum of money increases. Customers are more likely to pay for a complicated repair than just a trivial fix. When they come to pick up their consoles, customers want to know exactly what was wrong with their console and how it got fixed. At this point, if the trader says it was just about switching off the console and cleaning the motherboard, it is difficult to quote a hefty sum. One tactic that traders discovered is to show that they failed to repair the console independently. Instead, they had to send it to the official repair center to revive the console. Showing that the repair was so demanding that they needed help from a qualified technician opens the door to quote a high price. In reality, a company like Sony does not accept repair items from bazaar traders. Companies are more likely to deal with direct consumers or go through their official repair centers. In order for traders to simulate a possible official repair, they tamper with the barcode of consoles. By doing so, traders make it difficult to trace the product to a particular point of origin and consumers cannot easily contest traders' claims of such and such repair. Even if they try to take the console back to an official repair center, with a damaged code, it is unlikely that different transactions would be easily traceable. Such cosmetic tinkering creates income opportunities for traders in places that otherwise does not exist.

Tinkering with hardware and packaging or barcodes are all parts of the process of imagining new business opportunities in a gaming economy that is saturated by mobile phone gamers, official franchises, corporations, and online stores. In such a situation, the tweaks and modifications bring unique opportunities for bazaars to tap into the peculiar needs of ordinary gamers. Sometimes even the gamers do not realize that a specific tweak might be handy until they find it in the bazaars, like the time when Delhi's electronic bazaars started selling hard drives loaded with pirated games. Until then, gamers came to buy individual pirated DVDs. With the hard drive, they could get more games for a reasonable price. Also, for the traders this was a good business opportunity. It needed much less convincing for gamers to spend a certain amount to buy a number of games than a single one. There are several instances of tinkering that show the ingenuity of bazaar traders and street vendors. In some of them, technical knowledge and hard work are paramount. In other cases what counts is the capacity of bazaar actors to improve consumer experiences with minimal efforts and simple tweaks.

Mechanic

On any market day, alongside commodity exchange, some repair work or other is happening in the three marketplaces. As shown in the previous sections, repair work demands a particular skill set based on the complexity of a problem. By no means should such practices of tinkering be labeled inefficient and uncreative. But this is how traders and street vendors see their profession. One of the ways the traders speak about their own technical skills is with the term "mechanic." Traders refer to the term in a negative way. In their vocabulary, mechanics are inferior to engineers who have sophisticated knowledge and formal qualifications from recognized educational institutions. Lacking institutional knowledge, mechanics go for a trial-and-error method, literally, as their work is mostly experimental in nature, waiting for one of their efforts to bear fruit. The traders feel that qualified engineers and technologists have a much more systematic approach to a problem. Instead, many of the traders have learned things on the job. Simple things like not growing up with a computer at home have delayed the process of knowing information products firsthand. To make up for lost time, traders and street vendors use "shortcuts," which in their opinion do not carry the flair of a trained professional. Even street vendors use the word "mechanics" in a derogatory fashion to talk about the low status of their work. Sujit, a street vendor, says, "Jo software ka kam karta hain, usne kuch nahi sikha" (The one who does software work has not learned anything [here software alludes to selling pirated discs]).

Despite their knowing so many things about computers, a nihilistic attitude is visible among bazaar actors regarding their work. It is easy for traders and street vendors to dismiss what they do as useless as they have seen very few glorified accounts of their labor. A part of the disappointment comes from their immediate surroundings and the lack of a role model to analyze their performance positively. In a postcolonial context, attractive knowledge is the product of elite institutions and colleges. There is hardly any space to think progressively about informal learning. The post-secondary school courses at Industrial Training Institutes (ITIs) are ideally designed to provide vocational training to a large section of young people. But ITIs have not managed to emerge out of the shadows of the elite Indian Institutes of Technology (IITs). Those who graduate from ITIs are seen as "left outs," those who could not make it to other professional courses because of a lack of talent or economic resources, or both. The available ecosystem of technical knowledge systems does not provide any positive identities around technology apart from the figure of the engineer. The association of status with higher qualification is perhaps why the engineers are the dominant figures compared to whom traders and street vendors are inferior. "How can we get jobs elsewhere? We are not engineers with degrees from top colleges!" Saumya notes. "Mechanics are not creative; we are just doing timepass here." Whatever work they perform falls short of the standard and efficiency of trained professionals.

While mechanics do not develop as a respectable vocation in the traders' vocabulary, a few Hindu movies, particularly from the 1970s and 1980s, present them as a working-class icon.[6] An image from films of that era is the sight of a grease-laden mechanic emerging from the rear of a car to confront a well-dressed professional. Often justice and right are on the side of the hardworking mechanic, and the urban professional is morally vacuous. Nowadays, however, traders and street vendors cannot conjure the image of a justice warrior when they speak of their predicament. In post-liberalization India, movies don't frequently carry images of mechanics fighting injustices and class wars.

In such a situation where neither in popular media nor in the wider society is there glorification of informal technological work, tinkering with games appears as a last resort, not something that one does because it is creatively fulfilling but only because of the unavailability of other prospects. Is there no way to reclaim practices of tinkering as a formidable trait of popular knowledge? In the following sections, by contextualizing tinkering in local knowledge and also global movements, I present ways of mainstreaming fringe practices.

Tinker

In many ways, the fact that traders and street vendors struggle to find a positive way to talk about their repairing skills is linked to their inability to find allies in their external surroundings. The affluent urban life is ever-present in gated neighborhoods, advertisements, and hoardings. *Bazaari* style does not fit into an aspirational lifestyle. Historically this is not the first time that informal knowledge systems are in a marginal place. Tinkers in medieval Europe—Irish, Scottish, and Roma travelers—made a living by doing door-to-door repairs mending pots and pans. Soldering tin and metal vessels created a model of livelihood for marginalized communities as they had little competition. The locals did not see it as an attractive vocation to travel the length and breadth of a country doing odd repairs for survival. Tinkers were people on the fringes that migrated to a new place and could not secure traditional forms of employment (Stephenson 1948). One of the benefits of using the term "tinker" to portray traders' and street vendors' activities in the bazaar is to compare them with other historical figures who struggled to have a secure livelihood because of their marginal status. Their patterns of economic activities are similar: the use of everyday tools and embodied knowledge (Deka 2018). Such embodied knowledge included soldering pots and pans in the case of Roma tinkers and tricks and performances for jesters and street magicians. If we break down what Delhi's traders share with medieval tinkers, what stands out is the use of similar technology. Both groups use the soldering technique to repair and mend items. For one group the method of soldering was used to repair kitchenware and the other group uses it to fix electronic products. In each instance, one follows a trial-and-error method.

There is also an innovative use of bodies. We see this among street performers whose innovative use of their physical bodies guarantees them a livable income. Throughout history, street performers, tradespeople, and people doing informal labor have used their physical bodies to create traditions of knowledge and livelihood outside of formal structures of knowledge production (Serafini 2017). Of course, these modes of marginal knowledge came from the specific social-cultural universe. Their challenges and struggles depended on the type of people they came in contact with and the nature of their jobs. But what undoubtedly connects marginalized knowledge is the effective use of limited resources to survive in a competitive environment. When nothing else is available, performers and technicians used their bodies in novel ways to survive an otherwise inhospitable climate. In *Jadoowallah Jugglers and Jinns: A Magical History of India*, Zubrzycki (2018) gives a detailed account of street magicians in Delhi, like Tantric performers, for whom community knowledge gets mapped on the human body by painstaking training. In the British colonial era, street performers and magicians performed risky tricks to generate a livelihood out of sheer courage. The famous Indian rope trick, featuring a young man climbing a rope and disappearing in the sky or, alternatively, emerging out of a basket on the ground, exemplifies how ordinary people can use the resource that is fundamentally common to all, the human body (Deka 2021). The extent to which the physical body is a common resource for ordinary people is also visible in the tricks of the snake charmers who hang snakes on their necks. That there is not much that prevents people from making use of their physical body to produce exceptional results is what many communities on the fringes depend on to survive. A recurring image of electronic repair is that of a person working adroitly on a machine. The bent back and the eyes concentrated on the job produce a similarly effective image of the use of the physical body. Tinkers, street magicians, performers, and manual laborers make use of the human body when faced with new and old challenges. No doubt, we hear less and less of the laboring classes, but the sheer number of people who depend on innovative uses of bodily knowledge is evidence of their sustained power to produce an alternative to formal and institutional knowledge.

Analyzing the Local Context, Tinkering, and *Lokavidya*

The bazaar actors' lack of confidence about their skill and knowledge relates to contemporary urban class *distinctions*, and also to traditional knowledge hierarchies that unduly disadvantage popular knowledge systems. In India, the classical tradition builds on brahminical knowledge passed through primary Sanskritic texts such as the Vedas and the Upanishads. In many ways such knowledge is exclusive; the most obvious discrimination has come from the ritualistic division of the caste system into pure and impure castes. The higher the caste the purer they are; those on the lower rungs do not have duties that connect them with sacred knowledge. At the top of the ritualistic caste hierarchy, Brahmins have been the custodian of scriptural knowledge. As the opportunities to acquire scriptural terms have been largely unavailable to marginalized communities, large parts of traditional knowledge have been inaccessible to the layperson.[7] In contrast, however, the Indian philosophical tradition opens knowledge to subjective experience. There is a contradiction here. On the one hand, the possession of scriptural knowledge depends on the traditional occupation, which is inherited by birth. On the other hand, by stressing the experiential foundation of knowledge there is also a tendency toward its democratization. Focusing on subjective experience has been one radical way to look at people's everyday lives in a structurally exclusionary universe (Matilal 2015).[8]

Individuals' unique experience of the world has offered science and technology studies (STS) scholars an interesting lens through which to examine how the local context shapes scientific practice. Ashis Nandy and Sarukkai, among others, have analyzed how scientific knowledge is embedded in the cultural universe of practitioners, which is also influenced by religion, customs, and other things. For instance, Nandy's analysis of the scientist Jagadish Chandra Bose focuses on how his Brahmo Samaj upbringing and his mother's moral presence stayed with him as ethical influences throughout his life, also shaping his temperament as a scientist (Nandy 1972). Sarukkai and Guru (2012) take the scope of experience a little further when they criticize social theory as fixed and elitist because it privileges a particular point of view—whether it has to do with the self or the other. Ultimately what is problematic for them is the defined position of the knower. In their view, opening up knowledge to diverse personal experiences creates a space where non-elites can develop legitimate discursive positions. To think "that explanation from science regarding crops is more desirable than the explanation of a peasant woman is to be blind to the notion of lived experience. Even seen through categories of science, lived experience is empirical, perhaps more empirical than much of science. But this does not imply that science and tradition have to be mutually exclusive strategies—when they both shed their ideological masks, they can grow together" (Sarukkai 1999, 799). Any kind of knowledge is a complex combination of a subject's unique position, her struggles, along with influences from myriad sources, many of which may appear confused and rarely of significant value to a trained professional. But for the subject herself, such epistemologies of being are dynamic and profound. While the world of scientists and sciences have undergone critical analysis, particularly through the works of STS scholars, popular knowledge has not been scrutinized in the same way.

In the Indian context, one of the closest readings of popular expertise and its connection to traditional knowledge has come from Amit Basole (2014) and his notion of *lokavidya*, "the knowledge of peasants, artisans and *Adivasis* (indigenous people)" (370). He develops a genealogy of *lokavidya*, principally borrowing from the works of Mahatma Gandhi and his own ethnographic insights from weavers in Banaras. In Basole's view, popular knowledge has remained largely outside of institutional practices. "The locus of *lokavidya* is ordinary life as distinct from other (more visible) loci of knowledge production/organization/management such as the university or (academic or commercial) research laboratory. The *lokavidya* perspective recognizes that ordinary life is a center of knowledge production and not only an 'implementer' of knowledge generated elsewhere" (391).[9]

Indeed, the evocation of concepts such as *lokavidya* is a way to center in on ordinary knowledge. Keeping both categories, *lokavidya* and *jugaad*, side by side provides a way to build a political historiography of ordinary people's struggles and life chances. Whether this is about peasants with their meteorological knowledge and understanding of terroir, artisans weaving intricate designs, or phone mechanics using household objects to fix a phone, the avenues of livelihood of diverse groups of people are sources of relevant knowledge. But their consistent marginalization and struggles to find stable income sources are a testimony to unequal power structures. What is confounding in such practices of marginalization is that the actual number of people who are part of the popular knowledge system is exceptionally high. But the strength of numbers has not meant that the group of non-elites and their knowledge are taken seriously. This is true in the present context as was the case in the past. Gandhi's vision of *swaraj* (autonomy achieved through sustainable local manufacturing) provided the possibility of popular knowledge taking center stage. But the efforts did not lead to long-lasting change as independent India decided to modernize heavy industries and large-scale manufacturing. Artisans and their *lokavidya* got pushed back, a process of marginalization that was already under way during colonial rule through resource extraction, manipulating foreign currency conversion systems to benefit the British, and using taxation as one way to pressure local peasants to cultivate cash crops (Patnaik 2017). State apathy did not mean that popular knowledge disappeared altogether; it survived in the fringes.

Colonial and Postcolonial Manufacturing

Post-Soviet Russia, southern Italy, the marketplaces in central Asia, or knowledge workers in Bangladesh—each context has people and forms of livelihood that have faced systematic neglect from official bodies and policies. Svetlana Alexievich (2016, 106) describes two friends in post-Soviet Russia starting their own denim business by renting a launderette and turning it into an acid-washed jeans factory. "Their technique couldn't have been simpler (necessity is the mother of invention): they'd toss regular, boring jeans into a solution of bleach or chlorine, add broken up bricks, and boil them for a couple of hours. The jeans end up covered in all sorts of stripes designs, designs, patterns—abstract art! Then they'd dry them and stick on a label that said 'Montana.'" Not much separates such everyday practices of innovation from *jugaad*, apart from the intricate political arrangements of a particular local context. In post-Soviet Russia, economic constraints lead people to deploy informal infrastructure as they continue to pursue individual autonomy and entrepreneurship.

The same is the case with Naples in southern Italy, as described by Alfred Sohn-Rethel in the 1920s, where ordinary people "make do" with available scraps of resources as the region succumbs to pressures from criminal organizations, corruption nexuses, and mass poverty. In fact, Sohn-Rethel declares that the Neapolitan relationship to things technical is broken. In Naples, when something is working, he writes, people have the added worry of when it will stop working. Instead, when things are not working, people are in the middle of technology, or rather within it, working with every nut and bolt, changing course and discovering what is possible for a particular technology. It is like not knowing to which station the train will bring you—there is always a chance of finding something new. Isn't what Sohn-Rethel notices of Naples in the 1920s true of tinkering worldwide?[10]

Some proletarian brashness emerges from looking at life not as rosy-hued but as clouded as the severed existence, life on the fringes, where people have made their way through a murky political terrain and are making ends meet. The spirit of grit is a spirit of a damaged relationship with available infrastructure, power, and objects. Rather than feeling destabilized, one learns how to ace these challenges to the point that a functioning product is almost the most unworkable. It does not inspire us like many other things that want us to work with them from the start. "Resourcefulness, the ability to improvise, and the know-how required to work with odds and ends are products of poverty and can be therefore found in a wide variety of contexts and approached through different analytical models—in terms of the shrewdness with which people respond to the inefficacy of the state" (Goldgel-Carballo 2014, 114).

A certain type of discrimination that has affected how popular knowledge has been perceived in India can be connected to British colonialism. A significant factor was the political climate—taxation and drain of wealth—used by colonial rulers to exploit local peasants and skilled workers. On top of that, local factory owners did not do much to change the status quo. Tripathi (1996) argues that local textile factory owners hardly created independent innovative systems nor did they collaborate with existing manufacturing units. They were largely reliant on technology coming from Japan and spinning machines from Manchester. "The Indians developed an industry that was almost an exclusive preserve of Manchester which never looked kindly at the prospects of rising competition from a colony. . . . During the early years of the industry, when no alternative had yet been developed, this was understandable. But even subsequently, when mechanical devices, more compatible with the Indian conditions, were available, the Indians, by and large, continued to patronize the technology the British manufacturers favored" (81). The inability to harness local innovation systems along the lines of crafts and related cottage industries has created a distance between a formal structure and a large base of popular knowledge. The gap continued after independence as rather than building a completely bottom-up model of development, heavy industries were suddenly preferred. The traditional biases were not taken into account, like the importance of bringing together people who had skills to devise macro plans that fit the needs of the people. However, the mass aptitude—abilities, inclinations, traditional skills—was not taken as the basis of plans. It is not that the ordinary people were not part of official plans, but they ended up as a target of plans, rather than initiators of it. Instead, an elite group of scientists and technocrats aided the modernizing processes of the first prime minister, Jawaharlal Nehru. J. R. D Tata, P. C Mahalanobis, and Homi J. Bhabha were close confidants of Nehru. Under their stewardship, institutions such as the Tata Institute of Fundamental Research, the Indian Statistical Institute, and the Bhabha Atomic Research Centre were established.

Further down the decades, other elite institutes such as the Indian Institute of Technology (IIT) were established. The first IIT, established in Kharagpur, was modeled after the Massachusetts Institute of Technology in the US.[11] Along with the fresh crop of state and private engineering colleges, the elite technological institutes provided a pool of engineers and programmers that got absorbed into multinational corporations. The surge of qualified graduates gave India's information technology (IT) dream an identity as foreign and local companies put India on the global map of software and software-related services (Chandrasekhar 2005). Apart from qualified technological graduates, call-center workers became a strand of information technology in India. However, they were at the lower end of the spectrum. Their work and struggle came into the limelight to show the underbelly of India's IT success. In all these stories, bazaar tinkers and their backyard innovation do not figure. Theirs is a story of a complete outsider. For some, their brush with formal education amounted to high school or primary-level schooling. But a few of them do not know how to read and write. Bazaar-level practitioners still work with technology and create innovative fixes based on a pragmatic approach to technology, tackling each new challenge as a possible business opportunity. Their knowledge has suffered from the country's inability to transform available knowledge into stable, wide production systems.

This failure can be partly traced to small to medium enterprises not taking off in the same manner as big enterprises. If mid-level production units had grown (incorporating local demands, and sustainable infrastructure) skilled labor like bazaar practitioners could have got absorbed in such places. After more than sixty years of neglect towards local manufacturing cultures, the "Make in India" program launched in 2014 was thought to create the necessary infrastructure to fill the void. But the project received partial success. Rather than remedy the lack of people-friendly manufacturing systems, large-scale manufacturing (mostly with foreign investments), continued top-down intervention. Such initiative also did not do much to reach out to the streets.[12] Even in the most ambitious project of building a stable manufacturing base in the country, there wasn't much room for ordinary people's creative pursuits.

Postcolonial Tinkering, *Jugaad*, and Commons

After independence, the bazaar tinkers, ragpickers, and peddlers began to mark their territory in the urban space. In the case of Delhi's electronic traders, they set foot in state-supported modernist architecture that, over the years, has taken on the look of decaying buildings. A significant character of marginal lives in cityscapes has been their relationship to the street, to ruins, and to messy architecture. There would not be any marginal figures in global cities if it were not for the presence of a specific type of decadence that accompanies them. Take the example of the early modernist buildings in Delhi that are left in a kind of a limbo as the city expanded into new commercial spaces. The interstices do provide ordinary people spaces to use. The use of common spaces, alongside the pragmatic approach to technology, harnesses a unique innovative spirit. As mentioned earlier, *jugaad* is a word to describe bazaar-style tinkering. It points toward stylistic variations and frugal innovation. *Jugaad* does not follow a regular infrastructure. It does not come from a functioning system but from the cracks of a functioning system. It originates in urban decadence and commons and for the very reason that they do not fall under modern propriety regimes. As Nandita Badami observes,

> While Western practices of repair exist and negotiate for ever greater space within regimes of legitimacy, jugaad, by comparison, can never be truly legitimised. However, given the comparison, it might be prudent [to] not simply stick to the binary of legality and illegality, pirate and liberator. . . . In its core sense, jugaad is a shared set of sensibilities and practices of the relationship between materials and people that can be best understood in terms of a "commons" by defining it as preceding the legalities that make a concept like "open source" intelligible, jugaad can be understood as uniquely outside, yet always open to the proverbial enclosures erected through the ever-growing articulations

of the legal and formal "rights" to repair, of everything from individual objects, to floundering businesses, to the economy itself. (Badami
2018, 54)

Here, Badami highlights one of the crucial distinctions that separate bazaar-
level innovation from the do-it-yourself (DIY) cafes that are part of the Global
North. Although the "open source"–backed hacker and maker spaces are
radical alternatives to intellectual property regimes, as Badami argues, they
still function under the purview of the law. Instead, people involved in *jugaad*-style innovation, including bazaar actors, do not operate under a strict
legality as most of their jobs including tweaks and fixes do not fall under the
rigid boundary of the legal system. For instance, as we saw previously, tampering with the barcode, cracking, and jailbreaking consoles are not specifically
legal practices. But neither are they strictly illegal. In many ways, laws are out
of touch with the experimental nature of pirate practices. While under TRIPs
(the Agreement on Trade-Related Aspects of Intellectual Property Rights)
software piracy and copyright violation come under the purview of law, acts
of tampering are yet to be seen as criminal in nature.[13] Badami observes that
the liberal citizens' affinity for law puts them in a better place to dialogue with
formal spaces and practices, as these groups also benefit the most from the law's
implementation. The bazaar actor works under no such constraints of identity
and reputation.[14] As technological fixes are a way to earn an income, their
daily use of technology gives rise to unconventional practices. The boundaries
of laws do not define innovation. This spirit has been made possible by the
grit of individual market actors to survive a competitive urban sphere and by
their irreverent use of commons of everyday tools, abandoned and discarded
items, and claiming things and objects that have fallen out of elite circulation.
The relationship that marginal actors design with objects, practices, and tools
outside of a strict proprietary regime has historically allowed marginal actors
to earn a living. The relationship with commons essentially ties Scottish and
Irish metal tinkers of the medieval age to the street performers and jugglers
in colonial India and to Delhi's bazaar traders working with video games. The
commons that we talk about may vary. For the Irish tinkers, it was household
tools and objects. For the street performers and jugglers, the physical body is
a common resort to enchant large crowds. For contemporary electronic traders, their embodied knowledge together with their access to everyday tools,
the economy of waste, and recycling have given them a new lease on life. The

political and economic angles of working with secondhand, stolen, and abandoned products have attained new meaning in the age of the Anthropocene (Bonneuil and Fressoz 2016).[15] At the most basic level, ordinary people's relationship with non-proprietary entities has enabled them to survive. At a theoretical level, formal organization and state policies might have ordinary people's interests in mind. In practice, marginalized communities are left to their own devices because of the failed implementation of state plans and the lack of a more nuanced understanding of popular lives. In such a situation, popular lives have utilized objects around them, bodies, and practices whose appropriation does not require untangling extra resources from the bureaucratic and legal labyrinth.

Sharing within Bazaar Commons

In many ways, popular knowledge systems develop a system of knowledge transmission that on the surface can appear exclusionary, but digging deeper reveals complex mechanisms of sharing and participation. Take, for example, the weavers in Banaras where flexible specialization is enabled "via a caste- and family-based putting-out systems where master weavers supply raw materials and designs to weavers who weave at home and return the product to the master weaver" (Basole 2016, 159). Artisanal clusters of the Ansari community produce fabric such as *Chanderi* on handlooms from home, and loomless workers use small workshops for production. Within the community, men weave, and women prepare the yarn and do embroidery work on the textile. In every step, traditional knowledge of artisanal clusters in Banaras is openly exchanged in certain cases and kept secret in others. For instance, new creations are part of the *naqsheband* system, within which trained weavers create unique designs. The system sees to it that a simple "knowledge in the air" environment does not develop where everybody can freely copy master designs. Secrecy about the new design is one such mechanism to avoid the immediate circulation of new concepts.

On the other hand, there is a gradual wide imitation of original designs in the absence of patents. Such a contradictory system of knowledge production where there is openness through lack of patents but closure through secrecy and community-based hierarchies is a common element of popular knowledge. Assa Doron (2012) observes in Lucknow that mobile "repairwala" are mainly from the Sunni Muslim community. Most of them learn the trade by observing others in the shop, but some also acquire training from professional institutes. In this regard, there is openness in the marketplace to learn new skills and be part of the marketplace. But there are also ways in which skilled repair people keep expert knowledge to themselves. Doron observes that "more skilled repairers jealously guarded their knowledge, restricted access to their shops and barred others from viewing their work" (Doron 2012, 580). Similarly, repair people in Lajpat Rai Market, Palika Bazaar, and Nehru Place create tactics to prevent the wide circulation of trade secrets. Senior and skilled repair people place their hands strategically to prevent observers from quickly learning new tricks. They avoid sharing trade secrets to a vast network. But with shop assistants and helpers in the shop, the senior repair person readily shares a secret.

For example, Lalit from Palika Bazaar is impatient that his assistant Dev takes so much time to learn new skills. He wants Dev to become a trained "mechanic" so that they can share the workload. When Dev is unable to pick up skills, Lalit amuses himself by talking about the time when he worked under his *ustaad* (master) in Lajpat Rai Market. Lalit remembers how his *ustaad* humiliated the students apprenticing under him. The taunts about not finishing a task on time made many students leave the workshop before completing their apprenticeship. Lalit is happy that he is one of the few migrants from Uttar Pradesh who finished the course. He jokes about how young men these days (pointing to Dev) would not bear the humiliation that he faced training under his *ustaad*. He speaks about the sensitivity of today's youth who are not used to his generation's ethics of hard work. At least, there is trust between them that has led Lalit to share some of the trade secrets with Dev.

The attitude of sharing among master and assistant is opposite to the practices of a repair person hiding important repair work. The hide-and-seek approach to knowledge is possible because bazaars do not operate under strict legal sanctions of intellectual property rights, whether it has to do with copyright infringements or the implementation of patents. The lack of legal protection of new knowledge places bazaars as part of "peer learning" along with other participatory cultures, like the access to knowledge movement. Talking about bazaar knowledge in tandem with activist-led participatory knowledge movements highlights the practices these worlds share. There are also important differences, such as the embedded context of bazaar knowledge sharing: necessity, survival, and pragmatism. Activist-led movements ignore some of the subtleties of everyday practices of sharing because of their emphasis on ideology. The opposition to intellectual property rights seems profound in movements such as copyleft and among hackers, although individual and community-level interactions on a day-to-day basis are not always visible.[16] Whenever such efforts have been made, for instance, looking at the organizational structure of the Debian project, there is a more complex mechanism of autonomy for small tasks and recourse to some form of structure for decision-making. But all of these operational dynamics occur under the idealism of writing beautiful code, keeping the source code free, and sharing it extensively on community-based platforms (Coleman 2013).

The 1990s free software culture came out of a strong opposition to corporate control of knowledge and the gatekeeping of resources by powerful bodies. While there are different knowledge-sharing systems, the joint opposition to intellectual property rights has brought free software, open-source, and hacker cultures together under the umbrella of the access to knowledge movement "as a reaction to structural trends in technologies of information processing and in law, and as an emerging conceptual critique of the narrative that legitimates the dramatic expansion in intellectual property rights that we have witnessed over the past several decades" (Kapczynski 2010, 17).

The prevailing representation of advanced technological knowledge such as programming has difficulties in incorporating bazaar tinkering within peer-to-peer knowledge. Furthermore, to activists, the commercial aspect of piracy-related tinkering does not sit well with the agenda of participatory knowledge systems. Also, as the discussion above shows, bazaar tinkering does not promote indiscriminate sharing of trade secrets. All these incompatibilities beg the question of whether we can still talk about bazaar tinkering as part of a "peer learning" system. I think we should, if we want to have an inclusionary system of knowledge outside of intellectual property rights. After all, if bazaars restrict knowledge within specific networks, so do participants of access to knowledge movements through General Public Licenses (GPLs) such as those from GNU, and not least, through the cultural capital at their disposition.

The economic imperative of activist movements and bazaar tinkering starts from the same prerogative of meeting survival needs, like paying rent and meeting day-to-day expenses (Arvidsson et al. 2016). Exchange by itself even of an economic kind is not problematic; it is more gatekeeping and monopolistic accumulation that create inequalities. The examples that bazaar actors use to talk about being okay with other people copying their innovations speak a great deal about their predicament. While not being able to contest people who copy their creations did produce frustration, traders and street vendors in Delhi's bazaars still showed a sensitivity that went beyond simply accounting for profit and loss. Harish from Lajpat Rai Market, whose innovation of a TV console was copied widely, saw copying as something that everyone does in the marketplace. He confesses, "I could have been angrier with other people copying my innovation had I not done that myself. I came to the marketplace with nothing. What I achieved is because I borrowed and learned from other people. Now, all of a sudden, I cannot be selfish about sharing." Acknowledging the interdependent networks that non-elites are part of, Harish suggests that each innovation enjoys a small window of monopoly profit. While other shops will quickly copy an invention, the original creator has at least a month to enjoy price control over the product. (Arvidsson and Niessen [2015] observed a similar dynamic in Bangkok's fashion markets.)

From a practical and ethical point of view, it makes little sense for bazaar actors to close knowledge transmission channels. In this regard, something like the Access to Knowledge (A2K) movement and bazaar tinkering have a lot in common. Both systems have their specific ways to govern how and when such knowledge gets shared. Like in the public domain, bazaars have particular knowledge that is widely copied and circulated while other forms of knowledge, like trade secrets, get passed down with caution. Neither activist-led movements nor bazaars depend on intellectual property rights to restrict knowledge within known networks. Bazaars violate copyright laws by their software and game piracy, and even in small-time innovation bazaar actors do not patent their inventions. Instead of external agencies mitigating disputes and facilitating, it is interpersonal relationships that govern knowledge exchange.

Perhaps attention to the subtleties of how bazaar knowledge gets shared can make it easier for activist movements to discern the radical potential of piracy, rather than emphasizing its seemingly apolitical commercial nature. This could lead to new avenues of cooperation across class and geographical lines, based on how ordinary people's use of technology is enabling rather than restrictive, as proprietary regimes would like us to believe. Such forms of collaboration between the bazaar and digital peer communities have not developed yet. In the current climate, the ethical life emerges as a way to find momentary relief from overbearing structural and material struggles.

4   Bazaar Ethics and a Common Human Condition

> Greed is a sin.
> —*Govind, trader, Palika Bazaar*

Big Businesses and Bazaar Traders: An Ethics of One's Own

The image of elite lifestyles is ubiquitous in Indian cities. The lifestyles of high-rise apartments, valet-driven cars, shopping in exclusive outlets, and billboards with jewelry ads are symbols of a new elite. Much like the rest of the world, a "neoliberal" elite has taken control over political affairs formerly held by a traditional alliance. Alongside landlords and bureaucrats are the corporate elites who are influential actors shaping the country's future. Almost every new change to the urban skyline is thinking of the benefits of the city's rich, and the long-term impact on ecology and societal well-being take a backseat. Some call the new class with disposable income "neoliberalism's poster child" as India's upper-class consumers are moneyed enough to aspire to and materialize a global lifestyle of the affluent. Of course, seen in another light, business is business, and Delhi's traders discussed in this book could also one day be merchants who take their voyage abroad to China to get goods of specific kinds. But the status of Delhi's traders, despite some of them pocketing a good profit, does not take them to any level of success or the limelight.

It is not their world that inspires management literature about how the rich in India have a unique propensity to excel based on their cultural environment, particularly rooted in Hindu sacred texts. While the spotlight is on India's wealthy and successful businesses, and a lot is written about what makes them tick, the less successful actors of the same fraternity confront these success stories daily without being close to such a life. In such an environment, bazaar actors develop a particular way of seeing their successful counterparts in the same urban sphere. It appears they navigate the dualism of belonging to a business community yet not being successful by evoking ethics to justify their economic behavior.[1] Actually, in some sense, both groups are rather similar. Manoj, a trader from Lajpat Rai Market, says, "Everything is fair in business and war." He makes this announcement to justify acts of tricking consumers into buying lower-quality products. Or for instance, Manoj sees the true spirit of business as the possibility of making a profit at any cost. "Nobody is here for charity." The basic rule of economic life stands true. No matter the circumstances, sellers or capitalists want a profit that betters their income possibilities or, in the worst-case scenario, maintains the status quo.

Manoj, however, sees the list of similarities as not very long. In his opinion, capitalists have no limits to their profit-maximizing tendency. To drive his point home, Manoj gives the example of Reliance, a business venture of the Ambani group. In the beginning, he says, Reliance started selling plastic bags for as low as ₹ 40 per kilo, making it difficult for small competing businesses to maintain a profit at such a low margin. Many small competitors could not keep up with the market pressure. The company kept the price low for as long as it took to establish a monopoly and increased the price to ₹ 65 per kilo only after it gained control over the market.[2] Manoj observes, "Big businesses follow a weeding-out process. Small actors do not stand a chance." Bazaar actors acknowledge the ruthless attitude of capitalists. For them, it is unsavory that someone can go to any extent for profit even though it may mean destroying the livelihood chances of people. Instead, bazaars operate in an economy of precarity far from employing such discretion of increasing and decreasing prices; they are at the mercy of elite plans and schemes. Most of the bazaar actors' energy is spent in keeping up with the times. Rather than making decisions that others follow, they are playing catch-up. To produce a level playing ground of sorts, bazaar actors build an ethical register to transcend temporary and permanent setbacks. The ethical life of bazaar actors is intertwined with the everyday trials and tribulations of the competitive market environment. It is not always a self-serving mechanism as ethics is made out to be in its relation to big businesses and their propensity to succeed.

Bazaar Ethics: Between Weber and Geertz

Delhi's bazaars are not unique in developing an ethics that sustains and supports an economy of face-to-face exchange. The degree to which an ethical life promotes a certain kind of economic behavior differs from one economic system to another. For instance, the relationship of ethics to economic life in early capitalist systems in Europe has developed in a way that household assets included surplus that could be put to rational use, important among which was the generation of wealth from commerce and other activities. In the essay *The Protestant Ethic and the Spirit of Capitalism*, Weber (2005) gives a foundational role to the Protestant ethic, particularly followers of the reformer John Calvin, in developing a certain type of economic discipline that led to the development of a calculative market actor. The doctrine of predestination directing spiritual matters in everyday pursuits provided a moral register that supported a parsimonious and prudent attitude toward investments. Weber notes that with time, the religious ethics were routinized and what was left were time-honored habits among Protestant businesses without necessarily carrying the religious fervor of their ancestors. He quotes the Methodist John Wesley to show how "the whole history of monasticism is in a certain sense the history of a continual struggle with the problem of the secularizing influence of wealth" (118). What started as a unique approach to moneymaking continued to shape dominant economic behavior in Europe and North America despite losing a strong religious basis.

Herein lies the difference between ethics in the bazaar economy and ethics under capitalism. Unlike modern capitalism in Europe and North America, where Weber observes a gradual replacement of religious fervor by the secular spirit of moneymaking, the ethical register in the bazaar economy acts as a constant frame of justification. Whether this tendency is brought about by a genuine concern for doing good or rather as a way of valorizing small profit is up for debate. Nonetheless, ethical life is alive in the bazaar economy. In recent years, however, we also see a trend of giving a complex rendering of capitalist pursuits, not seeing accumulative tendencies as devoid of any form of ethical considerations. Arjun Appadurai (2012), for instance, addresses the problem of weakening ethics under capitalism by focusing on the world of uncertainty. This sphere, in his opinion, continues the *Geist* of capitalism through magic and chance best represented in the figure of the "charismatic" financial capitalist. He argues that "the spirit which informs today's heroic, charismatic players at the very high ends of the financial market lies not in an as yet undiscovered set of proprietary databases, screens, tools or models, to which lesser players in the market do not have access. Rather, these are players who have a different strategy of divination, of reading the signs, charts, trends, flows, patterns, and shifts in the market from those who are less willing to take their outsize bets on the certainty and timing of market downturns" (14). No doubt there is much more to the lives of capitalists than calculative actions of a certain kind. But any level of description of the ethical life of capitalists at least in contemporary times cannot be about virtuous action at the cost of economic prosperity. There is a shared experience of precarity that is mostly missing from the lives of successful capitalists. And there is a comparison to be made about the visibility of economic actors: bazaar actors and their rhythm of commerce are out there for people to observe and converse about; the zone of ethical life of marginal economic actors is much more accessible than that of capitalist actors. In the bazaars, conditions of insecurity and anxiety create a certain type of ethical life. Its most vivid manifestation is in the bargaining ritual.

Traditionally used to portray a lack of ethics as the battleground of "information asymmetry," bazaar bargaining, far from signaling a lack of ethical life, is a visible representation of it, as shown in studies today. In his study of traders in Indonesia, Geertz notes, "In fact, the general reputation of the bazaar-type trader for 'unscrupulousness, lack of ethics,' etc., arises mainly from this role asymmetry in the retail market in a bazaar economy, rather than from an uninhibited, normatively unregulated expression of the 'acquisitive impulse' as Max Weber and others seem to think" (Geertz 1963, 34). Here, Geertz highlights the same idea that Manoj was also talking about when he wanted to show how bazaar actors differed from capitalists. The difference lies not in the search for profit but in the values attached to profit making. And how at a certain level, bazaars don't work with information sureties that would put them in a position to be completely nonchalant about their futures and ways of making profit. There would always be an element of frailty with each and every exchange: What if things get called off at the last minute? What if the buyer or the seller is being cheated? Are there any checks to "acquisitive impulse" or can it develop unhindered? In bazaars, ethical life acts as a counterpoint to an accumulative logic. Other scholars have noticed the intricate fabric of ethical life in the bazaar economy; for instance, in Paul Anderson's work in Aleppo he observes traders' use of civility as "an intermediate sociability that stands between the rivalry of strangers and the intimacies of kinship and clan solidarities" (Anderson 2019, 384). In numerous situations, bazaar actors restrain rather than break their civility for economic exchange. They would not show their annoyance beyond a point even though they had to bring out many things from the counters for a shopper, and the buyer left the bargaining midway without explanation. In this way, thirty minutes or so are wasted, and traders patiently put back everything in its place and start with the same level of enthusiasm with another buyer.

The intimate connection of bazaar ethics with commerce is visible not just in the moment of bargaining but throughout the market day. Ethics provides a sense of purpose after a tough day at work. It reconciles the anxieties of a competitive market environment. Anderson (2019, 394–95) says the zone of contemplation of bazaar actors is ordinary ethics, "relatively tacit, grounded in agreement rather than the rule, in practice rather than rule or belief." The conversational nature of ordinary ethics that can easily move between light rebuke and serious allegations brings out its everydayness. Depending on the situation, certain behaviors of a trader can cause serious turbulence in the bazaar if he is found to be dishonest and disloyal. Not that every trader will use the same textual or religious reference to condemn such behavior, but there is a general agreement about the credibility of a specific action, for instance, the value of honesty. Actors have their stories to show how in the long run dishonesty does not produce desirable results. Some may quote personal experiences, others folk stories, but others use rumors to make a similar point that no profit is okay if earned by dishonest means. In Aleppo's bazaars, honesty ranked so high as to determine whether a person gets a place in heaven or hell, as Anderson (2019, 395) notes of the importance of "'honesty and trust-worthiness' (sidq wa amaneh), cautioning that a single false word would be weighed on the Day of Judgement." Is there a way to see why such virtues are central to a *bazaari* way of life? The following section looks at the experimental nature of bazaar actors to appropriate something collectively available—religious texts, folk stories, rumors—and make them their own.

Bazaar Ethics: Lessons from Comparable Examples

Ramanujan's (1989) essay, "Is There an Indian Way of Thinking?," is a preview into the intersubjective world of South Asian subjects. By decoding what makes an Indian attitude unique, compared to its opposite, the European approach, Ramanujan shares insights on the mental life of Indians and what drives their worldview. However, as one reads through the piece, it becomes evident that while Ramanujan premises an Indian way of thinking, he is basing it on an ethical approach. Or rather, there is not much that separate ethics from everyday life. To have an Indian predisposition is, in some sense, to have a highly ethical worldview. For Ramanujan, this is evident in the reliance of Indians on context-specific reasoning. Such an approach is different from a universal logic of the "West" that separates a subject's internal and external world. A telling example of context-specific reasoning that is common in many cultures is how, when someone meets a person for the first time, it is quite common to ask where she is from. Somehow the individual's identity does not exist outside of her social context. There are also problematic aspects of context-specific reasoning, for instance, in the Indian case, the formulation of hierarchies based on caste and religious prejudices. The problem of understanding classics like Louis Dumont's *Homo Hierarchichus* or Ramanujan's essay is that it requires recognizing the influences of certain strands of Indian thought that have their origin in caste-based hierarchies. As a researcher, a way to engage with this paradox is to chronicle what one sees in front of one's eyes without necessarily supporting those viewpoints. Such an emphasis means having to choose whether to leave inappropriate material entirely out of the discussion or include it, while at the same time pointing out the researcher's ethical position. Fortunately, I encountered a diluted view of Hinduism where scriptural examples, when used at all, were pointing toward personal ethics rather than vitriolic messages against particular communities. There were a few instances when unsavory statements were made. Still, those were one-off examples. On a regular day, the ethical life of *bazaaris* is a personal journey to provide frames of "justification" for economic activities that are out of place in a contemporary urban environment (Boltanski and Thévenot 2006).

In researching the ethical life of the bazaar traders, I was reading comparable literature where ethics is a mitigator of everyday disappointments and ideas of justice. I did this to see if marginalized communities elsewhere used everyday ethics to make sense of pervading inequalities: if other communities were falling back on cultural universes of religion and moral life to provide meaning to their existence, and if so, how those negotiations were made. Writings on villages and peasant communities are comparable examples where actors simultaneously make use of varied value systems grounded in material struggles. In the Indian case, Robert Redfield (1955) was able to identify two main cultural influences that ordinary people had to absorb—the great tradition, "the great community of priests, theologians and learned men," and the little tradition, which is parochial absorption of the great tradition. With time, he rectified his view on the relationship between the great and the little tradition by introducing elements from the fast-evolving literature on village studies. Rather than one tradition getting absorbed by another, a more realistic account stresses the openness of each tradition to adapting to the needs of the other. Redfield's analysis is still valuable as he provides a way to think of everyday appropriation of structural and institutionalized aspects of culture without completely blurring the influences of each sphere. For instance, Gananath Obeyesekere (1963) builds on Redfield's concept to talk about the localized adaptation of Buddhism in Sri Lanka. He writes,

> We recognize the utility of the terms "great tradition" and "great community"; these abstractions are useful for describing the intellectual thought and interests of civilisations, and groups of individuals who promote and further these interests. The little tradition by contrast we agree with Dumont and Pocock is the *whole* culture of the little community of peasant society. Peasant societies are "whole," but we agree with Redfield that they are not isolated. Peasant cultures or little traditions are linked with great tradition through a common cultural idiom, which established channels of communication between the two traditions and sets up standards of mutual reference and influence. (Obeyesekere 1963, 153)

Wisdom from anthropological insights in South Asia is to keep the immediate world of the community at the center. An emphasis on the ethical register of bazaar actors does this by visiting the "common idiom" used in a particular context. Bazaars are not peasant communities residing in villages, whose contact with the reflective community of urban centers is intermittent. Instead, bazaars are at the heart of urban life. The influences of the "great tradition" or their particular rendition enter through Facebook videos, WhatsApp messages, political rallies, religious festivals, and spectacles.[3] Each market day brings together stories and references, the so-called fragments of tradition (Pandian 2010), in the form of classical poetry from school and proverbs passed down by ancestors. The popular ethics of South Asia is a pastiche of influences that help individuals make sense of their world and make hardships appear bearable. As Anand Pandian (2008, 471) mentions, "Well over two millennia of Indian moral thoughts and practice have generated diverse and at times incommensurable ways of addressing the problem of how one ought to live." The individual's efforts to find meaning come out poignantly through a dream that one of Pandian's participants narrated to him. In the dream, the narrator saw her paddy fields wilting under the strong sun. In her dream was also the rain god whose appearance saved her from facing the worst nightmare of drought. A specific problem and its resolution happened almost immediately through recourse to an ethical register. Encounters with everyday Hinduism are how Delhi's bazaar traders get past temporary and severe trade disappointments. If a market exchange does not go their way, feel-good stories make the present obstacle worthwhile.[4]

Hindu Ethics

On many occasions, I heard stories and references to incidents that traders and street vendors thought to be motivational. One thing that stood out in these narratives was the recourse to a Hindu moral universe to project a virtuous action. Actors do not directly quote from religious texts, and most of the learnings appear to be passed-down wisdom, stories and incidents that traders and street vendors have heard from their elders and other people in the bazaar. There is an everydayness to Hindu ethics that circulate in the bazaars whereby it is open to interpretation and additions by individual actors. As there is no authority assessing fallacies, nobody is there to point out why a certain story is authentic and not others. In a way, anybody can put forth a moral tale as coming from the Hindu pantheon without having to show the exact reference. Such fluidity not only shows an actor's creativity and willingness to project personal ethics but also how as a religion Hinduism is flexible enough to absorb new ideas. Tulsi Srinivas (2018) calls this ability of Hinduism to adapt to the times an indication of the experimental nature of Hinduism. In her ethnography, priests are not hesitant to use modern technology like laptops to deliver sermons and helicopters to travel from place to place. Here, modern technology and religion are not in opposition to one another. Rather, practitioners find ways to show how the same logic that pervades Hindu ideals also extends to modern technology, an aspect that also comes up in the Conclusion of this book. Other scholars, like DeNapoli, have probed the complex interaction between modern technology and Hinduism to show how the

latter's mutability allows it to adapt to the times. She quotes *sādhu* Parashuram Das to articulate how North Indian sages view modern technology such
as mobile phones in their daily life.

> What is technology? It is when a person leaves behind all of his [or
> her] judgments, dispositions, and temperaments. Suppose we want to
> create a mobile phone, at that time we have to sacrifice all our judg-
> ments about phones. We have to give all our time and effort to our
> work, to creating a mobile. We have to apply all our attention [*dhyān*]
> in one place. . . . The making of a mobile is technology. In technology,
> we have to sacrifice everything [*tyāg*]. (DeNapoli 2017, 13)

Connections between separate universes are made possible by the force of an
argument. Secular matters, folk stories, gossip, and individual imagination;
everything has a place in religion. This experimental nature of Hinduism is
on wide display in the bazaars. After all, stories and incidents are the author's
interpretation and rendition, which may or may not have an exact textual reference. Almost anything can count as Hindu ethics if the story starts with the
action of gods or has an arbitrary reference to Hindu texts such as the Bhagavad Gita, the Upanishads, and the Puranas. It is not that this experimental
nature of Hinduism does not veer toward problematic areas. In "Recycling
Modernity: Pirate Electronic Cultures in India," Ravi Sundaram (1999, 60)
notes that a large part of experimentation, particularly with new technology,
has been possible because of an elite nationalist agenda. "Hindu nationalism
in India came to power using an explosive mix of anti-minority violence and a
discourse of modernity that was quite contemporary. This discourse appealed
to the upper-caste elites in the fast-growing cities and towns, using innovative forms of mechanical and electronic reproduction. Thus, it was the Hindu
nationalists who first used cheap audio-cassette tapes to spread anti-Muslim
messages; further giant video-scapes were used to project an aesthetised politics of hate. Some of the first Indian web-sites were also set up by the Hindu
nationalists."

It is institutional actors—priests and politicians—who mostly spread religious ideas through the use of modern technology. So much so that such
a version of Hinduism has been typecast as a Hindutva ideology making
careful use of political outfits, modern technology, private capital, and state
agents. Gopalkrishnan (2008) argues that an organization like Vishva Hindu

Parishad disguises neoliberal ideas and self-interests as a good Hindu virtue. "The importance of the 'Hindu community' was not a result of invocation of religious identities alone. Rather, this exploration postulates that it built on a partial satisfaction of a material-ideological need of its cadre and its base— while simultaneously converting those needs into a driving force for individualisation and the restructuring of social relations in favor of capital." Within such an emphasis, there is less possibility for heterogeneity and individual interpretation of religion to take center stage. After all, so much is at stake to follow a rigid version of religion that Hindutva ideology prefers less division within the religion and sees the thing that matters as the division between a unified society and the other. If we probe the basics of a unified Hindutva, Gopalkrishnan thinks that after scratching the surface, the secular, private, self-interested individual comes to the fore.

In fact, Hindutva ideology fits well with different elite groups, not just followers of a particular political party. Fernandes and Heller (2011) highlight the links between Hindutva ideology and capital through the elite group of the new middle-class (NMC) white-collar professionals. They argue that Hindutva sits quite well with the emerging middle class's neoliberal aspirations of producing order on one hand and keeping factions and hierarchy alive on the other. There is, however, a rift in the smooth translation of homogeneous identity with other groups. With the rest of the society, affiliations with a majority religion do not automatically translate into privileges. There are concerns of meeting survival needs. Within such a focus, Hinduism is experimental in other ways. Such experimentalism includes not just an appropriation of different objects and ideas to propagate self-interest but also a way to find solace during hours of struggle and courage to face failure. Here, Hindu ethics works in tandem with a survival ethics. Of course, in specific moments, ordinary people and their religious identity can take a problematic turn as evidenced by the backlash against protesters of the recent Citizenship Amendment Act, although it is difficult to say whether ordinary people acted alone or were led by specific organizations.[5] The chances of a Hindutva ideology eclipsing an everyday Hindu ethics is present. Some of the everyday ethics may have communal undertones, but most of their usage is about making sense of one's life, finding a more significant meaning behind living, and how it is often difficult in South Asia to broach these topics without looking to the example of some god or another. A great deal of anthropomorphizing happens even when talking about gods. Not all of them are equally celebrated, nor are all their actions exemplary. Everybody has to live up to specific standards; even gods have their good and bad days. For instance, in the marketplaces, there would be debates about which action was worth emulating, the hedonistic tendency of certain gods or the selfless and sacrificial direction of others.

There were no absolute ideas that just because it is in the sacred scriptures or about gods, it is beyond interpretation. In fact, the context and the reference were so loose that they invited multiple versions. Often, I felt that traders and street vendors enjoyed this open-ended discussion. In my last visit to the marketplace in April 2022, after the peak period of the COVID-19 pandemic, Paras, a street vendor in Nehru Place, spoke of a cosmological turn when he said nothing was in our hands and it all depended on our planets and their movements. In previous conversations with him on the same topic, his sentiment was that Lord Krishna decides our actions. Some of that agency has widened from the gods' purview to include astrological signs, individual will, discipline, and *karma* (duty). In Paras's discourse, astrological influence is strong; we must look to our charts to determine our course of action and then seize the day so as not to miss the opportunities presented by our planets' positions. And if one manages that balance, one achieves what one needs in life. The individual way of carving an ethical life and revising one's beliefs and ideas are part of the moral universe of bazaar actors. What hasn't changed is that all these discourses play out against the trials of a market day. It is the everyday and more undefined zone when ethics provide momentary relief to trade-related worries and a perspective to articulate life choices in a dignified manner.

Dhyan, Dakshina, *and Pilgrimage*

In Palika Bazaar, Govind's father scrolls his Facebook page to show me a post on meditation. He says that business is for taking care of material needs, but one has to also look after one's spiritual needs. The social media post is about the merits of meditation and how it is good for every individual to meditate for at least half an hour every day. Fondly known as Uncle Ji (respected uncle) in the marketplace, Govind's father mediates every morning.[6] Seeing the young people at the shop giggling while the conversation is under way, Uncle Ji remarks, "Their *Dhyan* (attention) is somewhere else. Instead of spiritual matters, it is toward the liquor shop." Overhearing our conservation, Vishal denies the allegation and points to the fact they are not drinking anymore. The conversations about going to the *theka* (local liquor shop) prompt responses from the young men gathered at the shop.[7] As a last bid to show that even the young traders care about spiritual matters, Vishal directs a question to his brother, "We are going to visit Vaishno Devi (Hindu goddess) temple this weekend, aren't we?" His brother responds, "Yes, we are going, and a few others are joining us."

The topic of pilgrimage makes the younger traders more involved in the discussion. It is a suitable topic to show their interest in things outside their business and how even as young men their interests are not as frivolous as Uncle Ji thinks. Going on the pilgrimage is a clear enough sign that they are ready to stay away from work to get a sight of the deity. While they are away, none of them will shut down the shops. Someone else will chip in to manage the shop. But being personally absent shows the young men's commitment to religious matters. I could not say whether these pilgrimages taken by the young lot in shops, often involving friends and relatives outside the marketplaces, were just ways to take time out or were from a sense of moral responsibility. But such trips frequently came up in conversations. Somebody at the shop will make jokes about the young men's drinking habits: they get annoyed by the accusation and retaliate by showing their participation in moral activities. Discussions about meditation and pilgrimage punctuate the market day and highlight the parallel universe these traders inhabit.

In a secular context, these discussions break the monotony of trade and create camaraderie among the traders. But it also opens their life to a set of goals that make their labor worthwhile. Some practices give the traders a higher purpose. Sujit is a street vendor in Nehru Place. His day starts at about nine when he comes with his friends on a DTC (Delhi Transport Corporation) bus to the marketplace. The rest of the day he pursues consumers wanting to buy a pirated DVD of games and software. Most consumers give a deaf ear to his shouts, "Software, Games." Once in a while, a consumer stops and browses the leaflet in his hand with the names of different software. If the person finds something interesting, Sujit brings the potential buyer upstairs to Raj, the leader of their group of street vendors. After leaving the consumer with Raj, Sujit is back at his spot waving the leaflet at passersby. Chewing *gutka* (tobacco-infused betel nut) gives the impression of the hollowness that Adorno (1967, 109) alludes to when he remarks, "not that chewing gum undermines metaphysics but that it is metaphysics." There is a repetitive nature to the street vendors' shouts and chewing of *gutka*, giving the impression that they are caught in a cycle. The mundanity of street vendors' incessant shouting of the same words reflects a far more profound state of exhaustion, despair, and hopelessness. It is not just the tone of attracting consumers to their side but also that the job demands only the passing of standard information. As if by habit, after selling pirated software, street vendors say, "Copy karke chalana, install ho jayega" (Copy the [key], the program will install on [your computer]). They do not even look up from their work or wait for the customer to pose any question; vendors utter the phrase mechanically. The day-in and day-out repetition creates a tonal quality of precarious work but also points to how the alternative is even worse. A monotonous job still brings an income home. But without the opportunity, young men are part of an unemployed underclass invisible to public life.

When I spoke to Sujit in late July 2013, it made sense to me that he was irritable and said he did not want to be bothered by any *inane* query. But there were days when I could break through his tough exterior and he gave me a peek into his frame of mind. Part of his disappointment came from selling pirated software, and how there was a general lack of respect for such activities in the public eye. According to him, pirate bazaars could not shake off the reputation of selling *chori ka maal* (stolen goods). He said no matter what they did, consumers negatively valued their trade of selling things illegally. Sujit would have liked to be part of some other business where carrying a moral dilemma was not a day-to-day affair. But getting used to quick money from quite early on in life kept him in the same trade for the past three years. He knew that in the immediate future, he could not do much to change his situation. But that did not dissuade Sujit from looking at alternative avenues of income. On different visits, I heard about his decision to buy a car. Sujit was taking driving lessons so the moment he had enough savings he could start his own taxi service. He had also been filing his income tax return for a few months, and he hoped that he could rent one of the shops by the book and start a lamination business there. These efforts were still at the planning stage. At the moment, Sujit tried his best to stay on the right course. He helped people as much as he could; for instance, he made accounting software available to young students at an accessible rate. If it were not for the pirated marketplace, economically disadvantaged students had little chance of acquiring the latest software at affordable prices. These were the times Sujit felt validated by his work. Although such moments were few and far between, they lifted his spirits. The knowledge that not all his group of vendors does is cheating, that aspects of their trade also helped those in need, gave Sujit a sense of pride. At the end of the day,

Sujit reconciled his doubts about selling ill-reputed items with the prospect of assisting people. He did not hesitate to give part of his income to his mother with the full knowledge that she would make offerings to the temple from that amount. Sujit did not feel his earnings were "dirty" enough to stop him from offering to the gods. That selling pirated games and software carried fleeting moments of joy made his job worthwhile.

Gods on Pillars

On one of my visits to Nehru Place, I notice that the pillar near which Sujit keeps his CDs and DVDs is covered with images of Hindu gods (see Figure 4.1). The faces of gods line the pillar from top to bottom. Sujit complains about the rise of thefts in the marketplace. "The picture of gods will dissuade people from grabbing our things. After all, when we are dealing with customers, our eyes aren't fixed on our goods at all times." In another instance, Sujit speaks about putting up the pictures to discourage people from urinating below the staircase. With gods in view, people hesitate to dirty the surroundings. In a matter of days, I see another group of street vendors attaching images of gods to a pillar next to their place of work. "It's nice to come in the morning and have a place to bow your heads to gods. Our day starts on a good note." The street vendors are cautious not to spit betel nuts on the pillar. The wall of the gods is an exceptional place where people stop, some bow their heads, and nobody disrupts the images. "Gods in the bazaar" assist traders and street vendors to restrict untoward behavior; they are also a conduit to speak about ambiguities of bazaar commerce. In fact, bazaar actors attach anthropomorphic characters to gods when they do not approve of some of their actions, and only when their action are worth emulating do they take divine form. For instance, Indra, the king of gods, appears as indulgent and excessive. In conversations in Palika Bazaar, I heard a comparison between the sage Narada and Indra, the former being the more exemplary figure as he dedicated his life to the praise of the almighty.

One of the many complaints of senior traders in Nehru Place is the reckless fashion in which many young street vendors lead their lives. As they see it, one such wasted expenditure is the money spent by street vendors to buy betel nuts. Nor is the mere chewing of *gutka* the end to their behavior criticized as hedonism: senior traders found it appalling that many of them used the park in the area to drink alcohol in the evening. For the more permanent shopkeepers who sold assembled and brand-name computers in the marketplace,

Figure 4.1. A pillar covered with images of Hindu gods in Nehru Place (author's image).

the behavior of young street vendors is condemnable. They do not comply with any of the older traders' accepted virtues, for example saving money to avoid problematic situations. Instead, the young street vendors have made the marketplace a party area and the daily wage gets spent on alcohol, drugs, and betel nuts. One elderly trader asks me, "How much do you think these young men save? Nothing. They do not think it is their responsibility to look after their parents. It is sad to see them wasting away their lives." From the point of view of cautious traders, the recklessness of street vendors is unwarranted. After all, their long-term association with the marketplace has taught them to be prudent with money and not take for granted their earnings. It is not that street vendors do not think of their reckless nature. Especially the ones who are doing well for themselves are worried for their younger friends who are sometimes so careless as to drink and dance on the top floor, and one of them fell from there and was recovering from a severe accident. Not much is available to the street vendors regarding their prospects as they have not picked up any life-changing skills from the job and have not trained elsewhere. Anyone who has managed to get past the basic requirement of scanning consumers and has developed a technological skill set thinks it is possible for other street vendors to turn their life around if they keep to a straight and narrow path and do not waste away their youth by just drinking and wandering. But from the viewpoint of these young men who see the marketplace as an endless repeat of the same day, the revelry with friends is one of the few opportunities to vent and have a good time. Their most pressing concern is aging, that they perhaps would end up just doing this the rest of their lives, and they do not see any radical change coming into their lives.

On one side are the cautious traders and street vendors who have made their way to establish more or less stable roots in the business. On the other side are what appears to them as fatalistic young men living by the day and not strengthening their position in the marketplace. Each side feels the forms of alienation experienced by market actors; for one group, the need to be frugal arises from a fear of persecution and instability, and for the other group, their lack of an ethical life and their excesses make them feel alienation of another type, a resignation to the present to such an extent that even ethics would not produce any kind of soothing balm.

To the group that still manages to see a certain continuity and for that matter a betterment of their prospects in the best-case scenario, frugality and devotion are optimal virtues. And gods and human action both get judged by how they meet these standards. One can see links between frugality, aversion to greed, and emphasis on honesty. These virtues guide the traders and street vendors to come to terms with their considerable lack of mobility. After all, it is preferable to have an ethical register to live one's life frugally rather than always feel helpless and anxious. Traders and street vendors face slow business hours, and there is a pervasive fear that their income opportunities are running dry. The fear manifests as worries about an inability to pay school fees for children and rent for the shops. Street vendors fear police raids. In many encounters, they flee the scene even if their goods get confiscated. But the absolute worst is when one of them gets caught. The fear of being in police custody awaiting bail is a situation that street vendors want to avoid at any cost. Whenever anybody is in police custody, there is a tense atmosphere in the marketplace even as people continue with their trade. A part of the anxiety is guessing when the next raid will be. That the traders are back so soon despite warnings increases the chances of meeting harsh punishments. They are also worried about their friend in custody. Someone from the group, usually a senior vendor, pays the necessary fine to free their friend, but the procedure takes time, and the wait further increases their anxiety. Of course, arrests are not an everyday occurrence. The under-the-table dealings with law enforcers usually reduce the frequency of such raids. But there is the overall stress of competitive market commerce, of meeting expenses and clearing debts. It is unsurprising that moral stories, anecdotes, and proverbs are widespread in Delhi's bazaars. Often these tales have a message that hints at the other side of struggles, at how there is another register where failures in material pursuits can include spiritual benefits as a resource to make sense of their daily struggles. Perhaps in no other discussion is the reconciliation more visible than in the conversations around greed, as if a subject's entire moral compass stands on their negotiations with desires, and outlining how much is too much.

Greed as Social and Spiritual Depravity

Lobh, as greed is commonly known in bazaars, leads to calamities. For some time in 2013, I heard a rumor in Palika Bazaar about a particular shop assistant getting greedy and going to work for his ustaad's competitor. Indeed, choosing to work for a competitor's shop is one of the worst examples of greed and such acts do not have a positive outcome. In one of the stories, the shop assistant incurred a considerable loss and never earned the trust of the new trader. In another story, the extent of humiliation that he faced was enough for the shop assistant to come back to his former employer and ask for his for-giveness. The popular opinion is that it is better to have fewer financial gains than face social humiliation. As if shame were not enough, several folk stories remind the traders of the adverse effect of being greedy. Vivek narrates a dark tale of two friends losing everything just because they were greedy. He says the story originates in one of the Puranas.[8]

There were two good friends. One of them went to the Himalayas to med-itate with the hope of eventually appeasing the gods. His friend learned of this and followed him to the Himalayas. In one of their conversations, the first friend realized that the second friend would ask from the gods more than what he had intended to ask for himself. This realization did not sit well with the first friend. He was unhappy to find out that potentially his friend might end up being more prosperous than him. After the first friend's prayers were answered by the appearance of a god, he made his request: "I want you to cut off one hand and one of my legs and blind me in one eye." The god granted his wish. When the second friend came, he said he wanted twice as much as what the first friend wanted. As a result, he was blind in two eyes and was left without hands and legs.

After telling the story, Vivek speaks about the risk-taking nature of his friend, highlighting the links between moral stories and business. His friend had a photography shop but sold it recently to try his hand in event manage-ment. It perturbs Vivek that his friend changed his business when the pho-tography shop was earning a decent income. Nothing but avarice pushed his friend to take the risky decision and Vivek hopes that his friend will not face any untoward consequences because of a hasty decision.

The caution against greed forms a strong ethical life for bazaar actors. Geertz, Geertz, and Rosen (1979) observed frugality in Morocco's *suqs* in the 1960s, based on Islamic ideas, and more recently, Ilahiane and Sherry share similar insights about bazaars in Morocco. Ilahiane and Sherry (2008, 251) note that the traders of informal electronics in Joutia in Morocco use "Islam as an ethical and cultural force." Their account of the trader Samurai encap-sulates the anxiety of being a moral trader. The fear of Allah guides Samurai to strike a balance in commercial transactions. He does not cheat a customer beyond propriety, as he feels he may escape the wrath of the customer but not that of Allah. There are also instances when contemplations about just eco-nomic action order an otherwise chaotic life. "Regarding relations with the shopkeepers, the Samurai says, 'yes, they are legitimate, but they are greedy.

They're never satisfied with how much money they make because they have to pay some to the state. As for me, I'm a nomad. If I make five bucks in a day, that's great. That's the mercy of Allah" (252). Are there specific ways to connect the concept of greed to economic action? After all, every type of economic system—capitalist or noncapitalist—conjures certain images regarding greed, lest we forget Marx's (1887, 163) idea of capital as "dead labor which, vampire-like, lives only by sucking living labor, and lives the more, the more labor it sucks." Perhaps in noncapitalist systems, the sanction against greed comes from the community itself, while there exists a societal critique of capitalism as an unequal system. Or rather, social sanctions are strong as noncapitalist enterprises work closely with family, community, and personal networks to get support of different kinds. It is not to say capitalists aren't part of the kin network for the same reason, but the interrelationship varies. The everyday influence of community sanctions falls much more heavily on competitive market actors as they are operating in the same field as their network. In contrast, more prominent players have a distance that does not always have them meeting their competitors daily.

Small Is Beautiful and the Fight against Monopolies

The idea that ethics create boundaries of commerce is a less popular view. In most accounts, ethics encourage successful business ventures. A value of bazaar traders is "creditworthiness, which depended on social, moral and religious as much as economic performance, such that the moral qualities of piety and frugality would somewhat paradoxically translate into wealth and status" (Jain 2007, 96). The causal relationship between ethics and profit is an accepted idea of bazaar commerce and Indian capitalists. For instance, Rita Birla (2010) alludes to the literature that establishes strong linkages between the preaching of the Bhagavad Gita[9] and the creation of a successful Indian businessperson. "Indian management consultants now promote philosophies of corporate governance that claim to employ ancient wisdom such as those found in the *Bhagavat Gita* to learn 'self-mastery' for leadership and attracting fortune" (Birla 2010, 83). While ethics propagating successful business ventures is an accepted idea, other views are also present. As Partha Chatterjee (2008, 58) points out, "There are many examples where, if the business is doing particularly well, the vendors do not, like corporate capitalists, continue to accumulate on an expanded scale, but rather agree to extend their membership and allow new entrants." This is precisely the type of interrelationship that

Delhi's bazaar traders and street vendors show when it comes to legitimizing their commercial actions based on ethics. In doing so, the bazaar actors distance themselves from a capitalist tendency based on the continuous accumulation of profit. A critical way bazaar commerce maintains its distinctiveness from the capitalist economic system is by keeping its competitiveness.

This focus on ethics is not to suggest that within the marketplace no hierarchies and animosities are present. Hostilities arise when one trader spreads rumors about another that lead to his action being seen in a new light. In such a case, as Durkheim pointed out long ago, collective consciousness is enhanced. Following an incident of so-called betrayal, marketplaces are buzzing with allegations. Observations are made by random strangers and also traders who claimed to know the object of the rumor well enough to see that his actions were lacking propriety. However, being found to have spread a false rumor is also punished. To avoid being the target of social shaming and having to personally reflect on one's actions as falling short of the standard, bazaar actors do not want to come across as someone who destroyed the life chances of someone else. I have never met someone who was facing accusations. In fact, the absence of those figures says a lot about how they have been avoiding the marketplace. For example, stories began to follow when a trader in Palika could not pay off the money he borrowed as microcredit. "Who would have thought a trader with such a reputation can run away with other people's money?" Someone else quipped, "I always knew there was something odd about him. I did not trust him, to be honest." It went around how he avoids his shop, and the assistant minds the business in his absence. It was a complete disaster as far as other traders were concerned, for someone so respected to run away with other people's money. Ultimately, it was about losing respect and being unable to be in the marketplace with one's head held high.

The ethical life coincides with bazaar commerce so that traders can tackle their everyday trials and tribulations at an individual level and manage their shortcomings at a structural level. Bazaar actors are largely out of the formal education system and professional workspaces. In such a scenario, as is the case with most actors in the informal economy, one uses the resources at hand. The majority of the traders in Delhi's bazaars use their household savings, similar to most small-scale economies worldwide, to sustain their commerce (Besley and Levenson 1996). Particular attention is paid to seeing that acquiring a new stock of goods doesn't entail enormous risks for individual traders. "No risk, no gain" is not the mantra of the bazaars. Instead, as an informal economy hinging on meeting survival needs, there is much to gain from managing an income from the tried and tested methods. Once in a while, a trader invests beyond his means and achieves success from such a venture. Most of the time risk-taking does not bear desirable results. Rather than attributing such failures to structural inequality, traders and street vendors take them to indicate some kind of moral shortcoming. By attaching a negative attribute to a risk-taking nature, they see virtues in maintaining the status quo. On the other hand, in their view, big businesses lack virtues as they do not maintain a balance between greed and coexistence. Govind alleges big companies have a "sabotage mentality." As the phrase suggests, the sabotage mentality is an attitude where individual success is at the cost of other actors, like a giant tree that stunts the growth of smaller plants. Instead, Govind uses the allegory of the tea garden to talk about the equanimity with which bazaar actors operate, everybody of the same stature. As a result, many of them can flourish and not simply one. One observes the coexistence of different bazaar actors when accepting new members. Instead of new members being pushed out from the get-go, they get a chance to prove their sincerity. In the case of the street vendors in Nehru Place, most of them come from the same locality but by no means do new entrants get dissuaded from finding a job in the marketplace. In fact, the street vendors would welcome someone with financial problems who wants to earn a living by securing a space for trade. The most they would do is ask why a new person was there, and if they were happy with the response and ascertained that the reasons were genuine, street vendors would not stop a new vendor from starting his trade.

We must take the idea that bazaar actors are satisfied with "small profits" with a pinch of salt. We cannot know if bazaar actors would still follow high ideals if they had the resources to invest in ambitious projects. To what degree would they refuse success and wealth if it meant that they could expand in some other marketplace and multiply their income? Perhaps each one would take that opportunity if the wealth were significant enough for them to rise above the ethical life of a bazaar economy and not have to face their competitors regularly. Previous community morals do not bind them if they amass wealth that puts them above and beyond their competitors' reach. Nobody is against money-making; their current situation poses many hurdles in securing a stable position, and they are on the same level as the others. Those facing similar concerns are also looking for a similar ethical justification to give them a register of not having to feel frustrated about not being the prime movers in the economy. But since bazaar actors work with limited resources, a "non-sabotage mentality" goes with their level of economic life. Further, what is apparent is that bazaar actors are not alone in emphasizing coexistence. Early economic theory, including that espoused by Adam Smith, proposed that economic systems could be virtuous even though individual elements acted selfishly. "Each individual's hunger for profit will be kept in check by a similar drive among other individuals. Rather than producing ruthless greed, self-interest will tend to make people polite, serviceable, and honest" (Fourcade and Healy 2007, 287). Why do we hear less and less about instances of coexistence in mainstream societies?

Bazaar Ethics versus Capitalist Ethics

The ethical life of powerful actors and ordinary life are two distinct domains. Following a certain type of ethic has improved elites' life prospects. Ordinary actors like those in the bazaar economy have not been able to use ethics similarly. More often than not in bazaars, ethics sustain humble pursuits rather than make substantial gains. One reason for the difference between capitalist ethics and bazaar ethics can be attached to the role of the state and institutions in propagating certain interests. In his book *Adam Smith in Beijing: Lineages of the Twenty-First Century*, Giovanni Arrighi (2007, 331–32) writes, "The capitalist character of market-based development is not determined by the presence of capitalist institutions and dispositions but by the relation of state power to capital. Add as many capitalists as you like to a market economy, but unless the state has been subordinated to their class interest, the market economy remains non-capitalist." The relationship between profit maximization and capitalism is undoubtedly connected to institutions supporting a particular group over others. Although the forms and organization of power have changed, elites' influence in governance has meant that their interests are protected.[10] And for the rest of the society, capitalist ethics determining a certain pace and style of life is felt more as a constraint than freedom. In other words, while the non-elites witness what privileges mean in a consumer- and real estate–driven society, their own experience is only a negation of that world. There is a long history of elite actors benefiting from particular arguments with the state. In medieval Europe, the elites' control of common land created a substantial amount of disposable income. The excess income went toward mercantile activities, and states were central in assisting such processes of capital accumulation by supporting merchant families and networks. Many of these expansionary networks would not have survived if home countries did not protect company trade in colonies. For instance, in the case of Britain, the East India Company extended its monopoly trading rights into trading networks within colonies and subsequently changed the political fabric of foreign countries. The support that the company received from the crown blocking other corporations from having trade rights essentially gave the East India Company control over resources to deploy in different areas including political control over the colonies. In contemporary times, the relationships between big banks and states are the same. This has created a situation of almost complete impunity for certain actors at the cost of the suffering of many more. Take the examples of banks getting bailed out after the 2008 Wall Street crash or, more recently, austerity measures sanctioned on countries for what is largely the result of erroneous financial decisions of global banks. Institutions, including states, are working for the interests of those at the top (Tooze 2018). We do not even have to look at a crisis to see such favoritism. The strong support that formal institutions provide to elites has allowed them to resolutely carve an ethical life that fits their pursuit of success. Here, success itself is a virtue.

What is different with bazaar actors? Is the state utterly absent in their life? The influence of the state in bazaar commerce creates an identity to marketplaces as central to the economy or less significant. In Mughal bazaars, and colonial bazaars (Banerjee 2019), the state's presence was through taxes and revenues, and intermediate groups of administrators and functionaries negotiated power by playing different actors against one another. When we concentrate on a postcolonial context, the state as a regulatory body does not disappear altogether. From guaranteeing subsidies to actors, particularly for agricultural produce, the state as a juridical body is quite prominent in mass marketplaces. Perhaps more discreet are the underhand dealings with the state when engagement with institutional actors is not just about power maneuvers and lasting changes but about state actors becoming part of the everyday life of a bazaar economy. Partha Chatterjee's (2004) use of the Gramscian concept "political society" shows how within electoral democracies, state and popular classes develop their network of mutual favors, often employing money or utilities in exchange for votes. The shadow economy enables even those at the margins to better their chances. But state actors hardly come to the rescue of non-elite actors in the same capacity as they do for elite actors. Elite control also extends to these places. Subletting practices are a prime example of that. Rent-seeking "landlords" who initially leased shops from municipal bodies at a nominal rate create a hierarchy in the marketplace. As a result of establishing control of the shops early on, landlords are in a position to inflate rent without much resistance. At the end of the month traders have to pay as high as ₹ 75,000 and ₹ 100,000 for a shop in a marketplace like Palika Bazaar. Most shops of Palika are now divided into a number of small operations to share the shop's rent. Even in the most competitive market sphere, landlords have managed to carve a rentier system. And much like the stories that we hear about elusive capitalists, landlords are not far from that image. First of all, they are never in the marketplace. Yet their mythical presence loomed large in stories of a meeting about the welfare of the marketplace when the landlords were present, and one of them presided over the gathering. At times when traders did not know how to meet their rents that were rising, landlords were part of the conversations but never quite there. This absence is a simple illustration of elite privilege: one group has to experience the grind of everyday commerce, and another can swoop away with a chunk of money through networks and access to capital.

Elite actors creating easy alliances with state actors help translate a profit-maximization tendency into a capitalist one, where capital accumulation is multiplied. The "landlords" of Delhi's bazaars have not established a rentier economy by operating legally, but their transgressions have allowed them to gain certain privileges over time. In India, illegal and semi-legal dealings with the state are as much a reality of the "political society" as they are for liberal citizens of the "civil society." But what separates the interrelationship between the two spheres is that elites can cross over to the other zone; ordinary people cannot. Bazaar traders, for instance, cannot set the agenda for public discourses in the same manner as so-called liberal law-abiding citizens. Their sphere of influence is immediate. Whatever hope, frustration, and morality they preach have meaning within the economy of face-to-face commerce. Often there is sustained pressure to curtail the bazaar's sphere of influence. As if bazaar actors' existing in the margins weren't enough, civic society members have to have their eyes on informal pursuits for their involvement in criminal and uncivil activities.

The experience of a lack of protection has meant that bazaar traders' relationship with ethics will be one of caution. Bazaars' ethical life cannot mimic those of big businesses and financial capitalists where a quote from a religious text valorizes their acquisitive spirit. Ethics in the bazaar economy is a bandage that provides temporary relief in hours of stress. In other words, prosperity as an ethical position is readily available to elite actors as their life chances give them the freedom to traverse different zones without the crippling fear of retribution. The situation is quite the opposite for bazaar actors. Facing economic, legal, and social constraints in different areas of their life, they find that ethics provides a way to accept their predicament of being in the shadows.

More than an actual material and monetary marginalization, it is the shared experience of catching up with a profoundly changing urban context that creates a proletarian bazaar ethics. Each new fable is about restricting flight and more about the benefits of keeping low and accepting their fate. In Meena Bazaar in Delhi, Ajay Gandhi (2016b) observes that it is unsurprising to find a scruffy-looking vendor owning a big house and a beggar having powerful connections. Power and hierarchy are part of the bazaar world. Big traders will always have a certain kind of influence over small traders and a new entrant to the marketplace is likely to feel trade vulnerabilities in a different way than seasoned actors. In fact, there are examples of traders who put their ethical life aside to find other opportunities in other avenues of transnational trade and political negotiations. There are also instances of traders and street vendors breaking out of the collective ethos to formulate their own politics and ambition. But as a common condition of being, ethical life—fragments of traditions—remains one of the most vivid manifestations of a precarious life. This is particularly true for a people who feel the anxieties that come from operating in a competitive economic sphere, who are not designers of the urban environment and who repeatedly feel misunderstood by consumers and officials. Even a conservative estimate puts street vendors' monthly salaries between 25,000 and 30,000 Indian rupees and those of traders at about 1 lakh. By no means are they the most economically deprived group in the city. Yet after following their lives for a while, the things that stand out are the complaints about trade and their frustration of not finding allies in government and bourgeois public life. Not one single day passed when traders and street vendors did not encounter some form of dejection and disappointment. The stories that they tell each other are a rendition of their common condition. Seen from one perspective, it is the predicament of not being at the center of urban economic and political life, but from another perspective it shows the spirit of reinvention and not giving up. This spirit comes out strongly in the next chapter describing the bazaar practitioners facing their toughest competitor to date—e-commerce platforms.

5

Bazaar Platforms: Encounters with a New Competitor

The online will drown us all.
—*Harish, trader, Lajpat Rai Market*

IN THE LAST DECADE, the academic literature and journalism have focused considerably on the platform economy.[1] From startups to internet giants and e-commerce aggregators, it is an efficient rentier system where one earns not just by creating a product but also by providing a platform for viewing and buying third-party products. In the Indian case the most visible representation of the platform economy came in the way of air-conditioned white mini cabs that suddenly began to crowd city roads. Drivers for companies such as Uber and Ola rubbed shoulders with drivers of Delhi's *kalapila* (black and yellow) taxis. Many of these new drivers were recruits from the enormous pool of unemployed labor in the city, and others gave up odd jobs to find flexible sources of income. Emerging scholarship analyzes the problematic intrusion of e-commerce giants into the informal economy.[2] The uberization of taxi drivers increased unpaid loans and the chances of layoffs, much like delivery drivers and courier personnel who were at the mercy of apps to secure an income. On top of the complexity of labor relations, e-commerce sites have shaken the local economy of corner stores and bazaars. When e-commerce sites first entered the retail scene in India, Delhi's bazaar did not have a ready-made plan to engage with the platform economy. What followed was a series of trial-and-error attempts. The survival instinct of the bazaar actors kicked in early. But that did not mean that the road ahead was simple. Traders and street vendors struggled to establish an empowering relationship with the platform economy. Only after a long period of struggle, bazaar actors managed to establish a relatively stable relationship with e-commerce platforms. The following excerpt sets a resilient tone about technology in the bazaar. And this is why the response to e-commerce sites, as is evident in subsequent sections, is so compelling.

Field notes, Palika Bazaar, February 10, 2013
I am at Rohit's shop at Palika Bazaar. We are eyeing the stream of people entering the marketplace. He is getting anxious for someone to enter the shop, and half-heartedly participates in the conversation. At some point, the conversation moves from games to the general state of the marketplace, what it is like for other traders who sell clothes and accessories. To my surprise, Rohit shows much more enthusiasm to comment on the trade of other shopkeepers. He says, "I am happy that I did not start by selling clothes. There is just not much innovation in that area. Can you imagine having to work with the same line of business over the years? With electronics, it is different. Look at me! I started by selling DVD players and now am selling games and smart phones." Rohit says he is grateful to have chosen a business that does not languish from the prospect of lack of innovation. The chances of him getting bored with such a trade is slim because, unlike clothes, in his opinion, there will always be a new gadget that will attract people. Rohit discusses the possibility of tinkering with the materiality of electronics that products like garments do not offer. Disassembling a mobile phone and a console, to know the hardware inside out, is a different experience from learning the cut and feel of a garment. No matter how much one can know about the texture of a garment, a clothes vendor is neither a tailor nor a weaver. A garment vendor's relationship with the product exists within certain boundaries. They are good with what is in front of them and are expert salespersons but according to Rohit are never as experimental with their products as electronic traders are in the marketplace. The ease that traders develop around technological products gives them the courage to evolve with each new product. They

establish a sense of ownership to make the product yield to local needs of consumers, either by repairing work or doing custom-made tinkering on products and accessories.

The conversation with Rohit comes to my mind in 2014 while sitting at Bharat's shop at Lajpat Rai Market. The mood that day about new technology is completely different from the optimism that Rohit showed toward electronics trade awhile back. Bharat is preoccupied with the impending threat of the rise of e-commerce platforms and how bazaars may cease to exist under pressure from their newest competitor. It's not just Bharat; many other traders share the same set of worries about how e-commerce platforms are going to be bazaars' nemesis. Given that it is not the first time that Delhi's bazaars have seen change, why does the internet evoke such nervousness in the marketplace? Is it because traders cannot dismantle the material infrastructure and remake it to their advantage? Or are the fears about online platforms misplaced? As we see in subsequent sections, it is a bit of both.

"Demon" Technology and Making Sense of the New

The "online marketplace" gained ground in the 2010s, putting the traders and street vendors of the popular marketplaces in Delhi in a very insecure spot. We are speaking of a time when suddenly the e-commerce market in India grew from 3.9 billion USD in 2009 to 12.6 billion USD in 2013 (ASSOCHAM and EY 2016). The general logic of the platform economy in India, like in the West, has been to produce aggregators that can mediate traditional B2C (business to customer) sectors including food, garments, taxi rides, hotels, and so on. We rarely see e-commerce venturing into new territories, which is why the informal economy feels threatened. The traditional *kirana* store (neighborhood grocer) has to compete with delivery apps and the "cash on delivery" option of e-commerce aggregators. Whatever now went wrong in small traders' businesses was due to the rise of the "online." The worn-out faces of the traders and street vendors, and dwindling consumers at the shops, were shreds of evidence of impending doom. "This online will drown us all. Tell me why someone would come out in the heat to buy something from our shops when they can get it delivered at their doorstep." The quality of the shopping experience is one of the many concerns of a trader at Lajpat Rai Market. He continues, "You can now sell anything online, also secondhand products."

The reference to the secondhand product is interesting as bazaars enjoy a secured clientele because they sell used and pirated products. E-commerce platforms such as OLX sell secondhand goods and target one of the last bastions of bazaar trade: the market for old and secondhand products.

In the different complaints, the e-commerce platforms emerge as a monster-like creature, an unknown danger against which the traders are helpless. Some obvious remarks made are about the English language, which alienates them from the technology. On popular social media platforms such as Facebook, the traders quickly switched to Hindi, an option that at the time was unavailable for e-commerce platforms. Further, with e-commerce platforms, negotiations are complicated. Unlike a face-to-face market exchange, there is little space for the bazaar traders to charm consumers. When I ask them if they have tried to sell something online, I received a resounding no. "How can we! We do not understand a head or tail about online marketplaces. Even to register, one has to fulfill several criteria. I can never become part of this world." Other responses are about how bazaar goods cannot sell online. A trader in the Lajpat Rai Market remarks, "We can never sell online. There are just too many regulations. It is not like here (in the bazaar), where you go and sell anything. You have to first register as a vendor. And they will never accept a person like me with my reputation for selling gray products." In all these perceptions, what stands out is the larger-than-life conception of the online platforms. It develops as an entity with an almost supernatural presence. Phrases such as "the online demon will bring us all down" are repeated in many conversations. The same traders and street vendors who spoke about the benefits of trading in electronics because they constantly find something new to sell looked utterly helpless before their latest competitor.

Sometimes the goddess Kali was brought into the conversation for her to intervene and kill the online demon. As they said, it is now up to divine intervention to get them out of the mess as the traders did not see much that they could do on their own to defeat the unfamiliar threat. In the ordinary world, *techne*, humans, and gods coexist. In Dipesh Chakrabarty's (2000) *Provincializing Europe*, he criticizes European universalism that puts forward a strict separation of the religious from the secular. In such a binary, Chakrabarty believes the hybridity of cultural practices get lost. Workers worshipping the Hindu god of craftsmanship, Vishwakarma, is a case in point. Although it is easy to see the religious rituals performed before tools and machinery to procure secular gains such as well-being and prosperity as irrational and superstitious to an outsider, Dipesh maintains that cultural meanings get in-scribed in rituals. The frequent evocation of gods in conversations and actual practices creates continuity between human, nonhuman, and supernatural beings. The traders bringing up gods in everyday conversations show the pos-sibility of connecting *techne* with gods in a non-Western cosmos.[3] Only per-haps in Western philosophical thought is *techne* of an instrumental nature where it becomes a means to an end. Here, technology appears as a challenge to overcome, as does nature. "The revealing that rules in modern technology is a challenging [*Herausfordern*], which puts to nature the unreasonable demand that it supply energy that can be extracted and stored as such" (Heidegger 1977, 14). Heidegger essentially sees this modern approach to technology as a shift from the original Greek *techne* related to *poiesis*, the "bringing-forth" of the multiple forms of an object.[4]

In the context of Delhi's bazaar, *techne* continues to exist within the messy terrain of usefulness and awe-generating entities eventually to be brought under control by supernatural forces. Often evocation of gods appears as the most accessible way to speak about the unspeakable. In a certain sense, under the aegis of gods, even the worst situation can turn into something bearable. The bazaar actors' reservations are about having a new competitor and more to do with the fact that they cannot comprehend the inner workings of this new "demon." I see the traders' changed demeanor when I utter the word "online." In subsequent visits to the bazaars, I am careful not to utter the word "online" too many times and upset the traders. This reaction is in sharp con-trast to their other competitors, like the traders of upscale marketplaces. Al-though disappointed with shopping malls diverting parts of their consumer range, bazaar traders use a dry sense of humor when they talk about traders at upscale marketplaces. Perhaps that's the reason why the phantasmic presence of the "online" is striking. The traders cannot humanize the new technology through humor. Also, the chance of tinkering with "online" technology ap-pears to be minimal, and the lack of that prospect makes them nervous about a technology where they cannot use regular tricks and cheats.

Looking for Answers

In 2013 and 2014, I thought that the physical marketplaces would not sur-vive their latest competitor. Even as I was under this impression, a few trad-ers took the following concrete steps toward understanding the operation of e-commerce platforms. Bharat tells me that his friend has recommended a chartered accountant who can assess his assets and income if need be to transport to an online business presence. The move helps Bharat as the accountant advises him to show part of his gray income as legitimate. A few months later, he has a different strategy. The chartered accountant costs him a lot of money, and he realizes that the only way he can show his transaction and goods as legal will be to change his line of business entirely. Bharat looks for other ways to get online without suspending his existing trade. He learns how to hide his personal computer's IP address, which gives him the confidence to sell gray goods online. His logic is that even if he gets caught, his identity will not be immediately traceable. He is betting on his chances now.

By 2016, their experience with the online economy has shifted for the traders. It is far from a mystifying world with impossible rules and demands. Somewhere in the middle of all sorts of concern, it has started to be familiar. At least, traders can strategize their moves on e-commerce sites. Ankit, a trader in Palika, is now a full-time delivery person and e-commerce vendor. His daily routine includes "whatsapping" different traders on his list and updating their demands. After getting their orders, he drives his worn-out Maruti van to different wholesale marketplaces in the city to acquire the required material. At the end of the day, Ankit delivers the goods to shops in different parts of the city. He is also a registered vendor on several e-commerce sites and is happy with the profit he is making. When I ask him about the prospects of online business, he says, "You would be surprised how much money you can make online. Like just the other day, I got a payment of ₹ 6000 from selling power banks. The original power banks are expensive. I found Chinese copies and uploaded them on the site. Almost within a day, most of them got sold out." Ankit thinks that e-commerce sites do not run very differently from the bazaars; the administrators do not care what products they sell. As long as products are attracting customers, the platforms aren't concerned about day-to-day affairs overseeing every minute detail. The days are over of bothering vendors when they had to answer for every little complaint made against them. Since eBay came into the picture and started selling a variety of commodities, administrative personnel react differently to the type of goods sold online. They can't be so precise any more about the quality of products, as online platforms now have secondhand and "Made in China" products in their repertoire of best-selling items. Ankit adds that he is doing a good job, and usually his reviews are between three and four

stars on a scale of zero to five. Also, to avoid complications, he has given
different bank account details so the administrators will struggle to connect
different transactions to the same person. Still, his action once comes to a
website's notice. He had to speak to someone in administrative personnel for
two hours to get things sorted. Ankit does not panic. All he does is exchange
some of the damaged items for good pieces. With his swift action, he avoids
getting too many bad reviews.

By now, traders have learned several ways to outwit e-commerce platforms.
They make the utmost effort to avoid getting bad reviews. To do that, traders
exploit every avenue available to them, to find loopholes in the online interface
and use additional services to their advantage. There are instances of traders
making informal arrangements with courier services to discharge fake "out
on delivery" receipts. The fake receipts help traders get extra time to acquire
products that are not in the shop. This tactic comes in handy to meet the delivery time requirement even when items aren't immediately available. The by-
passing of e-commerce rules through bazaar shenanigans is not merely about
fraudulent practices. It points to something else—bazaar actors negotiate the
infrastructure of a formal trade network that gravitates toward moneyed customers and vendors by opening a buffer zone of informal arrangements that,
among other things, give them extra time to complete transactions. If they
play according to the rules, platforms would not be a hospitable place for informal actors. As they import familiar tactics online, they create a temporary
trading corner in an otherwise "regulated" environment.

All Is Not Well, or the Struggles of Maintaining a Stable Business Online

Lulu is a legend in Palika Bazaar. Many conversations in the shop of Rajesh and
Rohit (two brothers who ran a game and mobile phone cover shop in Palika
Bazaar) mention Lulu. The two brothers are intrigued by Lulu spending hours
in his west Delhi rented room surfing the internet and learning new skills.
Growing up with similar backgrounds, Rajesh and Rohit are in awe of Lulu's
self-taught skills without prior knowledge of the English language. According
to them, Lulu has no problem accessing e-commerce sites. He can converse
with anyone online whether it is an administrator or a trader from China. The
two brothers trust Lulu to set up their shop's online account. Lulu travels to
China to get exclusive products, which he later uploads onto e-commerce sites.
The partnership is bearing fruit; the two brothers look after the business at the

shop, and Lulu takes care of the online business. The happy alliance does not last very long. One day in February 2017, Rajesh is visibly upset. He complains about how Lulu betrayed them and absconded with ₹ 1 lakh. The betrayal is a huge blow, and Rajesh says they lost most of their savings. When I ask them if they are willing to continue their online trade, Rajesh says that they are most certainly suspending all online transactions as Lulu handled everything. Another day that week, Rajesh is speaking to a young couple about online commerce. The couple are undergraduate students with a good grasp of digital technologies. They are willing to try their hands at becoming e-commerce vendors. After they leave the shop, I show enthusiasm about the two brothers finding people to manage their online account after Lulu left. Rajesh is not convinced: "Our eyes are no longer on the online business. We are just letting these kids try their hand, but it is not our focus."

In several other conversations a sign of resignation to the new competitor was palpable. Like the time when Rohit said that the dwindling number of consumers in the bazaars is nothing but an indication of the shifting allegiance of previously loyal customers to the e-commerce platforms. He was dejected to see that not much time had passed since e-commerce sites had made their presence felt in India and already old marketplaces are facing the brunt of them. "What can we do in this situation! Online has advantages that we cannot compete with. With smartphones and internet connection, who would not want to buy with just a click of the finger." Against the scorching Delhi heat, Rohit's statement rings true. Indeed, who would want to venture out of their home to buy things they are getting delivered at their doorstep at a reasonable price. The complaints and worries that on some occasions appear excessive, in the case of e-commerce platforms are justified.

Bringing the Platforms to the Bazaars

After that conversation with Rajesh in 2017, I come away carrying a bleak image of the bazaars. The traders' constant search to find a foothold in the platform economy is failing, in their own words; it is their biggest challenge to date. From the early days of 2013, the traders have moved from perceptions into making a real foray into the e-commerce business, but the checkered journey has exhausted them. When I visited the marketplaces in 2018, I expected a repeat of the doom and gloom narrative. I was wrong—there is a buoyant mood in the marketplaces. The usual complaints aren't there, and the body language of the traders is relaxed. I am back at Rajesh and Rohit's shop in Palika Bazaar. Rajesh says to me, "No, the online will not destroy places like this. We will always have customers coming to these markets." His rationale is that there are customers in India who do not have the money and information to purchase a new product immediately. Bazaars cater to the masses, those who have not upgraded to new technology at a fast pace. Further, he says that "impossible titles you will only find in the marketplace. You can buy anywhere but ultimately to sell things you are here." Both these observations point toward the thriving secondhand market for games. Even though a few e-commerce sites post secondhand items, it does not compare to an extended customer base of the bazaars. When there is a demand for particular games, bazaars can present limited editions and games that have been out of circulation for a while. Traders can call their regular contacts, and they can also rely on their inventory to produce rare titles in cartridge games, TV and console games stacked up in basements and storage areas in the shops. Contrast this scenario to e-commerce platforms—the reach of secondhand games is limited to what users list on the platform on a day-to-day basis. Even when consumers manage to find "impossible titles," they have to go through bureaucratic procedures of making payments online and wait for the delivery of items and see to it that everything is in order. Bazaar traders feel the hassle further discourages customers from shopping online.

It's not just the wide reach of the bazaars; something else relaxes the traders. They arrive at a comfortable place of negotiation. Rather than turning into vendors and delivery personnel, the best option, they feel, is to engage with the platform economy from the outside with their feet in the bazaars. This they do by making maximum use of bargains on e-commerce sites. E-commerce sites frequently have annual sales, such as Flipkart's "Big Billion Days" and Amazon's "Great Indian Sales." Taking the opportunity, traders buy materials online in bulk and sell them to direct customers at a higher rate. Opening up the platforms as another distributive network and interacting with the e-commerce sites as consumers gives bazaar actors agency. By finding the alternative space that neither governments nor e-commerce platforms predicted, bazaar actors engage with the platform economy on their terms. Government policies and e-commerce platforms foresaw the informal economy's transformation as delivery personnel and e-commerce vendors. Neither of these roles preserved the independence of the bazaar actors as small business owners. Engaging with the platforms' economy as consumers has opened up an advantageous position; they can continue their physical trade and turn their biggest competitor into an expansive supply network.

Bazaar Actors' Way of Confronting the Platform Economy

Some traders continue to act as occasional vendors on e-commerce sites. Yet others are courier personnel delivering warehouse goods door-to-door. However, none of the traders make e-commerce platforms their only way of seeking a livelihood. Both platform vendors and delivery personnel must play by the rules of the platform economy. These roles push traders away from their comfort zone and make them vulnerable to an external employer to earn a living. Being a vendor, the traders struggle to get an intimate understanding of a system that essentially privileges the English language and a specific type of computer literacy that is not readily available to them. The inadequacy is felt more with the platform economy than with social media. Facebook and WhatsApp are the most popular apps used by the bazaar traders. They are constantly on both these applications on their smartphones. The unprecedented popularity of these social media applications is because of the possibility of creating micro-worlds within large platforms. Depending on the community, Facebook home pages and WhatsApp messages will look different. The applications allow for their sociality to flourish with forwards from friends and memes, a welcome respite from their quotidian activities. On hearing a particular trader laugh at a post on Facebook, others in the shop gather to see what the joke is all about. The exchanges continue until they lose interest in that piece of information. Business dealings with Chinese counterparts on the QQ app is an additional trade network outside of face-to-face commerce.

Compared to these familiar social platforms, e-commerce is an imposition of an entirely different and unknown system. While a few traders master the new trade, the regulation and rating system are alien to their way of life. Creating an online persona based on the interface does not come naturally to the traders, which, unlike Facebook and WhatsApp, require a completely different sensibility. Bazaars are known to carry an ambiguous reputation when it has do with their products and codes of commerce. It is only by word of mouth and the shared intersubjective world of the traders and consumers that both parties navigate a slippery terrain. Contrasted to the messy world of the bazaars is the profile of the e-commerce vendor who comes across as a transparent, reliable vendor. To an extent, the traders manage the image-making by manipulating the rating system. They see through the loopholes of the system and how, beneath the surface, it is not significantly different from a physical marketplace.[5] Nonetheless, in the long run, it is not advantageous to be in a position where an external administrator and an algorithm are measuring one's performance.

As far as becoming delivery personnel for a global platform is concerned, delivery services do not guarantee a stable income. At some point or other, many traders operate as delivery personnel or are in contact with people who run the delivery services for the shop. Delivery services are an additional income source but are not the sole income-generating prospect. If delivery is the only means to earn a living, a trader has come down the economic and social hierarchy. In fact, there are instances when someone took a delivery job after losing a business at the marketplace. Ankit, who is a delivery person and part-time e-commerce vendor, only chose that route because he failed to keep his business afloat in Palika Bazaar. He is aware of the temporary nature of his current work and is saving enough money to pay back his debts and restore the business at the shop. In any given situation, having a physical shop is a desirable position. That advantage is why many traders feel frustrated with the platform economy as it targets their businesses and is, in their own words, looking to turn them into informal labor.

At the same time, the practical experience of engaging with the platform economy has been different. Apart from a few dire cases, traders and street vendors in the three marketplaces hold their own while negotiating with e-commerce platforms. The long-term experience of working in a competitive market economy has developed in the traders a sophisticated way of gazing at challenges and turning them into opportunities. Such negotiations are not a one-off strategy but a culmination of trial-and-error methods that enable bazaar actors to produce a desirable position vis-à-vis e-commerce platforms.

Being a Consumer and a Seller at the Same Time

The phrase "consumer is king" is also valid in the platform economy. Bazaar traders realize that their most advantageous position while dealing with e-commerce platforms is to take the place of an actor who is under minimum surveillance from the websites. As consumers, traders buys from e-commerce platforms without worrying about their reputation. They operate entirely under the radar—the e-commerce platforms seldom blacklist consumers for purchasing a certain amount of goods. In fact, such excess is welcome. Contrast this to a vendor that is trying to sell x amount of goods: there is a lot more scrutiny of the quality of his goods. The e-commerce platforms, according to the traders, are interested in maintaining a balance. They do not want one particular trader to monopolize the marketplace so as not to lose out on revenue coming from different vendors. There is no such pressure on the consumption side. The more platforms they sell, the better it is for the actors involved. Early on, bazaar actors learn of this differential treatment and use it to their advantage. Instead of worrying about ratings, they keep an eye on significant discounts to buy things in bulk. Even though individual buyers are still looking for discounts, they are less likely to be as strategic as bazaar traders. First of all, unlike bazaar traders, individual consumers are unlikely to check websites regularly for discounts. Bazaar traders and street vendors peruse e-commerce platforms daily to know which new item has been added, what is on sale on a given day, and which items are trending. Also, having a keen knowledge of products in the shop, they can easily spot things that need restocking. At times, while browsing discounted products, traders can spot new items. This is particularly true for accessories. The quick turnover of many accessories such as power banks, adaptors, and batteries provide an easy income source for traders. As accessories are not as high-priced as gadgets but can improve user interface, regular customers are happy to try new accessories without having to go through the deliberations of buying an expensive console. Traders and street vendors have a sound judgment about the types of accessories that have the potential of becoming best-selling items. They do not lose time to stock popular items at their shops.

Deleuze and Guattari's (1987) idea of "nomads" reflects traders' and street vendors' ingenuity of carving a third space of coordinating their physical business with distributive e-commerce networks. In *A Thousand Plateaus* (1987), they argue that "the life of a nomad is the *intermezzo*"; the nomad exists in the in-between space of two points, in the sense of never permanently exiting any point and also simultaneously inhabiting a "local" that brings together different places of "varying orientations." How Delhi's traders use the online and physical spaces of the bazaars gives us a glimpse of a nomad's life and their strategic position of working between mediums. In Deleuze and Guattari's work, nomads were like Genghis Khan, who challenged the Western idea of warfare and rational planning. The guerrilla strategy was clear opposition to state organizational models. In an entirely different era, Delhi's traders also inhabit some of the qualities of the nomads: to evade control of the state and private corporations. As such, they moved, "but while being seated and only seated while moving" (Deleuze and Guattari 1987, 381).

The guerrilla strategy that traders use to engage with e-commerce platforms—being a vendor, consumer, and physical trader at the same time— provide a shielding mechanism similar to the one produced by the steppe nomads' movement. Somehow existing in all three places yet not permanently being in one, traders continue their rhizomatic existence that has on previous occasions enabled marginal groups to resist state control. The position that Delhi traders find most advantageous vis-à-vis e-commerce platforms is to maintain a certain level of fluidity. Traders and street vendors keep different modes of interaction alive, but the most preferential status is still the one when traders do not give up their independent business status. Such a maneuver places marginal dependence on online presence to meet survival needs. The bazaar "war machines" do not develop out of the blue. They are the result of lengthy negotiations, stretching from phases when the traders were vulnerable and defeatist to reaching a stage when they became confident about holding their own ground in front of their newest competitor.

Seeing how much bazaar actors struggled to find a formidable space to engage with e-commerce sites, it begs the question, is the world of platform economy really that different from the bazaars? Are people involved in this field different from bazaar level practitioners? I was able to delve into some of these queries on a month-long study of a prominent co-working space in Delhi.

A Co-working Space in Delhi

I regularly visited a co-working space in South Delhi in February 2016. When I stepped into the reception room, I saw mood boards and companies' brand names in large fonts across the main hall. I had seen similar spaces in Milan and Bangkok where young entrepreneurs surrounded themselves with quirky furniture and motivational quotes. Apart from that, the other visible similarity was the "meetup" hour with mentors when young startuppers discussed fledgling ideas, and difficulties they faced in launching their projects. Not to make any simplistic assumption about the homogeneity of such places, but what struck me in all these places was how young graduates increasingly saw their future as digital entrepreneurs. Middle-class youths, many of them just out of engineering colleges and some still in college, began to use co-working spaces to develop their startups. Different groups wanted to create something that had the potential of scalability to make projects attractive to venture capitalists.

Most young entrepreneurs were not looking for a sustainable business model but rather something to develop that caught buyers' interest immediately. Their ambition was to strike a dream deal and retire as a millionaire. The successes of Flipkart and Paytm were business models that a lot of the young startuppers wanted to mimic. In their conversations, I found it interesting that the most exciting prospect for them was to see their project becoming a unicorn company, a privately held startup valued at more than 1 billion USD. The people at the co-working space did not show as much enthusiasm about the everyday operation of their ventures. Their enthusiasm dwindled when I asked them about how they are going to establish contacts with available businesses and coordinate with different sets of people. Instead, they liked to discuss the valuation of companies that started from the same place as them and within a year or so doubled or even tripled their profit. It was all about having that one good "idea." Some even spoke about getting ideas in their dreams and were waiting for that day when they struck gold. Not everyone came up with a unique idea; many of them wanted to replicate business models that have already done well in the past. I spoke to a group of young entrepreneurs who wanted to develop a tourism-related platform where one could book a hotel, a guided tour, a spa, and adventure rides on the same website. Another team was interested in starting an elite food delivery app catering to affluent clientele in South Delhi alone.

When I asked about logistics and how they were going to aggregate local businesses, many of their ideas about the informal economy appeared somewhat skewed. While discussing, for instance, custom-made food delivery apps, labor came up casually in conversations while talking about hiring delivery drivers. A startupper in his early twenties told me each driver would go through a careful selection process. One of the essential criteria listed was the ability to speak in English, in addition to being well behaved and trustworthy. Employing drivers was one of the main ways to engage with the informal economy. The same imperatives also came up when talking about hiring drivers for heavy utility vehicles. The need for an experienced driver was mentioned by startuppers who focused on building a platform for school stationery items. They would need someone to deliver goods from warehouses to sorting centers in the city. Other than employing informal labor for delivery and other needs, there was no long-term idea of collaboration with people from different segments of the urban economy.

Seeing the informal sector having an abundance of labor is not an ingenious idea per se when specific platforms such as food delivery apps already connect many street-level restaurants to local consumers. As far as the start-uppers are concerned, they are caught up in the financial side of the equation. Not much attention is given to understanding the scope of such businesses and how they influence the local economy, for instance, to know where the actual need for innovation is other than aggregating existing local businesses or hiring informal labor as delivery drivers.

There can be other novel ways to determine sustainable business models that capture the gap in existing infrastructure. To give an example: Very early in my fieldwork, one bazaar trader notes how unimaginative big business is when it comes to understanding the needs of local consumers. He refers to a company like Sony that does not know much about the finances of the average Indian household. English is still the main language or only option for most of the releases of big companies and they do not consider the precarious infrastructure of many countries. Their target consumer is only a tiny proportion of the actual population interested in gaming. That is the reason why in the trader's opinion modding consoles and selling secondhand games are important avenues for bazaars to develop a steady clientele. What this particular trader observes about foreign companies perhaps is true also for some of the digital platforms. Their assessment of the local market is not necessarily sophisticated enough to be swift and innovative regarding the actual needs of ordinary people. On the other hand, bazaars enjoy an upper hand over e-commerce platforms because of their keen understanding of ordinary life.

Falling Back on Familiar Faces

It is easy to understand why bazaar actors are taken by surprise by their newest competitor, and most of their initial plans are a reaction to those fears. At the crux is the keen sense that platforms are targeting their traditional consumer base: a section of the population looking for a good bargain, sometimes even at the cost of the quality of products. The e-commerce platforms penetrate the traditional customer base of the bazaar economy: urban non-elites and small-town consumers. It is not unusual to see bikers going to the remotest part of the country delivering to rural consumers everything from a refrigerator to games. Until a few years ago, consumers visited their nearest town or city marketplace to buy consumer durables. In a way, bazaars suffer competitively as it seems that e-commerce platforms can deliver everything that bazaars provide even better and more conveniently, to the consumer's benefit. Perhaps the only real advantage that bazaars still hold over platforms is their in-depth understanding of diverse lives in the local context. It is unlikely that employees at Flipkart and Amazon have detailed knowledge about neighborhood businesses, with their daily demands for commodities queued as WhatsApp feeds to the traders. The minute details of local trade are the type of information that bazaar actors have at their fingertips. Bazaar traders have detailed knowledge about their immediate marketplace, neighborhood shops, and roadside kiosks. This knowledge does not come from algorithms and aggregating information at one place but in a true Lefebvre fashion by walking the city. For instance, traders at Palika Bazaar, Nehru Place, and Lajpat Rai know the assets of the roadside kiosk to understand who their next-door competitors are. Traders have an avid sense of the surrounding atmosphere. If traders want to expand their business and establish new contacts, they know whom to approach.

Apart from vendors' knowledge of the immediate surroundings, they benefit from cities' popular meeting points under trees and strategic locations (close to government offices, for instance) where people gather for lunch and tea. In such gatherings, traders learn about what goes on in high places and what files are circulating in office corridors. Of courses, most of this information is gossip, but they gain knowledge about things outside their trade. I have on a few occasions accompanied traders from Palika Bazaar to have tea at a stall near the central secretariat in Delhi that has key ministerial departments. Clerks, rickshaw pullers, and roadside vendors eat at the same shop. Not everybody participates in the ensuing conversation, but chances of making a random acquaintance with people from different walks of life are high. When I was there with Vishal one day, he initiated a conversation with a roadside vendor close to the tea stall. He first spots the vendor selling mobile phone cases under a giant Peepal tree as we continue our two-way conversation. Vishal asks me about my day and simultaneously tries to weigh in on the vendor's trade. He wants to know if the roadside vendor would be willing to sample some of the mobile phone cases he recently acquired from Karol Bagh marketplace in Delhi. After hearing Vishal's talk about the attractive color schemes and reasonable price, the vendor agrees to see on his next visit what Vishal has to offer. The city has many places where people from all walks of life meet. One aspect of the conversation can take a commercial turn where both parties, strangers a minute ago, are in the position to enter into a mutually benefiting exchange.

The resilience of the bazaar economy comes from a messy and lived network of people, objects, and places. Here, relationships develop from chance meetings and sustained contact when business relationships change into friendships. The sociality of the bazaar economy is what keeps it afloat through various challenges. It may appear elementary: what ultimately makes a bazaar-level economy unique is again not proprietary acquisitions but habits, practices, and tools that are common to us. Conversations, networks of strangers, and familiar people who know the ins and outs of a city are a collective resource like no other. Taking inspiration from Dick Hobbs and Malin Akerstrom, Ruggiero and South (1997, 67) state, "In the bazaar, 'Jacks-of-all-trades' are common, and a high degree of independence is valued, people are constantly . . . on the outlook for every opportunity, for example moving around bars finding out 'what's up,' and 'connecting' with others." The insider knowledge is perhaps why informal economies in Lagos or Delhi emerge as radical spaces. Anthropological coverage of the network of an urban underbelly finds that is where radical social forms exist—the zone where a pure type of capitalism does not operate. Instead, there are possibilities for different ways of being modern. Perhaps what one needs is a change of focus, one different than the dominant understanding that inhabiting the modern world means existing in the corridors of power, and under the glitz and glamor of capitalist consumer spaces and private real estate. Instead, a rich way of being modern is also prevalent in the streets, mainly in the Global South where advanced technological products flourish alongside a traditional knowledge base, analog media, and dilapidated architecture.

In contrast, e-commerce platforms are doing everything in their reach to introduce a new way of life where the popular technological question would no longer be about the digital coexisting with other ways of acting but would make the digital the start of everyday exchange, surveillance, and work. And in many ways, they are succeeding. With the widespread use of smartphones, the traditional consumers that depended on cash can now use digital payment and shop from home. Further, as mentioned, the presence of different types of products online means that even consumers previously dependent on bazaars can find things online from one or two key platforms. There is an increasing tendency to establish monopolies in the retail sphere in India, and the digital platform is a critical centralizing force, as seen in the quick rise of Jio in India as a go-to provider for internet connection (Mukherjee 2018). It is a sure method, as not much pushes consumers to step out of the home; they have everything literally at their fingertips: they can use the same device, usually the smartphone, to shop, pay bills online, and trade in commodities.

To talk about a bazaar way of life is to see the flaws in its alternative that is introducing a more impersonal way of life as an imposition from above, an impoverished societal and ecological composition. Instead, the bazaar-level digital society is a mix of many things, the old and the new, the physical and the online world, but without one aspect pushing out the other. If in fact there has to be a priority, it will be on the side of people and seamless human, non-human technological interface. An easy way to register the difference between bazaar technological society and that brought about by e-commerce platforms is that in the former there is a horizontal dimension, people are constantly looking at each other, and in the latter they are adapting to a vertical platform. This difference was in fact brought out by Ajay, a trader from Lajpat Rai Market who is noticing a difference in the interaction in the marketplace already. He observes that before smartphones and platforms, there used to be far more face-to-face conversations; now when there is free time most of the traders are looking at their phone and scrolling mindlessly. Also, with consumers getting used to having a lot of services delivered at the doorstep, Ajay says it is a different energy altogether—it is as if people have forgotten spontaneous conversations.

To lose sight of the rich street economies and their myriad life forms is to continue to restrict the modern world to certain standards. We lose out on capturing available modes of existence that, because of a lack of interest from elite actors, are at risk of becoming obsolete, and we risk serious threats to people's life chances. Particularly under the current climate emergency and pandemic among other crises, these conversations are just beginning to take place. What we lose by physical bazaars becoming an ancillary to e-commerce platforms is that there is no longer a viable option for small independent actors to carve out their pace and rhythm of commerce; they are at the mercy of impersonal infrastructure and website admin personnel with whom they have few direct encounters. In fact, the new order of the platform economy introduces a vertical commerce where a small number of platforms employ a large pool of labor. In face-to-face commerce, interactions reveal the common human condition that might or might not impact the immediate economic transaction but goes on to inform the decision-making process of individuals to take note of their fellow actors. On the other hand is the logic of the platforms that work quite well with isolated actors connected from their devices performing tasks. Here, there is no real necessity to take note of each other's material and social reality; we are all on our own to fend for ourselves. Perhaps it is the missing social connection that is the real loss in the e-commerce takeover of urban economies. After all, money will come in to urban economies at a stagnant or decreased rate; the fear that traders are voicing, particularly after the pandemic, is that they will become dependent on a system that takes away a lot of decision-making autonomy and spaces to interact with one another.

Of course, critical theorists and scholars have been talking about the need to be cautious about short-term actions that are solely based on convenience. How little space is available to individuals and societal groups to act out of only selfish concern without taking into account rising inequality and a fragile ecology? This choice was perhaps still a reality in the postwar boom in the Global North and early years of independence in the postcolonial societies. Now, after centuries of unchecked development and the rising cost of living together with a degraded habitat, we face a different challenge to making a future that is more about repair and reset than surging forward at full steam. There is an awareness that the present order of the world is unsustainable and that capital accumulation at the cost of other parameters of well-being is untenable. While some scholars have gone back to connecting contemporary problems to historical injustices of colonialism, industrialization, and slavery, others have shown the existence of radical modes of being among us, such as the grassroots mobilization of activists influencing media cultures. These are networks that can make a considerable difference to our approach to the planet's ecosystem.[6] The bazaar economy can be one such node if some of its problems are addressed to produce not just survival politics but also a politics that is outward-looking and inclusive.

Conclusion

IN ANNA TSING'S BOOK, *The Mushroom at the End of the World: On the Possibility of Life in Capitalist Ruins*, she focuses on the radical potential of a mushroom, the matsutake. In her innovative ethnography, Tsing connects matsutake growing out of ruinous and hazardous places to how it involves an unexpected group of people—forest pickers, migrant workers, and communities—operating under a capitalist supply chain and yet outside of its accumulative logic. Tsing (2015) cleverly navigates the parallel world of globalized labor chains and capital while showing that despite capitalism's footprints, carbon and otherwise, matsutake build their assemblages, often remediating destructive aspects of deforestation and toxic waste into something useful. Tsing's account and Donna Haraway's (2016) *Staying with the Trouble* remain two of the most hopeful scholarly works of recent times. They paint the subversive potential of ordinary practices, which, however marginal, have stood the test of time and emerged as sustainable lifestyles. In Haraway's case, nonhuman animals show us a way forward to exist in harmony with the pace and demands of inhabiting a collective earth.

This book has been an attempt in the same light. It recounts the extra and different assemblages from capitalist structures, which are present at a meta-level but have not been able to subsume everything as part of private extraction. Bazaars have maintained a communitarian approach to resources, particularly objects and spaces that are in the public domain. They are part of knowledge exchange, tools, and speech that lie informally outside institutionalized knowledge systems. Ad hoc arrangements have absorbed a motley grip of urban non-elites producing commercial structures while at the same time being social and communitarian. What acts as a specific deterrent to a capitalist spirit is the embedded nature of a market actor. To be a respectable market actor, traders and street vendors earn a living but not at the cost of destroying the ethical fabric of such marketplaces. It is not to say that ethics set the boundaries of economic activity. Instead, it is the opposite. Ethics help market actors legitimize their economic activity. As a result, they lend a certain character to bazaar-level commerce as noncapitalist influenced by a sense of collective worth and self-esteem.

There is, in fact, nothing novel about Delhi's bazaars behaving a certain way. Historical accounts and contemporary examples have shown that bazaars exist because lived realities are diverse and in times of need this diversity of skills, people, and objects becomes a resource. Their distinctiveness is not because such popular economic systems are rare but rather because they do not readily conform to a bourgeois worldview despite such ideals appearing to be functional and productive. They exist outside liberal citizens' division of rights and encroachments, in a zone that is messy and chaotic. The inside and outside existence of bazaar economies is not their own doing, but more about how elites have built enough influence to move in different zones and bazaar actors are most comfortable in their immediate surroundings. In other words, while elite lives are not dependent on the bazaar economy, they have time and again participated in its revelry, whether in the carnival of medieval bazaars or "local" fervor of contemporary bazaars in expos and exhibitions. They also participate in the upper layer of bazaar-level commerce as landlords and big merchants. It is more difficult for small-scale bazaar actors to make that jump. Fictional accounts such as Aravind Adiga's *The White Tiger* or nonfiction such as Rana Dasgupta's *Capital* and Aman Sethi's *A Free Man* portray how challenging it is for ordinary lives to make that transition. Unlike elites' voluntary encounters with bazaars, the journey for bazaar actors to become part of an elite society is not simple and has its fair share of risks.

That difficulty is why ordinary people instead seek a livelihood in spaces and jobs that already have emerged as lucrative employment for people like them. New migrants to the city, urban poor, and unemployed exist in the cracks and fissures of cities that are otherwise segregated by gated neighborhoods, leafy avenues, and sleek office complexes. Taking a cue out of "pirate modernity," non-elites have survived at the very places that did not have any clear plans for their well-being. Working from a disadvantaged position, bazaar actors test the limits of urban existence by the unconventional use of available infrastructure built by the state and private capital. From high-voltage electricity posts, one sees numerous wires hanging to procure electricity for areas that are not on the official map, or even if they are recognized, their presence is temporary as planners look to relocate popular neighborhoods to the periphery. Even when popular lives face evictions and other legal sanctions, they manage to resurface, sometimes by activating old trade and at times starting new work close to their homes. Similarly, existing infrastructure is put to use. Out of necessity, popular lives create new use of available artifice that even the original creators did not have in mind when they first came up with the idea. Many popular innovations do not come from careful research and knowledge but rather develop from the spur of the moment inspiration and a do-it-yourself (DIY) approach to things. This is why assembled desktops produce copies of software and games for local marketplaces. Bringing slight variation in design and modification to media content, these products are closer to the aesthetic choices of ordinary people. The small tweaks and semi-legal arrangements are what governs the destiny of many non-elites in urban centers. As capitalist structures are dominant in modern times, ordinary lives continue to survive in bazaar-like places.

Bazaars as commercial places are also avenues to meet survival needs for almost anyone who manages to secure a spot. Such a practice is visible as bazaars latch on to the "commons" of collective ethical life, discarded products, and everyday skills and tools. The crowded and dense spaces and expressive use of embodied knowledge sustain a bazaar system. It is not that bazaars pre-exist their inhabitants. It is the people and their skills that create the rhythms and pace of bazaar life. One begins to notice how similar today's electronic marketplaces are to the bazaars of antiquity—the selling of trinkets and mismatched objects, together with tinkers and traveling salespersons, are part of both worlds. The remarkable feature of bazaars has been to mimic ordinary life and practices. They make valuable and productive what is otherwise banal and common to all. As Chapter 1 shows, bazaars look a particular way because of their reaching out to spaces and practices that are in many ways the recycled waste of middle- and upper-class consumption. Chapters 2 and 3 on price and bazaar tinkering are an in-depth way of investigating how bazaar aesthetics is put to work to create exchange relations. The ethical universe provides a vital component of behavioral equity and stability for bazaar actors, as Chapter 4 shows, guiding deals with competitors, customers, and fellow bazaar actors. Chapter 5 on the platform economy gives a glimpse of the future of the bazaar economy, how there is a good chance that, just as in the past, bazaars will continue to evolve with each new challenge.

While I have been enthusiastic about the subversive potential of the bazaars to the point of almost being romantic, I have to acknowledge the elephant in the room, how ordinary people and popular lives have globally receded to extreme conservatism and a problematic version of populism. How do we talk about people from a majoritarian religion without reproducing inequalities? How do we remain cautious about the pitfalls of such mass-based systems without sacrificing their radical character? All these questions do not have easy answers. I was unable to probe these questions in my fieldwork as biases and prejudices were not always obvious. But to highlight the bazaar economy as a credible alternative to capitalism, we also need to address some of the gray areas. What follows is some initial discussion about the problematic aspect of popular economies. It fleshes out possible challenges of building bazaar economic systems as emancipatory.

Bazaar Economy, Communal Sentiments, and Populism

Against the backdrop of the August 2020 *Bhumi Pujan* (Hindu ritual of worshipping earth) in Ayodhya to build a Ram temple on a site contested by Hindus and Muslims in India, deeper conversations about the place of secularism began. Although it is at the core of the Indian Constitution, secularism appeared out of place as the *Bhumi Pujan* was live telecast on television channels. Seeing the backlash by a section of liberal elites, political commentator Yogendra Yadav said that they are not in touch with the people because they espouse secularism in a country whose consciousness is embedded in religious ideas. Long before the secular versus religious debate sprang up in recent debates, Ashis Nandy wrote a piece in the mid-1990s to bring out the uniqueness of the Indian version of secularism. Nandy (1995) shows how freedom fighters recognized in the early days of the formation of the new republic that India's political self has religious influences. Not least of these is the writing of Mahatma Gandhi, whose ideas of justice were borrowed from Hindu philosophical and religious texts.[1] On top of this, the phenomenological basis of Indian philosophy is experience-based and not author-centric, adding a syncretic nature to pan Indian Hinduism with the mixing of influences from

Islam and other sources. While some have critiqued such stories of exchanges as representing superficial change, there is no doubt that communal issues in India are far more complex than framing groups as religious jingoists and secularists.

In such a charged atmosphere, probing religious identities in the bazaars was not easy. When I circulated a questionnaire requesting religion, caste, and income details, some traders and vendors responded to it. Others questioned why I needed such specific information, but after their refusal to provide exact information, through observation and a bit of information here and there, I had a rough assessment of such matters. Most traders and street vendors are Hindus. I noticed before Delhi's assembly election in 2016 how the traders by their religion are closer to the nationalist identity foregrounded by the Bharatiya Janata Party (BJP). Yet they were keen to vote for the Aam Aadmi Party (AAP) for issues around *roti, kapda, aur makaan* (bread, clothing, and housing). This gives a clear indication about priorities, how material concerns precede religious concerns. As one trader indicates, voting for AAP means securing better lifestyles, and there will be other times to fight religious battles if the need arises at all. It was a menacing statement, suggesting that traders were building their ground stronger to take care of religious differences later. But as far as the time of my fieldwork, such communal matters were still directed to the future and not an experienceable reality.

During my fieldwork, I have not directly confronted communal sentiments against any religion. Traders and street vendors are so focused on meeting their everyday material concerns that everything else takes a backseat. It will be interesting to see if bazaars take on a communal character when all actors feel economically stable. This concern pushes us to analyze religious identity as a meta identity that lurks in the background and that can at any moment take center stage. In casting bazaars as an alternative model, one cannot get past these concerns.

I leave this section with the position that William Mazzarella (2019) reserves for the anthropologist to tackle populism critically. As he mentions, an anthropologist has to heed the voice of the people: "One might also safely say that anthropology as a discipline, methodologically if not always ideologically, tends toward a populist stance, habitually aligning with the common sense of the common people, investing hope in 'unflagging popular ingeniousness'" (49). Mazzarella observes that criticism of populism has mainly come from "Western" ideations where a certain liberal life of privilege and order is standard. In the Global South, he says, there exists a far murkier terrain where it is not about plainly marking the legal from the illegal but more about capturing the so-called "residual savagery" of ordinary life. In his analysis, affect becomes the most vivid way of understanding populism, both in its manifestation of lived concerns and its rapid spread on online platforms. "The task, therefore, is to track the specific ways in which any given social and therefore political formation is always built on a (necessarily vain) attempt to manage—which is to say to mediate and thus to organize—collective sensuous potentials. To speak of a mattering forth of the collective flesh, then, means to note the moments in which the affective and corporeal substance of social life makes itself felt as an intensification that exceeds or has fallen out of alignment with prevailing institutional mediations" (50). What Mazarella proposes is exercising caution and the keen observational knowledge of anthropologists that guides them to unravel the intricacies of different situations, to contextualize spaces and groups that otherwise appear problematic. After all, the absence of nuances in many accounts of populism has been responsible for giving the impression that certain groups of people are easily swayed by propaganda politics or innately carry hate sentiments. Instead, a careful reading of individual contexts, to show the complex world of affect, what is temporary and intense and what flows much deeper, is going to be a central concern for anthropologists witnessing populist uprising. Diverging from recognized institutional practices does not necessarily make populism problematic; rather, insidious and sustained prejudices against certain groups need our attention. In my fieldwork, complaints were against the rationale of institutions and a dominant way of life and not so much about the invasion of religious freedom, at least that was not the towering concern of the actors' everyday life. In the spirit of the ethnographic present, I am leaving the bazaar's current position on divisive politics as mild and not visible at the surface level.

Bazaar Economy and Interpersonal Networks

The market economy displays a certain homogeneity in the employment of kin, family, and village networks to propagate trade interests. When Granovetter (1985) wrote about the embedded nature of markets, he was speaking about networks that actors use to meet commercial needs. Arguing against the under-socialized actor of neoclassical economics and the over-socialized actor of social theory at the time, Granovetter described the selective use of personal networks for economic gains. His emphasis was on the formal sector, especially looking at firms and their hierarchical management of "interpersonal" networks. In many ways, the reliance on interpersonal networks gets solidified in the bazaar-level informal economy. As there is a shortage of institutional support, most trust networks develop through personal channels—people from the same village and familial, religious, and caste networks. There is no one way of getting past these barriers. Popular economic systems rely on interpersonal relationships as a more secure network than trusting the government and state functionaries. Traders depend on interpersonal networks for trade partnerships, or when it comes to trusting someone with key business responsibilities, like employing a shop assistant who is from the same village as the main trader. Bazaar traders even let street vendors congregate outside their shops because they live in the same neighborhood. The use of familiar and kin networks to occupy key roles is why Assa Doron (2012) contests the open nature of popular marketplaces. If recruits are from the same religion, village, or family, is marketplace work open to strangers? This is a valid concern and one that does not have an easy answer. The everyday functioning of the bazaar carries sufficient examples of traders and street vendors welcoming strangers to their network and allies emerging by chance encounters.

One side of the story is the prevalence of interpersonal networks, particularly regarding new actors entering the marketplace. On the other side are material concerns. If traders see lucrative opportunities even with strangers, they won't let go of them just because such alliances are not based on traditional trust. As competitive market actors, they are forever searching for extra income. In the grain market Naya Bazaar, Delhi Vidal (2000) regularly observed caste groupings determine roles in the marketplace. Most traders are from the merchant caste, whereas among intermediaries and accountants, there are Brahmin. But this is not always the case; such arrangements can be overthrown if actors see that other affinities bring trade benefits. "Caste, religious origin and economic power are all significant factors of identity in the marketplace but their particular relevance varies in different professions. For instance, although the traders share a similar background in terms of religion and caste, it is their access to capital that gives them their distinctiveness in the market. Among coolies it is regional origin rather than caste identity that is emphasized. In each case what matters are the networks that one's identity enables one to tap both in terms of business and social relations" (Vidal 2000,

130). Rather than the prevalence of traditional hierarchies, what is important is their employment for specific gains.

Even though their reliance on traditional hierarchies can show bazaar economies to be of a closed nature, crisscrossing alliances create a certain elasticity. By default, bazaar actors prefer familiar ties of friends, kin, and regular customers to be part of most of their transactions to reduce risk. But there is that chance encounter that expands their social network. No matter how much bazaar actors find comfort in familiar networks, they are dependent on infrequent consumers, passersby, and visitors to give them information about products and new business opportunities. There is a little more caution about permanently including new members as shop assistants and partners, but these partnerships are not the entirety of bazaars. It is the large volume of people that make the bazaar, lending their energy and noise. Comments on the closed nature of bazaars for their dependence on traditional networks for recruitment have to be balanced with the extraordinary number of people visiting the marketplace every day and participating in the exchange. In that sense, bazaars have an open interface. From the perspective of the physical layout of the bazaars that often have several entrances for the varied people that gather there, bazaars are much more open than supermarkets and malls. The openness is about the sheer number of people that can enter the marketplace in different roles—as visitors, consumers and intermediaries, but who if need be can also find a trading spot in the porosity of such places.

Bazaar Economy and Gender

A lot of peasant marketplaces are women-led. Khasi marketplaces in Northeast India and indigenous marketplaces in the Bolivian Andes are good examples. Women vendors run these marketplaces, and they set the tone of commerce. Despite women being prime actors in face-to-face interaction, their role in bazaar commerce is still product-specific. Women vendors and traders are more active in agricultural products than, say, media. It is not in the scope of this book to explain why that is the case. One can speculate that STEM (science, technology, engineering, medicine) disciplines still see fewer women participating and that related biases prevent women from participating in electronic marketplaces. Women's absence in electronic marketplaces can be related to the range of skills and ease with technology that in popular assumptions women don't possess. Popular descriptions in TV shows and other places tend to show women having less interest in technological fields.

But there may be another factor for the marginalization of women from urban bazaars. In recent years, urban marketplaces have been getting typecast as unsafe for specific groups and communities, which also has to do with the current political and cultural climate. The seclusion of urban life into zones and the popular beliefs that the safety of women can be guaranteed within certain parameters have meant that crowded places are risky and unsafe. As a result, public spheres have become masculine, and these spaces are much more welcoming to men as opposed to women. There are safe and unsafe hours when women are free to move about in city spaces and when they need to be in the confines of their homes. Also, there is the impression that particular places are not safe for women, and when they are there, they need to be chaperoned by other people. There are many boundaries on the free movement of women in cities. Usually, women congregate more in the university campus and secured places and less in bazaars and town squares. In the light of the differentiated access to public spaces, protest movements such as Pinjra Tod (Break the Cage) want to make urban spaces equally habitable for people of different genders. Such movements highlight the surveillance of women's whereabouts that result in women receding further into the private zone. As a result, marginalization is compounded. Not only do certain spaces appear unsafe but the mandate of the dominant section of society is such that not much is done to contest the categorization of public spaces into suitable and unsuitable zones. Even if certain spaces are hostile to people from different sections, rather than continuing isolation of groups in neighborhoods and residential complexes, freer mobility carries the potential of making such places hospitable to different groups. But this level of intermixing is yet to be a reality in a city like Delhi.

Today, in electronic bazaars, women are mainly consumers. Just like with men, traders and street vendors crack jokes and establish a relationship of familiarity and trust with women consumers. Some women are friends, and they regularly visit the marketplaces. Their visits are so frequent that they are not hesitant to get something as intimate as a tattoo done in the shops. Rajesh and Rohit at Palika Bazaar ran a tattoo parlor in a separate room from their gaming trade. A woman consumer was friendly with the two brothers and wanted to get a tattoo from them in her next visit. Afterwards, she was happy with the job, and she also brought a friend with her the next time to get a

tattoo from the same place. This type of interaction between women customers and traders is a regular affair. As with a bazaar's dealings with men, interactions are ultimately about finding opportunities for customers to spend
some money at the shop. Many times, women consumers established contacts
with the shopkeepers on their own. Sometimes they also accompanied boy-
friends and family members. Together with increasing women's participation
in the workforce, more and more women are heading out of their homes and
also inhabiting public spaces. This has meant their wider participation also
in bazaars and street corners (Srivastava 2010).[2] The class-based movement of
women cannot be ignored. Women from elite groups hardly visit bazaar-like
places. While some of the dangers of bazaars are not paramount for working-
class women, the same places appear particular uncivil for bourgeois women.
One factor can be the general unruliness, chaos, and messiness of bazaars
that are a stark opposite to orderly upscale malls. Bourgeois women do not see
bazaars to be particularly safe nor do bazaars carry things that are attractive
enough for them to make the journey from clean neighborhoods to messy,
crowded marketplaces. The absence of women from different sections in the
bazaar creates the impression of bazaars as masculine spaces.

Thoughts on Bazaars as an Alternative Economy

This book examines what a noncapitalist economic system looks like. Despite
social sanctions, creating in-group solidarities, bazaars and mass marketplaces are highly competitive, densely populated, and inclusive spaces of the
urban underclass. My exposition of bazaars is not of a socially perfect system.
If continued unchecked and without ongoing dialogue with progressive ideas,
such places can turn populist and be exclusionary on grounds of gender and
religion. I have listed some of those prospective areas of concern to indicate
where the conversations need to happen to take face-to-face commerce seriously as an essential element of economic life. Of course, there is also the issue
of overproduction. One area where both bazaars and capitalist production are
guilty is the quick turnover of mass-produced goods. Bazaars use recycled
and secondhand goods, but they are equally part of fast production loops of
local and transnational manufacturing that create a tremendous amount of
waste. Waste, pollution, fast fashion, and so on are all conversations worth
having to incorporate planetary issues of our times. In their current form, bazaars still demand more academic attention than they are receiving right now.

Considering that most countries today have a neoliberal agenda at their core, perhaps it's not very surprising to see corporations and state actors refusing to see the potential in an economy of small profits. Their interest in the informal economy often is limited to favors of vote bank politics and rarely extends to long-term structural changes. On the other hand, activists and some scholarly literature have skillfully highlighted the plight of the urban underclass, emphasizing instances of evictions, criminalization of certain populations, and lack of diverse health and welfare schemes.

This book adds another layer to the life of the non-elite in a city like Delhi. It shows how, essentially, the existence of a diverse group of people engaged in face-to-face trading makes use of everyday resources. In doing so, bazaars have kept alive a way of life that extends back to the most elementary forms of commodity exchanges, the sociality of "higgle and haggle" and heterogeneous goods and people. The story of endurance is present in street marketplaces worldwide. Facing limitations of all kinds, ordinary exchange relations do not fade away. Instead, they morph into something else, into previously unimaginable social and economic forms. It is this spirit of the popular economies to surprise and shock bourgeois existence that needs our attention. What is unpalatable on the surface is an indication of the resilience of ordinary people to create livable income out of objects and situations that are not considered useful by conventional wisdom. Also, any serious analysis of economic theory today has to take into account how a large portion of the world population frames needs, desires, and disappointments. The current focus of government and private actors on a singular lifestyle is not just myopic but will soon run out of steam. Already protests by farmers, students, climate activists, and migrants have shown frustration with the current scheme of things where new proposals of growth and aspirations do not make much sense to their way of life. After all, bazaars have shown that what ordinary people value is the stability of their lifestyle and openness to experiment with their trade. Their disappointment is the lack of sensitivity toward their way of life and toward people like them. Modern democracies have taken on an uneven path of development where more often than not, they threaten existing structures rather than build on them. And to realize that existing structures are unique to a given context makes choices around selective developmental projects even more tragic when urban plans should have benefited a wide base.

If we center on bazaars as a microcosm of ordinary life, state developmental projects and plans will be different. There will be more heterogeneity and multiple uses of spaces and less segregation and artificial boundaries. There will be greater presence of needs-based employment rather than just stream-lined professional jobs. And there can be a spirit of recycling and reuse and not just production of the new. All these unconventional practices are among us, in urban fringes of cities in the Global South and also in parts of the Global North. The fear is not that such spaces will disappear in their entirety. Even during the pandemic (Deka 2022), many informal marketplaces continued their business, quickly adapting to the needs of the "lockdown" economy.[3] Yet things have changed, as people in the bazaars are weary about what this new life will look like. Someone at the bazaar mentioned how in the early days of finding oneself in the lockdown, there was no other option but to talk to one another, looking up from their phones. It was as if family members were there after a long time and had not checked out because of their phones. Rajat from Delhi's Lajpat Rai was enamored by this change of scene when he could have a conversation with his neighbors and children at home. He misses that, and coming to the marketplace after the lockdown, he realizes the pacing of com-merce had already changed. There was now less time for meaningless gossip, and everyone was constantly on their phone after being pushed to use the smartphone for trading and digital payment during the lockdown. The hustle and bustle of a bazaar is present even after the pandemic, but Rajat senses a strong sense of alienation. No one wants to communicate unless it is an ab-solute necessity. Everyone prefers to be on their phone, scrolling mindlessly on the screen. What Rajat is pointing out is an extreme. After the COVID-19 pandemic, bazaars are back in business. They are now navigating a new world when face-to-face consumers are fewer, and they are increasingly acting as distributors providing goods to e-commerce platforms and consumers through WhatsApp groups. The traders and street vendors survive even after a challenging three years of the pandemic. More problematic is the chances of the disappearance of bazaar sociability, and if sociality is not the core element, bazaars don't have to be there physically and can transform into warehouses. And we deduct another public space from our midst that carries the potential for collective discussion and mitigations.

Therefore, this book is more of an appeal for state actors and planners to open up to existing economic systems to solve many of the problems for which they have been using a borrowed framework. Instead, sustainable models are available in their backyard; what is missing is a will to see not as a state but as inhabitants and pedestrians of global cities. This vision would subvert the gaze from what is believed to be useful infrastructure based on a neoliberal model, instead engaging a keen understanding of local life and of practices that may challenge the existing legal framework, including proprietary rights. It is ultimately a teleological understanding of modernity that is of value to developmental projects of countries and global economies. Here, the contradiction of modernity lies in obstacles to growth and uninterrupted movement from one place to another. In fact, anything that deters the path—uncivil elements, nuisance, messy assemblages—needs displacement. In this dominant view, to be modern here is to progress from point A to point B without looking back. Instead, as Michel Serres (Serres and Latour 1995) argues, there can be fulfilling perspectives where the presence of elements from different times and fields is not a pathology but, like poetry, enriches our understanding of the world. Bazaars exist between the past and the present; their quick adaptations of the latest consumer products exist alongside age-old tools and skillsets. To be modern in the bazaars is to be adjusted to the needs of the time but without being fixated on destroying everything that came before.

Notes

Introduction

1. In colonial India, elites were landed aristocrats, bureaucrats, and politicians. In postcolonial India, what now emerges as the "the new middle-class" (Fernandes 2006; Saavala 2010), the white-collar English-educated professionals alongside the corporate and business elite, have joined the traditional elite category (Chatterjee 2008). The non-elites are groups of people who fall outside these categories.

2. The slum redevelopment colonies were in various parts of Delhi. The government provided an alternative place of residence to thousands of people who found their houses destroyed because of urban redevelopment projects. The street vendors in Nehru Place succumbed to such demolition drives. Many of them lived in slums close to the marketplace before they were relocated a few kilometers away.

3. Wasiak (2014) focuses on the link between the bazaar and the home through his account of the Polish hacking scene in the late 1980s. As an observer of personal computing, he points out that computer magazines created a culture of hacking among young people in the communist regime in Poland as the government censored other distribution networks. As a result, informal networks grew to surpass state sanctions. Hackers and bazaars worked together. But soon, the two entities were incompatible as the romanticism sometimes attached to hacking as a counterculture was disappointingly unavailable in bazaars as places of commerce. "In technology enthusiasts' view, computer bazaars should be sites where computer users instead of entrepreneurs sold their old computers and peripherals for a fair price. The software would be exchanged on a nonprofit basis. In reality, peddlers moved in from other bazaars and quickly took over the supply of hardware and pirate software. Hackers did not anticipate this transformation of a large part of the informal innovation to take the character of bazaar style exchange. Computer magazines and the popular press targeted the bazaars for their shady economic activities, even as sources of piracy software" (Wasiak 2014, 133).

4. See T. Roy 2012; De Vries 1994; Wolf 1982.

5. The transition from feudalism to capitalism did not happen overnight and was not without its challenges. In *Trading Spaces: The Colonial Marketplace and the Foundations of American Capitalism*, Hart (2019) argues that before British colonizers established capitalist trading places in America, much changed on the home front. Until about the eighteenth century, marketplaces were about an "industrious" local community who traded "quality wares" and cared about the common good more than private interest—"that bargains would be honest, prices fair, deals observed, and stolen goods prevented from entering the marketplace" (Hart 2019, 21). Many processes, such as guilds and traveling peddlers, eroded the links of local life to marketplaces and fairs. "Markets became more abstracted as places when these merchants were joined from the early eighteenth century by factors, who acted as brokers and transporters in the cheese, cattle, and grain trades" (27).

6. It is striking that much more than the exchange itself, the universe that early bazaars conjured brought people to participate in such spectacle. In a way, the exotic bazaars in Europe led to the development of a shopping habit, initially needing something spectacular to bring people into shops and eventually being replaced by more mundane commodities. This spirit of the unexpected is brought out quite forcefully in the 1845 edition of Douglas Jerrold's *Shilling Magazine*: "A 'Bazaar'—'tis a trite word for commonplace thing—often an idle mart for children's trumpery—brought forth of laborious idleness. But an idea can ennoble any its true sense, is an idea; and how grand is the idea which ennobles our bazaars which, even apart from its claims as an industrial exposition, makes it a great and holy thing. 'Free Trade.' These words form a spell by which the world will yet be governed. They are the spirit of a dawning creed—a creed which already has found altars and temples worthy of its truth. The Anti-Corn Law League Bazaar has raised thoughts in the national mind which will not soon die. As a spectacle it was magnificent in the extreme; but not more grand materially than it was morally. The crowd who saw it, thought as well as gazed. It was not a mere huge shop for selling wares; but a great school for propagating an idea" (Gurney 2006, 390).

7. See Said 1979.

8. The Braudelian understanding of the markets as distinct from capitalism is an influential strand in the literature on "market anarchism." Market anarchism builds on the complexity of everyday exchange. It focuses on the ideological benefits of the freedom of the market as a sphere of mutual dialogue and not of privilege. The supporters of market anarchism draw heavily from scholars like Proudhon, who saw the authoritarian laws enabling poverty, property, and alienation to be replaced by mutual systems of contract and dissolution of political privilege (Chartier and Johnson 2011).

9. With the birth of early industrial society, the common lands gradually came under the control of private individuals. In many parts of the world, and significantly in England, the land enclosures movement handed legal deeds to private owners. The protests against enclosures in England from the sixteenth century onward show the dependence of ordinary lives on common lands having legal protection under the Magna Carta of 1215 and Forest Charter of 1217 (Linebaugh 2008). Enclosures were

already present in the thirteenth century but accelerated in due course as more and more lands were allocated to private actors; eventually the size of commons was significantly reduced under a new order of production in Europe.

10. Adam Smith's early work ([1759] 1976), *The Theory of Moral Sentiments*, saw the human propensity to trade made possible by negotiating personal dependencies with the common good. Sympathy is an idea related to the common good; as individuals identify with one another, they can enter into a market exchange with mutually benefiting ideas about value and sacrifice. It is in Smith's later works that economic exchange takes on a more materialistic aspect. Even then, there was a concern for the consequence of money destabilizing existing relationships, leading to formulating exchange in new ways of being moral beings. It is much later that economic action takes a gloomy view of human beings as only capable of bettering one's chances without any other concerns such as that of collective well-being, expressed for instance by Garrett Hardin's ([1968] 2009) notion of the "tragedy of commons." His economic version develops from a rationale that community-level usage of public land leads to its depletion because individual actors do not care for its upkeep, and there is a gradual erosion of resources from over-exploitation. He concludes that for optimal use of public resources, the need is for self-interested actors who are motivated to look after things only if they know it is their property.

11. See Benkler and Nissenbaum 2006.

12. See Nancy Fraser (1990) for her analysis of counterpublics.

13. See Didier Fassin 2010.

14. A significant interest in Delhi's geography has grown out of urban plans and policies that have tried to implement a certain discipline on the urban sphere. The Delhi Improvement Trust (DIT) in 1936, followed by the Delhi Development Authority (DDA) established in 1957, shaped the city's geography. The New Delhi Municipal Corporation (NDMC) and the Delhi Municipal Corporation, respectively, supervised architect Edwin Lutyens' imperial capital and popular neighborhoods. The Delhi Development Authority (DDA), established in 1957 as the successor body to the DIT, also sought through a variety of means to "cleanse" Delhi of unwanted spaces such as slums. "The DIT also administered 'reclamation colonies', such as those near Karol Bagh in west Delhi, where members of 'criminal tribes' were confined within well-defined geographical boundaries, with their residents requiring permission from the police to travel beyond" (Srivastava 2011, 44). Although these plans were indicative of state control and interventions, as Diya Mehra (2013a) argues there was never a full-fledged execution of them as global events like World War II and the Partition of India in 1947 intervened. On top of that, profit and extra juridical interventions became part and parcel of the project of accommodating the rising influx of people into the new capital. From the beginning, Delhi's modern development was the product of excessive state regulations and underhand dealings that opened up spaces of negotiation for different groups of people.

15. Bazaars in precolonial and colonial times differed in the importance placed on patrimony and personal networks in the former and free trade in the latter (Saraf

2020). Rajat Kanta Ray (1988, 1999) observed that under British colonialism the powerful channels of Indian merchants lost their hold over the national and global economy as "European managing agencies" controlled the money market after the Suez Canal was built and London emerged as a center for international trade. Indian merchants were now taking a secondary position to their counterparts in their East India Company, limited to indigenous commissions of agents (*arhats*) and bills of exchange (*hundi*). To a great extent, Indian bazaars could not return to their position of being central economic actors even after independence. Tyabji (2007) points out that in the first half of the twentieth century, Indian industrialists were speculating in the grain bazaars of Bombay. Still, over the next few decades, bazaars took on a postcolonial character of catering mainly to the urban non-elites, with notable exceptions of bazaars for agricultural products that are an essential part of the food economy, connecting state actors with private traders, peasants, and intermediaries.

16. Writing about the bazaar economy in colonial India, Bayly (1983) and Yang (1999) showed how it linked village life to that of the town and the outside world. Such descriptions challenge the view of India as a stagnant society, unchanging and locked into the self-sufficient nature of village life, typical of the idea of an Asiatic mode of production (Habib 2006) that was central to European Enlightenment visions of the East from Hegel to (the early) Marx as well as later Gandhi. "The idealized opposition between the bazaar, a premodern arena of personalised exchange, and the market, a site of rationalized and impersonal transactions, has been put to rest especially by studies of indigenous merchants and industrial capitalists. As economic historians have argued, the Indian bazaar, the material domain of indigenous commerce and finance, was not peripheral, but central to the world system of the late nineteenth century; it was a vast intermediate network enabling the deep local penetration and extensive global reach of colonial capitalism" (Birla 2011, 9).

17. The design of the urban environment increasingly favors private capital and the educated new middle class through programs such as *bhagidari* (partnership) between government agencies and neighborhood organizations like resident welfare association (Mehra 2013b).

18. See Javed 2019.

19. The World Trade Organization's Trade-Related Aspects of Intellectual Property Rights (TRIPS) Agreement of 1995 tied international trade policy to intellectual property law. It signaled a new era in the globalization of trademarks, copyrights, and patents (Thomas 2012).

Chapter 1

1. Post-2008, the widespread use of *shanzhai* phones and cute imitations of Blackberry and Nokia phones crowded the global market. The official line toward *shanzhai* culture was to see such products as mere imitations. But in critical literature, it emerged as a uniquely local, bottom-up innovation sphere. Most importantly, such creative cultures were about reimagining the possibility of a single product once the legal restrictions around it in terms of intellectual property rights were not

stringently applied. Bai Gao (2011, 6) describes how introducing chip provider Media Tek in China spurred a new production logic: "Beginning in 2003, it began to produce both chips and software for cell phones and also provide technological support through turnkey service to its downstream clients who otherwise would not be able to overcome the entry barrier in cell phone production." In this way, Media Tek kept one foot in the formal economy and another in the informal economy, opening products to urban middle classes and customers in small towns and rural areas. Before *shanzhai*-style productive logic, it would be difficult to imagine a large pool of economically disadvantaged sections jumping on the bandwagon of globalization as their needs and channels of acquisition of goods were not the focus of official manufacturers.

2. Ghertner (2015) focuses on suppressing popular aesthetics by the emergence of a surveillance regime of the middle class and a specific type of bourgeois sensibility whereby owing private property, for instance, is a stabilizing feature of middle-class life. See Rohan Kalyan (2014) on his study of magicians in the Kathputli colony of Delhi and everyday struggles of combating evictions and surviving through odd jobs. *Chiragh Dilli* and *The Delhi Walla* are two blogs that have signposted Delhi's popular practices and sensory experiences, which are the city's pulse. *The Hindu* newspaper ran a column by R. V. Smith for a long time on the many facets of Delhi, drawing on its rich history. The ordinary spaces, ruins, and unsung people emerge as the heart of the city as they are the custodians of the unique use of shared spaces.

3. These noncapitalist forms of production consist of "self-employment-based production, household production with family labor or different forms of collective/communal organizations of production" (Gidwani and Maringanti 2016, 119).

4. Dipesh Chakrabarty (1991, 1992) looks at the construction of bazaars in the cultural milieu of colonial India. Bazaars emerged as the spaces for the messier and uncivil elements of urban lives, forms, and practices outside middle-class households. In his analysis, bazaars were a third space that co-opted the dualism of South Asian lives; everything that is unacceptable in a civilized society gets pushed to the streets. The uniqueness of bazaar life is that it can maintain a sense of the outside and the inside simultaneously. At times, bazaars became the core of social life amid religious festivals. At other times, bazaars were unsuitable because they carried out uncivil activities calling for, among other things, a restriction of bourgeois women's movements in the bazaars.

5. Constantine Nakassis (2013, 112) uses the word "surfeit" to talk about "the immaterial excess of social meanings that emerges out of engagements with branded goods ('original' or otherwise) but cannot be fully reduced to the brand concept (at least, not as formulated by marketing discourse or intellectual property law): appropriation, resignations, parodies, idiosyncratic associations, indifferences and ignorances." Such excesses overflow in popular marketplaces, as most commodities do not carry an original brand logo. They are cheap variations of a branded product with slight changes to the aesthetic, for instance, inverting a logo or adding another syllable to a brand name.

6. Hasan Karrar's (2019, 2020) work on bazaars in Central Asia (mainly in Kazakhstan and Kyrgyzstan) show how local bazaars adjust to geopolitical shifts in post-Soviet Russia.

7. Virno (2004) points to the generic capacity to communicate as what makes us part of the "general intellect," which, since the early days of the introduction of machines in factories, as shown by Karl Marx in *Grundrisse*, has been about employing collective wisdom to benefit productive enterprises of the few. In contrast, bazaar speech produces a particular tonality for everyday exchange, whereby one tries to sell a product through lucid storytelling. The virtuous bazaar trader is not acting on behalf of anyone else but using the generic linguistic ability to make his profit.

8. However, scholars have started to see carnivals, fairs, and so on as not just an occasional form of subversion but as examples of our ancestors having a far more flexible organization of life than we do. Different combinations of sociality administered in a state-led formation and community-style bonhomie coexisted, and people did not necessarily have to choose between either way of being in their life; there was experimentation with different types of social organization with none of them taking a perverse turn for lack of a societal alternative. See Graeber and Wengrow 2021.

9. Craig Jeffrey's (2010) book *Timepass* provides a sociological analysis of leisure practices. The book focuses on unemployed youth in Meerut, who spend hours chatting to cope with the lack of gainful employment. Jeffrey connects the desperate situation of urban youth to a corrupt network of local politicians and to student politics that have highlighted the sense of being in limbo and not finding something meaningful to do with one's time. A broader connotation of *timepass* is wastefulness, of not using time productively. In some cases, it does carry a genuine sense of having ample time to gossip and socialize with people.

10. Walter Benjamin's (1999) flaneur walked the passages and arcades of Paris. The flaneur became part of the bohemian lifestyle, shared by artists, intellectuals, and people who walked the city as a form of experience and to nurture an artistic temperament. However, not much literature is available about the flaneur underclass and people who don't belong to the urban elites. There could be aimlessly wandering even for those whose material conditions are precarious, but who find walking to be a mode of distraction from everyday affairs. The segmented world of the two types of flaneur emerges in Ajay Gandhi's writing: "On Fasil Road, the adda-seeking poet, in search of bourgeois company, would find a different scene: workers from the countryside congregating in ganja addas, huddled circles of hashish smokers. Capitalism, no doubt, would be deficiently realised——and the canon of verse may not extend to Bengali poets. Adda in Old Delhi is a male activity associated with unemployment and undesirables" (Gandhi 2015, 267). Specifically, many social gatherings occur in bazaars, where aimless wanderers meet others of their kind. It is here that, amid card playing and sharing joints, possibilities of future work are discussed. An underclass flaneur walks the city with a precarious disposition of lacking stability, but such exploration isn't entirely bereft of friendship, joy, and camaraderie. The flaneur's sentiments may

include both loss at the moment and hope of gaining a foothold in a new place through contacts made by aimless wanderings.

11. See Stephen Legg (2007) and Emma Tarlo (2003) on the spatial map of Delhi with emphasis on colonial India and also subsequent periods like the emergency period between 1975 to 1977.

12. The Master Plan for Delhi 2021 has among its consultant members representatives from the "Government of NCT [National Capital Territory] of Delhi, public sector agencies, professional groups, resident welfare associations, elected representatives, etc." http://52.172.182.107

13. See Tabassum et al. 2010, *Trickster City*, for a detailed account of how bazaars accommodate marginal lives in a city like Delhi.

14. In the introduction to *South Asian Governmentalities*, Stephen Legg and Deana Heath (2018), taking a Foucauldian perspective, provide an extensive background to understand subaltern self-governance and dominant formations. According to works of scholars such as Prathama Banerjee and Indrani Chatterjee, precolonial governmentality was about divided Hindu kingdoms and local monastic units that could convert their influence into control of large swaths of land. The king became part of a pastoral care network based on kinship lineage. In the Mughal and colonial times, centralized control became more prominent along with bureaucracy for everyday governance. All these and more elements of the racialization of colonial subjects, liberal universalism, and economic extraction created an elite network that could continue in the same form, if not in substance, in a postcolonial context. Colonial governmentality and independent India's developmentalism set the rules of the game. Small spaces to negotiate are available to ordinary people to find their footing under an elite principle of governance.

Chapter 2

1. See Jorion 1998.

2. Emma Rothschild's analysis of Adam Smith's *The Wealth of Nations* situates the book in the larger political environment in Europe to investigate the change of tone in Smith's writings from his earlier works. Crucial was Louis XVI's presentation of Turgot's six reform edicts of 1776, where he proposed the abolition of the mastership guilds and limited the 'inalienable right of humanity' to choose where to work. Rothschild connected Turgot's reform to a change in European labor relationships, which involved servility with a degree of equality in labor and product markets (Eltis 2004, 148).

3. For someone like Karl Polanyi, it was not a simple question of one system of economic organization replacing another. Instead, he was more interested in showing that there are concerns for the human condition, even in so-called rational atomized societies. He borrowed this idea from Marx's humanism and empirically bases it on the Speenhamland system of wage subsidies of late eighteenth-century England. Polanyi's narrative emphasized the so-called double movement; as soon as there was a

decline of the last vestiges of the medieval settlement, the self-protection of society set in, as was visible in the writings of Ricardo. Factory laws and social regulation, and a political and industrial working-class movement sprang into being to resist the worst of liberal capitalism, in particular to ensure that "its 'utopian' aim of hiving the economy off entirely from broader social norms was never completely realized" (Rogan 2017, 80).

4. See E. Thompson (2011) for details of *hawala* operations in Afghanistan.

5. The effects of the demonetization measures in India, particularly their impact on the informal economy, become apparent considering the complexity of credit relationships. It is challenging for bazaar actors to import all their transactions to a banking system immediately. The more imminent problem is that the capital remains spread in a complex network of local and transnational borrowers and debtors. On the other hand, unlike banks, informal credit facilities allow heterogeneous arrangements based on the needs of individual actors. People can borrow and lend small sums of money. Often these transactions also can be quite a last-minute thing. Based on the density of social interactions between a debtor and a creditor, rules are less stringent. At other times, lenders use force and social sanctions to retrieve loans. For actors engaged in the informal economy to use formal banking systems gainfully, those systems would need to adapt to their nuances of everyday calculation. At the present moment, a complex understanding of their needs is missing.

6. The market for TV games is a hidden side of the gaming industry in India. While revenues came from selling new games and consoles, a substantial share of the informal economy of video games is in selling and purchasing TV games. Informal networks of bazaars almost exclusively cater to the market for TV games. Local distributors from small towns visit marketplaces like Lajpat Rai to order TV games. The sustained popularity of these games says a lot about a common kind of consumer in India—one who does not have a steady electricity connection or own a computer. Many traders pointed out that the idea of an average consumer in India having a laptop is misplaced. Most consumers likely have a television, particularly those outside big cities.

7. Informal arrangements include bribes and passing goods through familiar officials at check posts. Ledeneva's (2008) work in China and Russia examines the practices of *Guanxi* and *Blat* as informal networks used by ordinary people. In formerly communist countries, state regulations and bureaucracy, along with poverty, often lead people to use kinship networks to get by. It is now accepted in academic scholarship that corruption and informal networks of favors are never just about moral deficiency vis-à-vis the responsibilities of a good citizen. Corruption is embedded in economic transactions, social hierarchies, and mobility conditions, making a group lacking ready service channels highly likely to resort to corrupt practices.

8. Television shows and web series attest to the extravagance of Indian weddings as portrayed in shows like "The Great Indian Wedding," "Made in Heaven," "Band Baaja Bride," to name a few. Many of these shows portray the rituals of an elite wedding. A basic level of expenditure for a wedding remains the same for everyone across classes to invest in a wedding trousseau, jewelry, venue, gifts to kin, and food, apart from

making it a four- or five-day affair and destination wedding that is affordable only for the country's affluent.

Chapter 3

1. Michael Polanyi (1958) draws from Gestalt psychology to show "personal knowledge" as a way to envision knowledge once the separation between experience and reason is not there. Polanyi sees Euclidian geometry as the starting point when the capacity of stating anything beyond sets of tautologies is minimal. He attempts to put the person back into knowledge. After all, one of the crucial truths of any knowledge, including scientific knowledge, is that the knower knows more than the person is aware of at a given time. The interest in personal knowledge takes Polanyi to look into traditional knowledge systems such as guilds as having a more holistic approach to forms of knowledge. He touches on two critical aspects of traditional knowledge subscribing to embedded knowledge. First is the depth of such knowledge, which private channels of transmissions can only pass down. "An art which cannot be specified in detail cannot be transmitted by prescription since no prescription for it exists. It can be passed on only by examples from master to apprentice" (Polanyi 1958, 53). Another point Polanyi emphasizes about personal knowledge is the prevalence of trust and how certain unique forms of knowledge transmission are present in such systems. "To learn by example is to submit by authority. You follow your master because you trust his manner of doing things even when you cannot analyse and account in details for its effectiveness. By watching the master and emulating his efforts in the presence of his example, the apprentice unconsciously picks up the rules of the art, including those which are not explicitly known to the master himself. These hidden rules can be assimilated by a person who surrenders himself to that extent uncritically to the imitation of another. A society which wants to preserve a fund of personal knowledge must submit to tradition" (55).

2. In his classic work on knowledge management, Ikujiro Nonaka shows how the transformation of tacit wisdom to explicit knowledge is crucial for innovation. Through different examples in Japanese firms, Nonaka illustrates that after tacit knowledge gets external expressions, employees have a better image of the concept, helping them transform it into a saleable product (Nonaka 1994). The firm cannot benefit as a whole if the knowledge is within an individual. To get an idea to a larger public, it has to be in some way codified. Codification happens by keeping written records of innovations on paper or electronically.

3. Not everything produced in China is also conceived there from start to finish. In China, street-level innovation gets criticized for its lack of creativity. Such perspectives view *shanzhai* as a matter of creating copies and not as something potentially cutting-edge and visionary. The criticism comes mainly from a new generation of designers who visit international exhibitions and workshops and find their own country lacking a sense of direction. For them, a city like Shenzhen, with its small productive units, looks messy and does not have the technical rigor of design they see in exhibition spaces in Milan and other European cities (Chumley 2016).

4. To know more about the techniques of reballing, see Deka 2017.

5. Recycling is also about shuffling through the "graveyard" of e-waste to find used parts. In the Seelampur area of Delhi, for instance, the urban underclass searches for tiny amounts of gold, silver, nickel, and so on from used smartphones (Corwin 2018). When I speak of recycling in Delhi's bazaars, it is mainly related to product-specific readjustments to bring old products to the marketplace in a workable condition.

6. Hindi movies such as *Zanjeer*, 1973, and *Avtaar*, 1983, develop auto mechanics as redemptive figures.

7. See Hunter 2020.

8. See Scott Lash (2018) on the subject of experience.

9. *Lokavidya*, as traditional knowledge, is not a predecessor of scientific tempera-ment but is the continuation of skills and craftsmanship passed down through gen-erations and between communities. In contrast is *jugaad*-style knowledge, which has a more contemporary basis where individuals/collectives create knowledge to solve a problem. The transmission of *jugaad*-style innovation is far more accidental, pointing to discreet, indiscreet, and even unintentional copying practices, and might not have the same character of crafts skills passed down in traditional guilds.

10. https://hardcrackers.com/ideal-broken-neapolitan-approach-things-technical/?f bclid=IwAR0AYuCW3VEyT0LeKd4iDztLyGAa55_RllQa1xj265F7fAVKimc6IZgxj0U.

11. See Bassett 2016.

12. Startups were the bridge between the local manufacturing base and the "Make in India" initiative. The ASSOCHAM and E&Y (2016) report identifies startups as possible partners to bring the real spirit of the Make in India initiative to the fore by acting as a kind of bridge between different small and medium business ventures and informal sector enterprises (Deka 2017).

13. The legal case between Sony Computer Entertainment America and George Hotz in 2011 targeted the latter's jailbreaking and reverse engineering. These cases are not straightforward, and legal systems do not have exact laws on transnational tinkering and tweaking electronic products. Neither are there specific laws that can encompass varied ways of transgressing a product, and often, the original creators didn't think these products were amenable to such changes in the first place (Badami 2018).

14. Often an entire economy gets developed around the cult status of a particular creator or digital entrepreneur. Television series around founders like Adam Neu-mann of WeWork or Elizabeth Holmes of Theranos are a testament to knowledge workers capitalizing on the reputation they build for themselves as risk-takers or mav-ericks. See Gandini 2016.

15. It's important to note that recycling and repairing practices fit with the politics of the Anthropocene of creating sustainable and local cultures of innovation. I do not stress this aspect of recycling because such discourses were absent from the traders' vocabulary.

16. Hackers' skepticism toward piracy brings to light an age-old debate of alter-native knowledge production systems ranging from copyleft to commercial piracy.

Practitioners such as Lawrence Lessig have been highly critical of pirating practices, including bazaar-level copying of software and movies. Such practices go against the "copyleft" culture of knowledge production and sharing without commercial motives. Media theorists, particularly from the Global South, have shown how complicated the relationship between piracy and urban lives is, especially when we consider the limited means available to ordinary people to acquire media products through legal means. Moreover, the piracy debate (Dent 2012) in the Global South projects a more complex idea of a political subject that, unlike a civic citizen, has to circumvent legal routes to create survival opportunities. The unconventional use of semi-legal infrastructure makes media scholars such as Lobato (2014) focus on "what piracy does" rather than what piracy is.

Chapter 4

1. I use the term "ethics" as distinct from morality. The subjective interpretation of arete, or virtue, might come from religion and scriptures but is not a straightforward adaptation of commandments and prescriptions. Instead, ethics in a Foucauldian register is about how one ought to live "in accordance with certain principles through practices of enquiry, reflections, and self conduct" (Pandian and Ali 2010, 3).

2. News reports validate what Manoj said about the Reliance company wanting to establish a monopoly in the retail sphere. The Ambani group has a stake in the Walmart group and in 2021 was negotiating a deal with the Future group of retailers that would open up their chances to control the retail economy of household purchases through physical stores and online shopping. As traditional distributors compete with the low prices of big companies, the struggles of "mom and pop" businesses to stay afloat are a reality. https://indianexpress.com/article/india/princes-to-paupers-indias -salesmen-face-ruin-as-ambani-targets-mom-and-pop-stores-7636274/

3. The term "WhatsApp university" shows the role of social media in creating cultural clusters, often by using materials from unverified sources. It has received critical attention, mainly after communal riots and disturbances, as forwarded messages on family group chats are seen as valid news sources and are known to perpetuate sentiments of hate and fear. There isn't a culture of verifying forwarded messages on WhatsApp, giving its viral news feed near impunity.

4. An ethical life based on religious and moral influences differs from how Marx sees religion as a seductive possibility to misconstrue social inequalities. There is some truth to such conceptualization of religion as reproducing social inequality. Rather than take an absolute stance, a more challenging role is to rescue some of the nuances of social lives even though they take refuge in texts and stories that are part of a dominant framework. In other words, it would be nice to see informal actors and bazaar traders not having to resort to moral stories to negotiate anxieties of precarity. As it stands, storytelling creates bonds of solidarity that impact South Asian subjectivity.

5. The Citizenship Amendment Act of 2019 proposes relocating Hindu political refugees from neighboring countries to India. Protesters have noted the unconstitutional

character of the proposed law as the Indian Constitution does not confer citizenship based on an individual's religious affiliation.

6. In South Asia, it is common to use avuncular terminology to develop fictive kinship relations. Usually, fictive terms of uncle and aunty establish relationships of familiarity. The suffix "ji" is attached to elders in north India as a sign of respect.

7. As unethical behavior, alcohol or illicit product consumption is a common trope of the bazaar economy. Among street vendors in Joutia, Ilahiane and Sherry (2008) notice how their interviewee Samurai responds to such behavior: "These people just sell to make ten bucks or so to go get drunk or get high. Make their ten bucks and go. They are the 'Satan.'"

8. Whether the story came from the Puranas is not the main issue. It illustrates how ordinary people legitimize their stories by plotting them in one religious text or another—a classic example of everyday Hinduism where anecdotal references are a way to justify subjective experiences. Here, the search for a virtuous action does not rest on institutionalized morality but on how the subject can project superior acts by using religious symbols and texts arbitrarily.

9. The Bhagavad Gita, a sacred religious text in Hinduism, records a conversation between Krishna and his prodigy Arjuna about the ethics of going to war. The paradox of participating in violent behavior is explained through *karma* (duty) and commitment to an action without thinking about consequences. Such emphasis creates an elasticity to Hindu moral life as activity can acquire new meaning through a cosmological reading, not an ethical one in worldly terms.

10. Paul Veyne's (1990) analysis of "euergetism" argues how elite privileges and ordinary life do not follow the same logic. The measures taken by elites to alleviate the suffering of ordinary people do not disturb the existing status quo. For instance, Veyne (1990) analyzes the Roman practice of distributing bread and hosting circuses to keep the ordinary people content. Such practices of generosity were not only a way to establish order in the early Hellenistic period but also promoted an imperial class ruling an empire.

Chapter 5
1. See Paul Mason 2015; Nick Srnicek 2017.
2. See Aditi Surie 2020, Chhavi Sharma 2019.
3. Yuk Hui (2016) argues that Chinese thought does not follow the modernist separation of *techne* from nature. He refers to the Greek myth of Prometheus, who "became the father of all techne and master of all crafts to show that the West had an understanding of technology that separated the sphere of men from gods. Instead, in China, no such separation took place; it had already 'naturalised the divine.'" Hui writes, "Compared to Presocratic and classical Greek philosophy during the same period of history in China, neither the question of Being nor the question of *techne* comprised the core questions of philosophy. Rather than 'Being,' what was familiar to Confucian and Daoist teaching was the question of 'Living' in the sense of leading a moral or good life'" (Hui 2016, 63).

4. When seen as poiesis, "technology is therefore no mere means. Technology is a way of revealing. If we give heed to this, then another whole realm for the essence of technology will open itself up to us. It is the realm of revealing, i.e., of truth" (Heidegger 1977, 12).

5. Byung-Chul Han (2015) connects iPhone screens and Jeff Koons's images to the propensity of the modern subject to value smooth surfaces as an innate attraction to consumer goods. He is skeptical of the rising tendency to like everything undisturbed, as slick surfaces do not develop an alert spectator. Often ugly, undisciplined, and imperfect compositions provoke deeper contemplation, an element marginal in modern images of beauty.

6. See Yusoff 2018; Bauwens, Kostakis, and Pazaitis 2019; Appadurai 2011; Latour 2005.

Conclusion

1. Sheldon Pollock (2009) picks up on cosmopolitanism much earlier in the subcontinent's history through the Sanskrit language. He writes about the prevalence of Sanskrit cosmopolitanism as the language spread from Afghanistan to Bali in the common era without any particular territorial and imperial motive but instead through consent. He compares Sanskrit as a written language to vernacular languages in the eighth and ninth centuries that communicated regional and geographical happenings.

2. Sanjay Srivastava (2010) notices that Hindi women's magazines such as *Grihasobha* (Home Beautiful) and *Meri Saheli* (My Girl-Friend) allow greater freedom among working-class women to have discussions on sexuality and mobility in urban spaces.

3. The long-term impact of COVID-19 on the informal economy is not known. In 2020, Amazon increased its profit by almost 200 percent, and other platforms are also doing relatively better than before the lockdowns (Takefman 2021). In this scenario, when an increased number of people have gotten used to shopping online, and there is a push by e-commerce giants to capitalize on new delivery networks, bazaars would have to present unique benefits for consumers to choose them as a point of business.

References

Abu-Lughod, Janet L. 1989. *Before European Hegemony: The World System, A.D. 1250–1350.* New York: Oxford University Press.

Adorno, Theodor W. 1967. *Prisms.* London: Neville Spearman.

Akerlof, George A. 1970. "The Market for 'Lemons': Quality, Uncertainty and Market Mechanism." *Quarterly Journal of Economics* 84, no. 3: 488–500.

Alexander, Jennifer, and Paul Alexander. 1987. "Striking a Bargain in Javanese Markets." *Man,* n.s., 22, no. 1: 42–68.

Alexander, Jennifer, and Paul Alexander. 1991. "What's a Fair Price? Price-Setting and Trading Partnerships in Javanese Markets." *Man,* n.s., 26, no. 3: 493–512.

Alexievich, Svetlana. 2016. *Second Hand Time.* London: Fitzcarraldo Editions.

Amin, Samir, Giovanni Arrighi, Andre Gunder Frank, and Immanuel Wallerstein. 1990. *Transforming the Revolutions: Social Movements and the World.* New York: Monthly Review Press.

Anderson, Paul. 2019. "Games of Civility: Ordinary Ethics in Aleppo's Bazaar." *Ethnos: Journal of Anthropology* 84, no. 3: 380–97.

Anjaria, Jonathan Shapiro. 2016. *The Slow Boil: Street Food, Rights and Public Space in Mumbai.* Stanford, CA: Stanford University Press.

Appadurai, Arjun. 2011. "Cosmopolitanism from Below: Some Ethical Lessons from the Slums of Mumbai." *Johannesburg Salon* 4: 32–43.

Appadurai, Arjun. 2012. "The Spirit of Calculation." *Cambridge Journal of Anthropology* 30, no. 1: 3–17.

Arrighi, Giovanni. 1994. *The Long Twentieth Century.* London: Verso.

Arrighi, Giovanni. 2007. *Adam Smith in Beijing: Lineages of the Twenty-First Century.* New York: Verso.

Arvidsson, Adam. 2019. *Changemakers: The Industrious Future of the Digital Economy*. London: Polity.

Arvidsson, Adam, and Bertram Niessen. 2015. "Creative Mass. Consumption, Creativity and Innovation on Bangkok's Fashion Markets." *Consumption Markets and Culture* 18, no. 2: 111–32.

Arvidsson, Adam, Alessandro Caliandro, Alberto Cossu, Maitrayee Deka, Alessandro Gandini, Vincenzo Luise, Brigida Orria, and Guido Anselmi. 2016. "Commons Based Peer Production in the Information Economy." https://www.academia.edu/29210209/ Commons_Based_Peer_Production_in_the_Information_Economy.

Aspers, Patrik. 2009. "Knowledge and Valuation in Markets." *Theory and Society* 38, no. 2: 111–31.

ASSOCHAM and EY. 2016. "'Turning the 'Make in India' Dream into a Reality for the Electronics and the Hardware Industry." https://www.slideshare.net/MalayShah9/ eyassocham-reportturning-the-mii-dream-into-a-reality-for-the-electronics-in dustryfinal-report.

Badami, Nandita. 2018. "Informality as Fix: Repurposing Jugaad in the Post-Crises Economy." *Third Text* 32, no. 1: 46–54.

Bakhtin, Mikhail. 1968. *Rabelais and His World*. New York: Anthem Press.

Bandyopadhyay, Ritajyoti. 2012. "In the Shadow of the Mall: Street Hawking in Global Calcutta." In *Globalization from Below: The World's Other Economy*, edited by Gordon Mathews, Gustavo Lins Ribeiro, and Carlos Alba Vega, 171–85. London: Routledge.

Banerjee, Sumanta. 2019. *The Parlour and the Street: Elite and Popular Culture in Nineteenth-Century Calcutta*. Calcutta: Seagull Books.

Bang, Peter F. 2011. *The Roman Bazaar: A Comparative Study of Trade and Market in a Tributary Empire*. Cambridge: Cambridge University Press.

Barthelmes, Lisa. 2012. "Peasants or Peddlers: Mobile Street Vendors in Hanoi, Vietnam." Max Planck Institute for Social Anthropology PhD Proposal.

Basole, Amit. 2014. "Whose Knowledge Counts? Reinterpreting Gandhi for the Information Age." *International Journal of Hindu Studies* 18, no. 3: 369–414.

Basole, Amit. 2016. "Informality and Flexible Specialization: Apprenticeships and Knowledge Spillovers in an Indian Silk Weaving Cluster." *Development and Change* 47, no. 1: 157–87.

Bassett, Ross. 2016. *The Technological Indian*. Cambridge, MA: Harvard University Press.

Bataille, Georges. 1985. *Visions of Excess: Selected Writings, 1927–1939*. Minneapolis: University of Minnesota Press.

Bauwens, Michel, Vasilis Kostakis, and Alex Pazaitis. 2019. *Peer to Peer: The Commons Manifesto*. London: University of Westminster Press.

Baviskar, Amita. 2020. *Uncivil City: Ecology, Equity and the Commons in Delhi*. New Delhi: Sage.

Bayly, Christopher Alan. 1983. *Rulers, Townsmen and Bazaars: North Indian Society in the Age of British Expansion, 1770–1870*. Cambridge: Cambridge University Press.

Beckert, Jens. 2013. "Imagined Futures: Fictional Expectations in the Economy." *Theory and Society* 42, no. 3: 219–40.

Beckert, Jens, and Patrik Aspers, eds. 2011. *The Worth of Goods: Valuation and Pricing in the Economy*. Oxford: Oxford University Press.

Belshaw, Cyril S. 1965. *Traditional Exchange and Modern Markets*. Englewood Cliffs, NJ: Prentice Hall.

Benjamin, Walter. 1969. "The Work of Art in the Age of Mechanical Reproduction." In *Illuminations*, edited by Hannah Arendt, 1–26. New York: Schocken Books.

Benjamin, Walter. 1999. *The Arcade Project*. Cambridge, MA: Harvard University Press.

Benkler, Yochai, and Helen Nissenbaum. 2006. "Commons-Based Peer Production and Virtue." *Journal of Political Philosophy* 14, no. 4: 394–419.

Berger, Peter L., and Thomas Luckman. 1966. *The Social Construction of Reality: A Treatise in the Sociology of Knowledge*. London: Allen Lane.

Bernstein, Basil. 1964. "Elaborated and Restricted Codes: Their Social Origins and Some Consequences." *American Anthropologist* 66, no. 6: 55–69.

Besley, Timothy, and Alec R. Levenson. 1996. "The Role of Informal Finance in Household Capital Accumulation: Evidence from Taiwan." *Economic Journal* 106, no. 434: 39–59.

Beunza, Daniel, Iain Hardie, and Donald Mackenzie. 2006. "A Price Is a Social Thing: Towards a Material Sociology of Arbitrage." *Organization Studies* 27, no. 5: 721–45.

Bhabha, Homi. 1984. "Of Mimicry and Man: The Ambivalence of Colonial Discourse." *October* 28: 125–33.

Bhattacharya, Neeladri. 2018. *The Great Agrarian Conquest: The Colonial Reshaping of a Rural World*. Ranikhet: Permanent Black.

Birla, Rita. 2010. "Vernacular Capitalists and the Modern Subject in India: Law, Cultural Politics, and Market Ethics." In *Ethical Life in South Asia*, edited by Anand Pandian and Daud Ali, 83–100. New Delhi: Oxford University Press.

Birla, Rita. 2011. *Stages of Capital: Law, Culture, and Market Governance in Late Colonial India*. New Delhi: Orient Blackswan.

Boltanski, Luc, and Laurent Thévenot. 2006. *On Justification: Economies of Worth*. Translated by Catherine Porter. Princeton, NJ: Princeton University Press.

Bonneuil, Christophe, and Jean-Baptiste Fressoz. 2016. *The Shock of the Anthropocene: The Earth, History and Us*. London: Verso.

Boym, Svetlana. 1994. *Common Places: Mythologies of Everyday Life in Russia*. Cambridge, MA: Harvard University Press.

Braudel, Fernand. 1977. *Afterthoughts on Material Civilization and Capitalism*. Baltimore: Johns Hopkins Press.

Braudel, Fernand. 1983. *Civilization and Capitalism, 15th to 18th Century*. Vol. 2, *The Wheel of Commerce*. London: Book Club Associates.

Caliskan, Koray. 2007. "Price as a Market Device: Cotton Trading in Izmir Mercantile Exchange." *Sociological Review* 55, no. 2: 241–60.

Callon, Michel, Yuval Millo, and Fabian Muniesa, eds. 2007. *Market Devices*. Malden, MA: Blackwell.

Chakrabarty, Dipesh. 1991. "Open Space/Public Place: Garbage, Modernity, and India." *South Asia: Journal of South Asian Studies* 14, no. 1: 15–31.

Chakrabarty, Dipesh. 1992. "Of Garbage, Modernity and the Citizen's Gaze." *Economic and Political Weekly* 27, no. 10/11: 541–47.

Chakrabarty, Dipesh. 2000. *Provincializing Europe: Postcolonial Thought and Historical Difference*. Princeton, NJ: Princeton University Press.

Chakrani, Brahim. 2007. "Cultural Context and Speech Act Theory: A Socio-pragmatic Analysis of Bargaining Exchanges in Morocco." In *Texas Linguistic Forum: Proceedings of the Fifteenth Annual Symposium about Language and Society, Austin*, vol. 51, 43–53. Austin: University of Texas at Austin Department of Linguistics.

Chandrasekhar, C. P. 2005. "Who Needs a Knowledge Economy? Information, Knowledge and Flexible Labour." *Indian Journal of Labour Economics* 48, no. 4: 763–776.

Chartier, Gary, and Charles W. Johnson, eds. 2011. *Markets Not Capitalism: Anarchism against Bosses, Inequality, Corporate Power, and Structural Poverty*. London: Minor Compositions.

Chattaraj, Durba, Kushanava Choudhury, and Moulshri Joshi. 2017. "The Tenth Delhi: Economy, Politics and Space in the Post-Liberalisation Metropolis." *Decision* 44: 147–60.

Chatterjee, Partha. 2004. *The Politics of the Governed: Reflections on Popular Politics in Most of the World*. New York: Columbia University Press.

Chatterjee, Partha. 2008. "Democracy and Economic Transformation in India." *Economic and Political Weekly* 43, no. 16: 53–62.

Chaudhary, Manjula. 2000. "India's Image as a Tourist Destination—A Perspective of Foreign Tourists." *Tourism Management* 21, no. 3: 293–97.

Chubb, Andrew. 2015. "China's Shanzhai Culture: 'Grabism' and the Politics of Hybridity." *Journal of Contemporary China* 24, no. 92: 260–79.

Chumley, Lily. 2016. "Seeing Strange: Chinese Aesthetics in a Foreign World." *Anthropological Quarterly* 89, 1: 93–122.

Cochoy, Frank. 2007. "A Sociology of Market-Things: On Tending the Garden of Choices in Mass Retailing." *Sociological Review* 55, no. 2: 109–29.

Coleman, Gabriela. 2013. *Coding Freedom: The Ethics and Aesthetics of Hacking*. Princeton, NJ: Princeton University Press.

Corwin, Julia Eleanor. 2018. "'Nothing Is Useless in Nature': Delhi's Repair Economies and Value-Creation in an Electronics 'Waste' Sector." *Environment and Planning* 50, no. 1: 14–30.

Daryaee, Touraj. 2010. "Bazaars, Merchants, and Trade in Late Antique Iran." *Comparative Studies of South Asia, Africa and the Middle East* 30, no. 3: 401–9.

Davis, William G. 1973. *Social Relations in a Philippine Market: Self-Interest and Subjectivity*. Berkeley: University of California Press.

de Certeau, Michel. 1986. *Heterologies: Discourse on the Other*. London: University of Minnesota Press.

Deka, Maitrayee. 2016. "Bazaars and Video Games in India." *Bioscope* 7, no. 2: 172–88.

Deka, Maitrayee. 2017. "Street Level Tinkering in the Times of 'Make in India.'" *Ephemera* 17, no. 4: 801–17.

Deka, Maitrayee. 2018. "Embodied Commons: Knowledge and Sharing in Delhi's Electronic Bazaars." *Sociological Review* 66, no. 2: 365–380.

Deka, Maitrayee. 2020. "Bazaar Aesthetics: On Excess and Economic Rationality." *International Journal of Cultural Studies* 24, no. 3: 470–84.

Deka, Maitrayee. 2021. "Postcolonial Peer Production." In *Handbook of Peer Production.* Edited by Mathieu O Neil, Christian Pentzold, and Sophie Toupin, 322–333. Wiley-Blackwell.

Deka, Maitrayee. 2022. "Three Years into the Pandemic: What Changed in Delhi's Electronic Bazaars." *Contributions to Indian Sociology* 56, no. 1: 88–93.

Deka, Maitrayee, and Adam Arvidsson. 2022. "Names Doing Rounds: On Brands in the Bazaar Economy." *Journal of Consumer Culture* 22, no. 2: 495–514.

De Landa, Mannuel. "Markets and Antimarkets in the World Economy." *Alamut*, 1998. http://www.alamut.com/subj/economics/de_landa/antiMarkets.html.

Deleuze, Gilles, and Felix Guattari. 1987. *A Thousand Plateaus: Capitalism and Schizophrenia.* Minneapolis: Minnesota University Press.

DeNapoli, Antoinette Elizabeth. 2017. "'Dharma Is Technology': The Theologizing of Technology in the Experimental Hinduism of Renouncers in Contemporary North India." *International Journal of Dharma Studies* 5, no. 18: 1–36.

Dent, Alexander S. 2012. "Introduction: Understanding the War on Piracy, or Why We Need More Anthropology of Pirates." *Anthropological Quarterly* 85, no. 3: 659–72.

Dertouzos, Michael L. 1997. *What Will Be: How the World of Information Will Change.* San Francisco: Harper Collins.

De Vries, Jan. 1994. "The Industrial Revolution and the Industrious Revolution." *Journal of Economic History* 54, no. 2: 249–70.

Doron, Assa. 2012. "Consumption, Technology and Adaptation: Care and Repair Economies of Mobile Phones in North India." *Pacific Affairs* 85, no. 3: 563–85.

Dursteler, Eric R. 2011. "On Bazaars and Battlefields: Recent Scholarship on Mediterranean Cultural Contacts." *Journal of Early Modern History* 15: 413–34.

Dyer, Gary. 1991. "The 'Vanity Fair' of Nineteenth-Century England: Commerce, Women, and the East in the Ladies' Bazaar." *Nineteenth-Century Literature* 46, no. 2: 196–222.

Dyer-Witheford, Nick, and Greig de Peuter. 2009. *Games of Empire: Global Capitalism and Video Games.* Minneapolis: University of Minnesota Press.

Ekwall, Eilert. 2008. "The Etymology of the Word Tinker." *English Studies* 18, no. 1–6: 63–67.

Eltis, Walter. 2004. "Emma Rothschild on Economic Sentiments: And the True Adam Smith." *European History Journal of Economic Thought* 11, no. 1: 147–59.

Fanselow, Frank S. 1990. "The Bazaar Economy or How Bizarre Is the Bazaar Really?" *Man*, n.s., 25, no. 2: 250–65.

Fassin, Didier. 2010. "Ethics of Survival: A Democratic Approach to the Politics of Life." *Humanity: An International Journal of Human Rights, Humanitarianism and Development* 1, no. 1: 81–95.

Federici, Silvia. 2004. *Caliban and the Witch*. New York: Autonomedia.

Federici, Silvia. 2018. *Witches, Witch-Hunting and Women*. Oakland, CA: PM Press.

Fernandes, Leela. 2006. *India's New Middle Class: Democratic Politics in an Era of Economic Reform*. Minneapolis: University of Minnesota Press.

Fernandes, Leela. 2009. "The Political Economy of Lifestyle: Consumption, India's New Middle Class and State-Led Development." In *The New Middle Classes: Globalizing Lifestyle, Consumerism and Environmental Concern*, edited by Lars Meier and Hellmuth Lange, 219–36. Dordrecht: Springer.

Fernandes, Leela, and Patrick Heller. 2011. "Hegemonic Aspirations: New Middle Class Politics and India's Democracy in Comparative Perspective." *Critical Asian Studies* 38, no. 4: 495–522.

Fourcade, Marion, and Kieran Healy. 2007. "Moral Views of Market Society." *Annual Review of Sociology* 33: 285–311.

Fox, Richard G. 1969. *From Zamindar to Ballot Box: Community Change in a North Indian Market Town*. Ithaca, NY: Cornell University Press.

Frankopan, Peter. 2015. *The Silk Roads: A New History of the World*. London: Bloomsbury.

Fraser, Nancy. 1990. "Rethinking the Public Sphere: A Contribution to the Critique of Actually Existing Democracy." *Social Text*, no. 25/26: 56–80.

Gandhi, Ajay. 2015. "The Postcolonial Street: Patterns, Modes and Forms." In *Cities in South Asia*, edited by Crispin Bates and Minoru Mio, 265–86. New York: Routledge.

Gandhi, Ajay. 2016a. "The Language of the Crowd: Public Congregation in Urban India." *Distinktion* 17, no. 3: 308–15.

Gandhi, Ajay. 2016b. "The Hermeneutics of the Bazaar: Sincerity's Elusiveness in Delhi." *South Asia: Journal of South Asian Studies* 39, no. 1: 126–48.

Gandini, Alessandro. 2016. *The Reputation Economy: Understanding Knowledge Work in Digital Society*. London: Palgrave Macmillan.

Gao, Bai. 2011. "The Informal Economy in the Era of Information Revolution and Globalization: The Shanzhai Cell Phone Industry in China." *Chinese Journal of Sociology* 31, no. 2: 1–41.

Geertz, Clifford. 1963. *Peddlers and Princes: Social Change and Economic Modernization in Two Indonesian Towns*. Chicago: University of Chicago Press.

Geertz, Clifford. 1978. "The Bazaar Economy: Information and Search in Peasant Marketing." *American Economic Review* 68, no. 2: 28–32.

Geertz, Clifford, Hildred Geertz, and Lawrence Rosen. 1979. *Meaning and Order in Moroccan Society: Three Essays in Cultural Analysis*. Cambridge: Cambridge University Press.

Ghertner, David Asher. 2015. *Rule by Aesthetics: World-Class City Making in Delhi*. New York: Oxford University Press.

Gibson-Graham, J. K. 2008. "Diverse Economies: Performative Practices for 'Other Worlds.'" *Progress in Human Geography* 32, no. 5: 613–32.

Gidwani, Vinay, and Anant Maringanti. 2016. "The Waste-Value Dialectic: Lumpen Urbanization in Contemporary India." *Comparative Studies of South Asia, Africa and the Middle East* 36, no. 1: 112–33.

Goldgel-Carballo, Victor. 2014. "The Reappropriation of Poverty and the Art of 'Making Do' in Contemporary Argentine Cultural Production." *Global South* 8, no. 1: 112–27.

Goffman, Erving. 1959. *The Presentation of Self in Everyday Life*. New York: Doubleday.

Gopalkrishnan, Shankar. 2008. "Neoliberalism and Hindutva: Fascism, Free Markets and the Restructuring of Indian Capitalism." *Monthly Review Magazine*, November 14, 2008. https://mronline.org/2008/11/14/neoliberalism-and-hindutva-fascism-free-markets-and-the-restructuring-of-indian-capitalism/.

Graeber, David. 2014. "On the Moral Grounds of Economic Relationships: A Maussian Approach." *Journal of Classical Sociology* 14, no. 1: 65–77.

Graeber, David, and David Wengrow. 2021. *The Dawn of Everything: A New History of Humanity*. London: Allen Lane.

Granovetter, Mark. 1985. "Economic Action and Social Structure: The Problem of Embeddedness." *American Journal of Sociology* 91, no. 3: 481–510.

Gréine, Pádraig Mac. 1934. "Some Notes on Tinkers and Their 'Cant.'" *Béaloideas* 4, no. 3: 259–63.

Gurney, Peter J. 2006. "'The Sublime of the Bazaar': A Moment in the Making of a Consumer Culture in Mid-Nineteenth Century England." *Journal of Social History* 40, no. 2: 385–405.

Guyer, Jane I. 2004. *Marginal Gains: Monetary Transactions in Atlantic Africa*. Chicago: Chicago University Press.

Habib, Irfan. 2006. "Introduction: Marx's Perception of India." In *Karl Marx on India*, edited by Iqbal Husain, 19–54. New Delhi: Tulika Books.

Halberstam, Jack. 2013. "The Wild Beyond: With and for the Undercommons." In *Undercommons: Fugitive Planning and Black Studies*, edited by Stefano Harney and Fred Moten, 2–13. Wivenhoe, UK: Minor Compositions.

Han, Byung-Chul. 2015. *Saving Beauty*. Cambridge: Polity.

Hannerz, Ulf. 1989. "Notes on the Global Ecumene." *Public Culture* 1, no. 2: 66–75.

Haraway, Donna J. 2016. *Staying with the Trouble: Making Kin in the Chthulucene*. Durham, NC: Duke University Press.

Hardin, Garrett. (1968) 2009. "The Tragedy of the Commons." *Journal of Natural Resources Policy Research* 1, no. 3: 243–53.

Harney, Stefano, and Fred Moten. 2013. *Undercommons: Fugitive Planning and Black Studies*. Wivenhoe, UK: Minor Compositions.

Harriss-White, Barbara. 2013. "Inequality at Work in the Informal Economy: Key Issues and Illustrations." *International Labour Review* 142, no. 4: 459–69.

Hart, Emma. 2019. *Trading Spaces: The Colonial Marketplace and the Foundations of American Capitalism*. Chicago: University of Chicago Press.

Haug, Wolfgang Fritz. 1986. *Critique of Commodity Aesthetics: Appearance, Sexuality, and Advertising in Capitalist Society.* Polity Press.

Heidegger, Martin. 1977. "The Question Concerning Technology." In *The Question Concerning Technology and Other Essays*, 3–35. New York: Garland.

Hénaff, Marcel. 2002. *The Price of Truth: Gift, Money, and Philosophy.* Stanford, CA: Stanford University Press.

Hennessey, William. 2012. "Deconstructing Shanzhai—China's Copycat Counterculture: Catch Me If You Can." *Campbell Law Review* 34, no. 3: 609–60.

Heslop, Luke. 2016. "Catching the Pulse: Money and Circulation in a Sri Lankan Marketplace." *Journal of the Royal Anthropological Institute* 22, no. 3: 534–51.

Hill, Sarah. 2011. "Recycling History and the Never-Ending Life of Cuban Things." *Anthropology Now* 3, no. 1: 1–12.

Hoek, Lotte, and Ajay Gandhi. 2016. "Provisional Relations, Indeterminate Conditions: Non-Sociological Sociality in South Asia." *South Asia: Journal of South Asian Studies* 39, no. 1: 64–72.

Horkheimer, Max, and Theodor W. Adorno. 2002. *Dialectic of Enlightenment: Philosophical Fragments.* Stanford, CA: Stanford University Press.

Hui, Yuk. 2016. *Cosmotechnics: The Question Concerning Technology in China.* London: Urbanomic.

Hunter, Michael. 2020. *The Decline of Magic: Britain in the Enlightenment.* New Haven, CT: Yale University Press.

Hüwelmeier, Gertrud. 2018. "Ghost Markets and Moving Bazaars in Hanoi's Urban Space." In *Traders in Motion: Identities and Contestations in the Vietnamese Marketplace*, edited by Kirsten W. Endres and Ann Marie Leshkowich, 69–80. Ithaca, NY: Cornell University Press.

Ilahiane, Hsain, and John Sherry. 2008. "Joutia: Street Vendor Entrepreneurship and the Informal Economy of Information and Communication Technologies in Morocco." *Journal of North African Studies* 13, no. 2: 243–55.

Jackson, Steven J., Syed Isthiaque Ahmed, and Mohammad Rashidujjaman Rifat. 2014. "Learning, Innovation, and Sustainability among Mobile Phone Repairers in Dhaka, Bangladesh." In *DIS '14: Proceedings of the 2014 Conference on Designing Interactive Systems*, 905–14. New York: Association for Computing Machinery. https://doi.org/10.1145/2598510.2598576.

Jackson, Steven J., Alex Pompe, and Gabriel Krieshok. 2012. "Repair Worlds: Maintenance, Repair, and ICT for Development in Rural Namibia." In *Proceedings of the ACM 2012 Conference on Computer Supported Cooperative Work, Seattle, February 11–15, 2012*, 107–116. New York: Association for Computing Machinery. https://doi.org/10.1145/2145204.2145224.

Jain, Kajri. 2007. *Gods in the Bazaar: The Economies of Indian Calendar Art.* Durham, NC: Duke University Press.

Jameson, Fredric. 1983. *The Political Unconscious: Narrative as a Socially Symbolic Act.* London: Routledge.

Javed, Umair. 2019. "Ascending the Power Structure: Bazaar Traders in Urban Punjab." In *New Perspectives on Pakistan's Political Economy*, edited by Matthew McCartney and S. Akbar Zaidi, 199–215. Cambridge: Cambridge University Press.

Jeffrey, Craig. 2010. *Timepass: Youth, Class, and the Politics of Waiting in India*. Stanford, CA: Stanford University Press.

Jorion, Paul J. M. 1998. "Aristotle's Theory of Price Revisited." *Dialectical Anthropology* 23, no. 3: 247–80.

Joseph, Manu. 2018. "'Jugaad,' India's Most Overrated Idea." *Livemint*, August 18, 2018. https://www.livemint.com/Leisure/2c3sntdHfJ8Py2tWxEqgcN/Jugaad-Indias -most-overrated-idea.html.

Jullien, Francois. 2004. *A Treatise on Efficacy: Between Western and Chinese Thinking*. Honolulu: University of Hawai'i Press.

Kalyan, Rohan. 2014. "The Magicians' Ghetto: Moving Slums and Everyday Life in a Postcolonial City." *Theory, Culture and Society* 31, no. 1: 49–73.

Kapczynski, Amy. 2010. "Access to Knowledge: A Conceptual Genealogy." In *Access to Knowledge in the Age of Intellectual Property*, edited by Amy Kapczynski and Gaëlle Krikorian, 17–56. New York: Zone Books.

Karrar, Hasan H. 2017. "Do Bazaars Die? Notes on Failure in the Central Asian Bazaar." *Working Paper Series on Informal Markets and Trade*, no. 4: 1–10.

Karrar, Hasan H. 2019. "Between Border and Bazaar: Central Asia's Informal Economy." *Journal of Contemporary Asia* 49, no. 2: 272–93.

Karrar, Hasan H. 2020. "The Bazaar in Ruins: Rent and Fire in Barakholka, Almaty." *Central Asian Survey* 39, no. 1: 80–94.

Keith, Michael, Scott Lash, Jakob Arnoldi, and Tyler Rooker. 2013. *China Constructing Capitalism: Economic Life and Urban Change*. London: Routledge.

Khuri, Faud I. 1968. "The Etiquette of Bargaining in the Middle East'." *American Anthropologist* 70, no. 4: 698–706.

Knight, Frank H. 1921. *Risk, Uncertainty, and Profit*. Boston: Houghton Mifflin.

Kracauer, Siegfried. 1995. *The Mass Ornament: Weimar Essays*. Cambridge MA: Harvard University Press.

Krishnamurthy, Mekhala. 2012. "States of Wheat: The Changing Dynamics of Public Procurement in Madhya Pradesh." *Economic and Political Weekly* 47, no. 52: 72–83.

Kumar, Akshaya. 2014. "The Aesthetics of Pirate Modernities: Bhojpuri Cinema and the Underclasses." In *Art and Aesthetics in a Globalising World*, edited by Raminder Kaur and Parul Dave-Mukherjee, 185–203. London: Bloomsbury.

Lamieri, Marco, and Enrico Bertacchini. 2006. "What If Hayek Goes Shopping in the Bazaar." *MPRA Paper* No. 367, University of Munich, Germany.

Langlois, Richard N., and Metin M. Cosgel. 1993. "Frank Knight on Risk, Uncertainty, and the Firm: A New Interpretation." *Economic Inquiry* 31, no. 3: 456–65.

Larkin, Brian. 2004. "Degraded Images, Distorted Sounds: Nigerian Video and the Infrastructure of Piracy." *Public Culture* 16, no. 2: 289–314.

Lash, Scott. 2018. *Experience: New Foundations for the Human Sciences*. Cambridge: Polity.

Latour, Bruno. 2005. "From Realpolitik to Dingpolitik or How to Make Things Public." In *Making Things Public*, edited by Bruno Latour and Peter Weibel, 4–31. Cambridge, MA: MIT Press.

Ledeneva, Alena. 2008. "'Blat' and 'Guanxi': Informal Practices in Russia and China." *Comparative Studies in Society and History* 50, no. 1: 118–44.

Legg, Stephen. 2007. *Spaces of Colonialism: Delhi's Urban Governmentalities*. Malden, MA: Blackwell.

Legg, Stephen, and Deana Heath, eds. 2018. *South Asian Governmentalities: Michel Foucault and the Question of Postcolonial Orderings*. Cambridge: Cambridge University Press.

Lemire, Beverly. 1988. "Consumerism in Preindustrial and Early Industrial England: The Trade in Secondhand Clothes." *Journal of British Studies* 27, no. 1: 1–24.

Liang, Lawrence, and Ravi Sundaram. 2011. "India." In *Media Piracy in Emerging Economies*, edited by Joe Karaganis, 339–98. New York: Social Science Research Council.

Linebaugh, Peter. 2008. *The Magna Carta Manifesto: Liberties and Commons for All*. Berkeley: University of California Press.

Lindtner, Silvia. 2014. "Hackerspaces and the Internet of Things in China: How Makers Are Reinventing Industrial Production, Innovation and the Self." *China Information* 28, no. 2: 145–67.

Lobato, Ramon. 2014. "The Paradoxes of Piracy." In *Postcolonial Piracy: Media Distribution and Cultural Production in the Global South*, edited by Lars Eckstein and Anja Schwarz, 121–34. London: Bloomsbury Academic.

Lu, Miao. 2021. "Translating a Chinese Approach? Rural Distribution and Marketing in Ghana's Phone Industry." *Media, Culture and Society* 43, no. 2: 309–25.

Lysack, Krista. 2005. "Goblin Markets: Victorian Women Shoppers at Liberty's Oriental Bazaar." *Nineteenth Century Contexts* 27, no. 2: 139–65.

Manuel, Peter. 1993. *Cassette Culture: Popular Music and Technology in North India*. Chicago: Chicago University Press.

Marazzi, Christian. 2008. *Capital and Language: From the New Economy to the War Economy*. Los Angeles: Semiotext(e).

Marx, Karl. 1887. *Capital: A Critique of Political Economy*, vol. 1. Edited by Frederick Engels. Translated by Samuel Moore and Edward Aveling. Moscow: Progress Publishers. https://www.marxists.org/archive/marx/works/download/pdf/Capital-Volume-I.pdf, 163.

Mason, Paul. 2015. *PostCapitalism: A Guide to Our Future*. London: Allen Lane.

Mathews, Gordon. 2011. *Ghetto at the Center of the World Mansions, Hong Kong*. Chicago: University of Chicago Press.

Mathews, Gordon, Gustavo Lins Ribeiro, and Carlos Alba Vega, eds. 2012. *Globalization from Below: The World's Other Economy*. London: Routledge.

Mathews, Gordon, and Yang Yang. 2012. "How Africans Pursue Lower-End Globalization in Hong Kong and Mainland China." *Journal of Current Chinese Affairs* 41, no. 2: 95–120.

Matilal, Bimal Krishna. 2015. *Mind, Language and World.* Vol. 1 of *The Collected Essays of Bimal Krishna Matilal.* Edited by Jonardan Ganeri. New Delhi: Oxford University Press.

Mazzarella, William. 2019. "The Anthropology of Populism: Beyond the Liberal Settlement." *Annual Review of Anthropology* 48: 45–60.

Mbembe, Achille. 2004. "Aesthetics of Superfluity." *Public Culture* 16, no. 3: 373–405.

Mehra, Diya. 2012. "Protesting Publics in Indian Cities: The 2006 Sealing Drive and Delhi's Traders." *Economic and Political Weekly* 47, no. 30: 79–88.

Mehra, Diya. 2013a. "Planning Delhi ca. 1936–1959." *South Asia: Journal of South Asian Studies* 36, no. 3: 354–74.

Mehra, Diya. 2013b. "What Has Urban Decentralization Meant? A Case Study of Delhi." *Pacific Affairs* 86, no. 4: 813–833.

Messias, José. 2020. "Emergent Precariousness Game Modding in the Context of a Decolonial Philosophy of Technology." In *FDG '20*, September 15–18, 2020, Bugibba, Malta.

Mintz, Sidney W. 1960. "Peasant Markets." *Scientific American* 203, no. 2: 112–23.

Moore, Jason. 1997. "Capitalism over the Longue Duree: A Review Essay." *Critical Sociology* 23, no. 3: 103–16.

Mukherjee, Rahul. 2018. "Jio Sparks Disruption 2.0: Infrastructural Imaginaries and Platform Ecosystems in 'Digital India.'" *Media, Culture and Society* 41, no. 2: 175–95.

Naik, Abhayraj. 2015. "'Wizards at Making a Virtue of Necessity': Street Vendors in India." *Socio-Legal Review* 11, no. 1: 1–60.

Nakassis, Constantine V. 2012. "Counterfeiting What? Aesthetics of Brandedness and BRAND in Tamil Nadu, India." *Anthropological Quarterly* 85, no. 3: 701–21.

Nakassis, Constantine V. 2013. "Brands and Their Surfeits." *Cultural Anthropology* 28, no. 1: 111–26.

Nakassis, Constantine V. 2016. *Doing Style: Youth and Mass Mediation in South India.* Chicago: Chicago University Press.

Nandy, Ashis. 1972. "Defiance and Conformity in Science: The Identity of Jagadis Chandra Bose." *Science Studies* 2, no. 1: 31–85.

Nandy, Ashis. 1995. "An Anti-Secularist Manifesto." *India International Centre Quarterly* 22, no. 1: 35–64.

Nayanjyoti. 2020. "Worker's Playtime: A Definitive Guide to Proletarian TikTok." *Raiot.* https://raiot.in/author/nayanjyoti/.

Nonaka, I. 1994. "A Dynamic Theory of Organizational Knowledge Creation." *Organization Science* 5, no.1: 14–39.

Obeyesekere, Gananath. 1963. "The Great Tradition and the Little in the Perspective of Sinhalese Buddhism." *Journal of Asian Studies* 22, no. 2: 139–53.

Orr, Winnie W. F. 2007. "The Bargaining Genre: A Study of Retail Encounters in Traditional Chinese Local Markets." *Language in Society* 36, no.1: 73–103.

Ostrom, Elinor. 1990. *Governing the Commons: The Evolution of Institutions for Collective Action*. Cambridge: Cambridge University Press.

Pandian, Anand. 2008. "Tradition in Fragments: Inherited Forms and Fractures in the Ethics of South India." *American Ethnologist* 35, no. 3: 466–80.

Pandian, Anand. 2010. "Interior Horizons: An Ethical Space of Selfhood in South India." *Journal of the Royal Anthropological Institute* 16, no. 1: 64–83.

Pandian, Anand, and Daud Ali, eds. 2010. *Ethical Life in South Asia*. New Delhi: Oxford University Press.

Pati, Sushmita. 2019. "The Productive Fuzziness of Land Documents: The State and Processes of Accumulation in Urban Villages of Delhi." *Contributions to Indian Sociology* 53, no. 2: 249–71.

Patil, C. B, and Purnima Ray. 1997. *Delhi, a Bibliography: Urban Studies*. Delhi: Sharada.

Patnaik, Utsa. 2017. "Revisiting the 'Drain' of Transfers from India to Britain in the Context of Global Diffusion of Capitalism." In *Agrarian and Other Histories: Essays for Binay Bhushan Chaudhuri*, edited by Shubhra Chakrabarti and Utsa Patnaik, 277–313. New Delhi: Tulika Books.

Pawlett, William. 1997. "Utility and Excess: The Radical Sociology of Bataille and Baudrillard." *Economy and Society* 26, no. 1: 92–125.

Pine, Jason. 2012. *The Art of Making Do in Naples*. Minneapolis: University of Minnesota Press.

Polanyi, Karl. 1944. *The Great Transformation: The Political and Economic Origins of Our Time*. Boston: Beacon Press.

Polanyi, Michael. 1958. *Personal Knowledge: Towards a Post-Critical Philosophy*. London: Routledge.

Pollock, Sheldon. 2009. *The Language of the Gods in the World of Men, Culture, and Power in Premodern India*. Berkeley: University of California Press.

Preda, Alex. 2009. *Information, Knowledge and Economic Life: An Introduction to the Sociology of Markets*. Oxford University Press.

Prochaska, F. K. 1977. "Charity Bazaars in Nineteenth-Century England." *Journal of British Studies* 16, no. 2: 62–84.

Radjou, Navi, Jaideep Prabhu, and Simone Ahuja. 2012. *Jugaad: A Frugal and Flexible Approach to Innovation for the 21st Century*. London: Random House.

Rajagopal, Arvind. 2001. "The Violence of Commodity Aesthetics: Hawkers, Demolition Raids and a New Regime of Consumption." *Social Text* 19, no. 3: 91–113.

Ramanujan, A. K. 1989. "Is There an Indian Way of Thinking? An Informal Essay." *Contributions to Indian Sociology* 23, no. 1: 41–58.

Rappaport, Erika Diane. 2001. *Shopping for Pleasure: Women in the Making of London's West End*. Princeton, NJ: Princeton University Press.

Ray, Rajat Kanta. 1988. "The Bazaar: Changing Structural Characteristics of the Indigenous Section of the Indian Economy before and after the Great Depression." *Indian Economic and Social History Review* 25, no. 3: 263–318.

Ray, Rajat Kanta. 1999. "Asian Capital in the Age of European Domination: The Rise of the Bazaar, 1800–1914." *Modern Asian History* 29, no. 3: 449–554.

Raymond, Eric S. 1999. *The Cathedral and the Bazaar: Musings on Linux and Open Source by an Accidental Revolutionary.* O'Reilly Media.

Redfield, Robert. 1955. "The Social Organization of Tradition." *Far Eastern Quarterly* 15, no. 1: 13–21.

Rogan, Tim. 2017. *The Moral Economists: R. H Tawney, Karl Polanyi, E. P. Thompson, and the Critique of Capitalism.* Princeton, NJ: Princeton University Press.

Roy, Tirthankar. 2012. *India in the World Economy: From Antiquity to the Present.* Cambridge: Cambridge University Press.

Ruggiero, Vicenzo, and Nigel South. 1997. "The Late-Modern City as a Bazaar: Drug Markets, Illegal Enterprise and the 'Barricades.'" *British Journal of Sociology* 48, no. 1: 54–70.

Saavala, Minna. 2010. *Middle Class Moralities. Everyday Struggle over Belonging and Prestige in India.* New Delhi: Orient BlackSwan.

Said, Edward W. 1979. *Orientalism.* New York: Vintage Books.

Sanyal, Kalyan. 2007. *Rethinking Capitalist Development Primitive Accumulation, Governmentality and Post-Colonial Capitalism.* New Delhi: Routledge.

Saraf, Aditi. 2020. "The Market and the Sovereign: Politics, Performance and Impasse of Cross-LOC Trade." In *Rethinking Markets in Modern India: Embedded Exchange and Contested Jurisdiction*, edited by Ajay Gandhi, Barbara Harriss-White, Douglas E. Haynes, and Sebastian Schwecke, 206–33. Cambridge: Cambridge University Press.

Sarukkai, Sundar. 1999. "Science, Knowledge and Society." *Economic and Political Weekly* 34, no. 13: 779–84.

Sarukkai, Sundar, and Gopal Guru. 2012. *The Cracked Mirror: An Indian Debate on Experience and Theory.* New Delhi: Oxford University Press.

Sayeed, Mohammed. 2017. "How Many Houses Can You Count in Jhabvala's Portrayal of This Old Delhi Lane?" *Chiragh Dilli*, March 17, 2017. https://chiraghdilli.word press.com/2017/03/17/how-many-houses-can-you-count-in-jhabvalas-portrayal -of-this-old-delhi-lane/.

Scalco, Patricia. 2019. "Weaving Value: Selling Carpets in the Liminal Space of Istanbul's Grand Bazaar." *Anthropology Today* 35, no. 5: 7–10.

Scott, James C. 1976. *The Moral Economy of the Peasant: Rebellion and Subsistence in Southeast Asia.* New Haven, CT: Yale University Press.

Serafini, Luca. 2017. "Beyond the Person: Roberto Esposito and the Body as 'Common Good.'" *Theory, Culture and Society* 34, no. 7–8: 215–28.

Serres, Michel, and Bruno Latour. 1995. *Conversations on Science, Culture, and Time.* Ann Arbor: University of Michigan Press.

Sharma, Chhavi. 2019. "Aggregators, Driver-Partners and the State: Administrative and Legal Conundrum." *Economic and Political Weekly* 54, no. 46.

Sharma, Yashraj. 2021. "Instagram Has Largely Replaced TikTok in India and Erased Working-Class Creators." *Rest of World*, October 2021. https://restofworld .org/2021/instagram-and-class-in-india/.

Smith, Adam. (1759) 1976. *The Theory of Moral Sentiments*. Oxford: Clarendon.

Spivak, Gayatri Chakravorty. 1988. "Can the Subaltern Speak." In *Marxism and the Interpretation of Culture*, edited by Cary Nelson and Lawrence Grossberg, 271–313. Basingstoke, UK: Macmillan Education.

Srinivas, Tulsi. 2018. *The Cow in the Elevator: An Anthropology of Wonder*. Durham, NC: Duke University Press.

Srivastava, Sanjay. 2010. "Fragmentary Pleasures: Masculinity, Urban Spaces, and Commodity Politics in Delhi." *Journal of the Royal Anthropological Institute* 16, no. 4: 835–52.

Srivastava, Sanjay. 2011. "A Hijra, a Female Pradhan and a Real Estate Dealer: Between the Market, the State and 'Community.'" *Economic and Political Weekly* 46, no. 51: 44–52.

Srivastava, Sanjay. 2014. "Shop Talk: Shopping Malls and Their Publics." In *Consumer Culture, Modernity and Identity*, edited by Nita Mathur, 45–70. New Delhi: Sage.

Srnicek, Nick. 2017. *Platform Capitalism*. Cambridge: Polity Press.

Stallybrass, Peter, and Allon White. 1986. *The Politics and Poetics of Transgression*. Ithaca, NY: Cornell University Press.

Standing, Guy. 2011. *The Precariat: The New Dangerous Class*. London: Bloomsbury Academic.

Stephenson, Carl. 1948. "*In Praise of Medieval Tinkers*." *Journal of Economic History* 8, no. 1: 26–42.

Sundaram, Ravi. 1999. "Recycled Modernity: Pirate Electronic Cultures in India." *Third Text* 13, no. 47: 59–65.

Sundaram, Ravi. 2010. *Pirate Modernity: Delhi's Media Urbanism*. New Delhi.

Surie, Aditi. 2020. "On-Demand Platforms and Pricing: How Platforms Can Impact the Informal Urban Economy, Evidence from Bengaluru, India." *Work Organisation, Labour and Globalisation* 14, no. 1: 83–100.

Tabassum, Azra, et al. 2010. *Trickster City: Writings from the Belly of the Metropolis*. New Delhi: Penguin Viking.

Takefman, Bruce. 2021. "Amazon Profit Increased Nearly 200% Since Start of COVID-19 Pandemic." *News and Media*, January 6, 2021. https://researchfdi.com/amazon-covid-19-pandemic-profits/.

Tarlo, Emma. 2003. *Unsettling Memories of the Emergency in Delhi*. Berkeley: University of California Press.

Tarrius, Alain. 2015. *Étrangers de passage: Poor to poor, peer to peer*. Avignon: Éditions de l'Aube.

Telles, Vera da Silva. 2012. "Illegalisms and the City of Sao Paulo." In *Globalization from Below: The World's Other Economy*, edited by Gordon Mathews, Gustavo Lins Ribeiro, and Carlos Alba Vega, 86–100. London: Routledge.

Thomas, Kedron. 2012. "Intellectual Property Law and the Ethics of Imitation in Guatemala." *Anthropological Quarterly* 85, no. 3: 785–815.

Thompson, Edwina A. 2011. *Trust Is the Coin of the Realm: Lessons from the Money Men in Afghanistan*. Karachi: Oxford University Press.

Tooze, Adam. 2018. *Crashed: How a Decade of Financial Crises Changed the World.* New York: Viking.

Tripathi, Dwijendra. 1996. "Colonialism and Technology Choices in India: A Historical Overview." *Developing Economies* 34, no. 1: 80–97.

Tsing, Anna Lowenhaupt. 2015. *The Mushroom at the End of the World: On the Possibility of Life in Capitalist Ruins.* Princeton, NJ: Princeton University Press.

Tyabji, Nasir. 2007. "Jawaharlal Nehru and Science and Technology." *History and Sociology of South Asia* 1, no. 1: 130–36.

Veyne, Paul. 1990. *Bread and Circuses: Historical Sociology and Political Pluralism.* London: Penguin.

Vidal, Denis. 2000. "Markets and Intermediaries: An Enquiry about the Principles of Market Economy in the Grain Market of Delhi." In *Urban Space and Human Destinies*, edited by Denis Vidal, Emma Tarlo, and Veronique Dupont, 125–39. New Delhi: Manohar.

Virno, Paolo. 2004. "Ten Theses on the Multitude and Post-Fordist Capitalism." In *A Grammar of the Multitude for an Analysis of Contemporary Forms of Life*, 46–51. Cambridge: MIT Press.

Wasiak, Patryk. 2014. "Playing and Copying: Social Practices of Home Computer Users in Poland during the 1980s." In *Hacking Europe: From Computer Cultures to Demoscenes*, edited by Gerard Alberts and Ruth Oldenziel, 129–50. London: Springer.

Weber, Max. 2005. *The Protestant Ethic and the Spirit of Capitalism.* London: Routledge.

Weiss, Allen S. 1989. *The Aesthetics of Excess.* Albany: State University of New York Press.

Willis, Paul E. 1977. *Learning to Labour: How Working Class Kids Get Working Class Jobs.* Farnborough: Saxon House.

Wolf, Eric R. 1982. *Europe and the People without History.* Berkeley: University of California Press.

Yang, Anand A. 1999. *Bazaar India: Markets, Society and the Colonial State in India.* Berkeley: California University Press.

Yatmo, Yandi Andri. 2008. "Street Vendors as 'Out of Place' Urban Elements." *Journal of Urban Design* 13, no. 3: 387–402.

Yusoff, Kathryn. 2018. *A Billion Black Anthropocenes or None.* Minneapolis: University of Minnesota Press.

Zubrzycki, John. 2018. *Jadoowallahs, Jugglers and Jinns: A Magical History of India.* New Delhi: Picador India.

Index

Aam Aadmi Party (AAP), 177
Access to Knowledge (A$_2$K) movement, 126
Adam, Robert, 23
Adiga, Aravind, 174
Adorno, Theodor, 39, 140
aesthetics, 9, 36, 43, 47, 64; commodity, 63, 67; of congestion, 56; of elite groups, 54; mass, 38; of modernity, 38; popular, 38, 191n2; as process, 35. *See also* bazaar aesthetics
Afghanistan, 199n1
Africa, 14
Age of Enlightenment, 71
agency, 65–66
agrarian economies, 98
Akerlof, George A., 73
Akerstrom, Malin, 170
Aleppo (Syria), 132–33
Alexander, Jennifer, 73, 84
Alexander, Paul, 73, 84
Alexievich, Svetlana, 120
Amazon, 199n3

Ambani group: Reliance, business venture of, 130, 197n2
Anderson, Paul, 132–33
Anjaria, 54
Ansari community, 125
Anthropocene, 124–25, 196n15
Anti Corn Law League Bazaar, 188n6
Appadurai, Arjun, 131
Arjuna, 198n9
Aristotle, 71
Arrighi, Giovanni, 11–12, 150
Art of Making Do in Naples, The (Pine), 43
Arvidsson, Adam, 128
Asia, 11, 14, 20, 44, 47, 120, 133, 135–36, 138, 192n6; avuncular terminology, use of, 198n6
Avtaar (film), 196n6

Badami, Nandita, 123–24
Baghdad (Iraq), 11
Bakhtin, Mikhail, 46
Bali, 199n1
Banaras, 119, 125

Baneerjee, Prathama, 193n14
Bangkok (Thailand), 128, 166
Bangladesh, 120
Bang, Peter, 11
bargaining, 90; chicanery, 87; as com-
    plex process, 87; foreign tourists,
    88–89; miserly customers, 89–90;
    risk-averseness, 98; as social act,
    85–86; trust and reputation, 88. See
    also bazaar bargaining
bargaining rituals, 98; fragile social
    bonds, representative of, 86; social
    character of, 85; surviving tendency, 98
Basole, Amit, 119
Barthelmes, Lisa, 44
Bataille, Georges, 40
Bath (England), 23
Baviskar, Amita, 18
Bayly, Christopher Alan, 190n16
bazaar actors, 20, 32–33, 64–65, 68, 70,
    92, 114, 149, 151, 158, 169, 194n5; agency
    of, 162; capitalists, as different from,
    132; chance encounters, 180; dualism
    of, 130; e-commerce platforms, 36–37,
    155, 164–66, 168; economic behavior,
    evoking ethics for, 130; elite society,
    174; ethical life, 130, 135, 146; ethics,
    133, 148, 175–76; excesses, use of,
    35–36, 42; ghost markets, 44; gossip
    and storytelling, reliance on, 99;
    immediate surroundings, comfort-
    able in, 174; information asymmetry,
    99; infrastructure, unconventional
    use of, 175; innovations, copying
    of, 127–28; lack of confidence, 118;
    nihilistic attitude of, 115; non-sabo-
    tage mentality, 150; online demons,
    158; physical and emotional toll on, 6;
    resilience of, 9; risk-averse nature of,
    98; as small business owners, inde-
    pendence of, 162; spending, aversion
    to, 92; as traders and street vendors,
    26; urban commons, 21

bazaar aesthetics, 38–39, 50, 62; back-
    yard innovation, as integral to, 61;
    commodity, 67; of congestion, 56;
    exchange relations, 175; as excess, 40;
    as lived experience of popular classes,
    68. See also aesthetics
bazaar art, 42
bazaar bargaining, 84; clientalization,
    73; collective sentiment, reliance on,
    96; ethics, 132–33; icebreakers, 85;
    information asymmetry, 132; rituals,
    85–86, 93–94, 98, 132; shared codes, as
    crucial, 73; sociality of, 85; and story-
    telling, 96–97. See also bargaining
bazaar commerce, 29; capitalistic prac-
    tices, as different from, 36, 148; com-
    petitiveness of, 148; ethical life, 148;
    Hindu ethics, 35; price, genealogy of,
    36; state, influence of, 151; women,
    role in, 180–81
bazaar consumers: money, frugal with,
    91–92
bazaar dealers, 9
bazaar economy, 4–8, 35, 41, 47, 59, 98, 172,
    190n16; and agency, 9; capitalism, as
    alternative to, 37, 176; capitalism, rela-
    tionship with, 10–11; collective worth
    and self-esteem, 174; commons, 19;
    commons-based resources, 37; elastic-
    ity of, and crisscrossing alliances, 180;
    as emancipatory, 176; ethical life, 131,
    149–50; ethics in, 131, 150, 152–53; in-
    formation asymmetry, 84; innovations
    in, 101; as non-capitalist, 174; political
    and economic role, changes in, 10;
    popular aesthetics of, 38; precarity of,
    132; resilience of, 170; shared culture,
    73; sociality, refuge in, 9; stories, as
    part of, 95; symbiotic relationship of,
    10; unethical behavior, 198n7; urban
    commons, reliance on, 35
bazaar ethics: 150; and commerce, 133;
    proletarian, 153

bazaaris, 48, 56; ethical life of, 134

bazaar innovation: state support, lack of, 36; and tinkering, 102

bazaar knowledge: 29, 100, 126; products, in-depth knowledge of, 100–101; sharing of, 128

bazaar pricing, 71–72, 90, 100; backstage, 77, 80, 84; boomerang effect, 93–94; bookkeeping, absence of, 74; cash transactions, 74–75; chicanery, stereotype about, 73; as complex, 94; deceit, 94; friendships, developing of under, 75; front stage, 77; information asymmetry, 73; maximum market price, 84; minimum price, underlying logic of, 77; price negotiation, 77, 79–80; for pirated products, 87–89; price setting, 94; for secondhand products, 78–80; shared codes of contact, 87; shared culture, 73; as unique system, 36; video games, and intermediaries, 82–83

bazaars, 28, 34–35, 51–52, 62–63, 66–67, 100, 116, 188n6, 190n16, 192n6, 199n3; adaptability of, 185; aesthetics of congestion, 56; aimless wandering in, 192–93n10; alienation, 184; bargaining ritual, 132; bourgeoisie environmentalism, 47; capitalism, 8, 17; capitalism, as antithetical to, 13; colonial, 151; commons, 70; commons, as physical manifestation of, 40; communitarian approach to, 173; copyright law, violating of, 128; as deceptive, reputation of, 86; as depraved places, 4; digital peer communities, 128; digital society, as mix of many things, 171; distinctiveness of, 174; diversity of, 50; domestication, 64; e-commerce, 153–56, 161–62, 168–71, 184; electronic, 77, 80, 88, 101, 110, 114, 181; endurance of, 183; ethical life, 132, 175; ethics of, 131, 150, 153; everyday Hindu ethics, 136–37; evolving with the times, 58, 176; excess of, 68–70; foreign tourists, 86, 88–89; greed, 145–47; and hackers, 187n3; heterogeneous mix of people, 59; as in-between, 8; informal economy, 179; as innovative places, 102, 122, 124, 128; as irrational places, 13; knowledge in, as copied and circulated, 128; knowledge exchange, 173–74; leg pulling, 45; during lockdown, 184; as masculine spaces, impression of, 182; as misunderstood, 8; new and used objects, 112–13; Mughal, 151; noise and din of, 36; nonstandardized goods, 4; online demons, 158; ordinary life, important feature of, 13; ordinary life, as microcosm of, 183; "oriental," 12; patrimony, 189–90n15; peer learning, as part of, 126–27; as physical, 2, 4; physical layout of, 180; pirated goods, 15, 141; power and hierarchy, 153; precarity, operating in, 130; price and innovation, 36; pirated goods, 157; recycling, 175, 182; religious identities, 177; Roman, 11; secondhand products, 157, 162, 182; sensory of, 36; and sharing, 126–27; sociability, fear of disappearance, 184; sociality of, 2, 45–47, 94, 183; software and game piracy, 128; storytelling, and bodily aesthetic, 40; subversive potential of, 176; survival needs, 175; technology, 155; as third space, 191n4; timepass, 48; uniqueness of, 191n4; urban underclass, spaces of, 182; Victorian, 12; video games, 104; waste, creation of, 182; women in, 180–82; women, class-based movement of, 182; as word, 2, 7; word of mouth, 163. *See also* Delhi bazaars, individual bazaars, marketplaces

bazaar speech, 192n7; as unregulated, 45

bazaar space: elasticity of, 57

bazaar tinkering, 122–23, 128, 175; as complex, 102; and grooming, 102; peer-to-peer knowledge, 127; *shanzhai*, as comparable, 103; street-level innovation of, 102; as vibrant and creative process, 105. *See also* tinkering

bazaar traders, 4, 6, 14, 20, 29, 33, 44, 48–49, 51, 57–58, 69, 91, 106, 111, 128, 136, 142, 156, 168, 192n7; alienation, 144; autonomy, fear of loss, 172; body language, 30; bookkeeping, absence of, 74; civility, use of, 132–33; consoles, repair of, 113–14; day-to-day accounting of, on pieces of paper, 74; "deceits," web of, 79; detailed knowledge, of neighborhood, 169; delivery services, 164; e-commerce platforms, 158–59, 163–66; e-commerce platforms, outwitting of, 160; electronics, selling of, 23, 25–26; ethical life of, 134, 152; ethics, 36, 174; extra income, search for, 179; face-to-face conversations, 10; fear of persecution, 27; gods, evocation of, 157–58; gossip, 169; guerrilla strategy of, 165–66; Hindu texts, interpretation of, 36; image-making, 163–64; informal credit systems of, 75–76; informal language of, 31; interpersonal networks, reliance on, 179; jokes, as alternative knowledge system, 31–32; liquidity of, 97–98; loiterers, 50; marginal status of, 116; marginalization, sense of, 28; as masculine space, 34; and mechanics, 114–16; merchant class, 179; mobility, lack of, 145; monthly earnings of, 26; as moral actors, 86–87, 89; moral stories, and precarity, negotiating of, 197n4; negotiation, comfort with, 162; networks of, 110, 112; new migrants, 26; as nomads, 165–66; online demons, 158;

online persona, difficulty of creating, 163; online technology, 158; partition refugees, 26; payment, postponement of, 76; pilgrimage, interest in, 140; platform economy, 155, 164; precarity of, 153; psychological warfare, 94; repairing skills, 116; religious identity, 177; risk-taking, 149; security, 97; shrewdness of, 93; slow business hours, 145; sociality, dependence on, 99; status quo, maintaining of, 149; tinkering, assisting of, 112; tinkering, ingenuity of, 114; video games, 9; vulnerability of, 26–27; whatsapping, 159; and women, 181–82

bazaar vendors: storytelling capacity of, 94–95

Beckert, Jens, 95–96

Benjamin, Walter: flaneur, 192–93n10; mechanical reproduction, 38–39

bhagidari (partnerships), 190n17

Bhabha Atomic Research Centre, 122

Bhabha, Homi J., 122

Bhagavad Gita, 137, 147, 198n9

Bharatiya Janata Party (BJP), 177

Bhattacharya, Neeladri, 18

bheed (cramped public spaces), 51

Bholakpar (India), 41

Bhojpuri, 69

Bhumi Pujan ritual, 176

Birla, Rita, 147

Bolivia, 180

Bombay (India), 189–90n15

Bombay Municipal Corporation, 54

Bourdieu, Pierre, 46

bourgeois environmentalism, 18–19

Boym, Svetlana, 64

brainstorming, 101

brandedness, 63, 66–67; branded products, 77–78, 191n5

brands, 96; authenticity, markers of, 66

Braudel, Fernand, 8, 10–11, 15–17, 188n8

Brazil, 52, 111
Britain, 151. *See also* England
B₂C (business to customer) sectors, 156
Buddhism, 135

Calvin, John, 131
"Can the Subaltern Speak?" (Spivak), 18
Calcutta (India), 21
Callon, Michel, 96
capitalism, 7–9, 15, 17, 96, 131, 170, 173, 188n5, 192–93n10, 193–94n3; bazaar economy, as alternative to, 37, 176; bazaar economy, relationship with, 10–11, 13; center-periphery approach, 13; colonial, 190n16; commons, as alternative to, 18; entrepreneurial, 95; ethics, 131; excesses of, 40–41; *Geist* of, 131; global, 39; letters of credit, 12; double-entry bookkeeping, 12; market anarchism, 188n8; marketplaces, as distinct from, 188n8; as monopolistic system, 16; precarity, missing in, 132; profit maximization, relationship between, 150; origins of, 16; as unequal system, 147; "window shopping," 12
cash transactions, 75, 94; *hafta* (protection money), 76
Certeau, Michel de, 31
Chahamana dynasty, 21
Chakrabarty, Dipesh, 157–58, 191n4
Chanderi, 125
charity bazaars, 12
Chatterjee, Indrani, 193n14
Chatterjee, Partha, 147, 151
chicanery, 71, 73, 87
China, 2, 11, 14, 27–28, 80–81, 86, 110–11, 129, 160, 190–91n1, 194n7, 195n3, 198n3; Chinese phone producers, adaptability of, 104; Chinese traders, 104; copycat culture, 103; intellectual property, 103; "Made in China,"

63–64, 82, 159; Robin Hood-style guerrilla tactics, 103
Chubb, Andrew, 39
Citizenship Amendment Act, 138, 197–98n5
city-states, 11
Civilization and Capitalism (Braudel), 15–16
collective bargaining, 13–14
collective consciousness, 148
collective creativity, 104
colonial bazaars, 2, 7, 151
colonialism, 2, 12–13, 54, 172; British, 121, 189–90n15
Columbia Sportswear, 63
common good, 71, 188–89
common lands, 17, 150, 188–89n9
commons, 70; bazaar economies, 19; capitalism, alternative to, 18; community ownership of land, 17–18; of everyday tools, 124; popular, 39; under threat, from elite bodies, 18–19
Commonwealth Games, 54
communalism, and gender, 37
consumer culture, 12; globalization of, 39
consumer goods, 12, 19, 78–79, 199n5
consumerism: bazaar, 65, 67; elite, 54; global, 65; posh, 66; proletarian, 50
contraband, 42
copyleft, 127, 196–97n16
cosmopolitanism: and Sanskrit language, 199n1
COVID-19 pandemic, 139, 172, 184, 199n3
co-working spaces, 166–67
critical theory, 16–17
Cuba, 62
culture industry, 38–39

Dambulla (Sri Lanka), 75
Dasgupta, Rana, 174
Debian project, 127
dehadi (daily wages), 76
Deleuze, Gilles, 165

Delhi (India), 8–9, 18–19, 63, 64, 66–67,
74, 78, 84, 88, 111, 161, 170, 177, 183,
191n2, 196n5; bazaar economy, 35;
British colonial expansion, 21–22;
"cleansing" of, 189n14; Connaught
Place, 21–23; co-working space in,
166; electronic bazaars, 114; excesses
of, as newness and waste, 68; Indian
rope trick, 117; Karol Bagh marketplace, 25–26, 169, 189n14; Khan
Market, 89; Lajpat Rai Market, 6,
10, 22, 24–25, 28–29, 31, 48, 51–52, 57,
61–62, 69, 71, 80–81, 83, 90–91, 93–94,
106, 109, 113, 126, 128, 130, 154, 156–57,
169, 171, 184, 194n6; Lutyens Delhi,
21–22; Meena Bazaar, 47, 51, 153; messiness of, 22; Naya Bazaar, 82–83, 179;
Nehru Place marketplace, 6–7, 23–26,
28–29, 31, 33, 48, 52, 55–58, 69, 76–77,
83, 87, 89, 97, 100, 105–6, 108, 126, 139–
41, 149, 169, 187n2; origin of name, 21;
Palika Bazaar marketplace, 6, 23–26,
28–29, 31–33, 45, 48–49, 52, 57, 69, 76,
79, 83, 90–93, 104–6, 109, 113, 126, 129,
139, 142, 145, 148, 152, 155–56, 159–60,
162, 164, 169, 181; Sadar Bazaar, 25–26;
Select City Walk, 55–56; Shahjahanabad (Old Delhi), walled city of,
21–22; slum redevelopment colonies,
187n2; South Delhi, 22–23, 54, 166–67;
street magicians in, 117; terrorist attacks, 49; traders and street vendors,
25–26. *See also* Delhi bazaars
Delhi bazaars, 128, 131, 148, 152, 156, 174;
as competitive, 112; diversity of, 50;
and Hinduism, 136; innovations, as
tinkering, 105; moral stories, as widespread, 145; new products, reinventing of, 112; platform economy, 154–55;
recycling in, 196n5; *techne*, 158
Delhi Development Authority (DDA),
52, 189n14
Delhi Improvement Trust (DIT), 189n14

Delhi Municipal Corporation, 189n14
DeNapoli, Antoinette Elizabeth, 136–37
Dertouzos, Michael L., 101
Dhaka (Bangladesh), 61
digital commons: of hackers, 19
digital economy: of e-commerce plat-
forms, 9
digital technologies, 6
do-it-yourself (DIY) cafes, 124
Doron, Assa, 125–26, 179
Dubai, 2
Dumont, Louis, 134–35
Durkheim, Emile, 148

East India Company, 151, 189–90n15
e-commerce platforms, 1, 5, 9, 17, 35–37,
153–54, 158–59, 163, 170, 184, 199n3;
annual sales, 162; bazaar actors, 155,
162; bazaars, interaction between,
6, 156, 161–62, 169; digital economy,
9; guerrilla strategy, used against
by traders, 165–66; as monster-like
creature, 157; negotiations with, as
complicated, 157, 164; online demons,
157–58; outwitting of, by traders, 160;
secondhand goods, 157, 162; shifting
allegiances, 161; traditional customer
base of bazaar economy, penetrating
of, 168–69; as vertical platform, 171
economic life: trickle-down economics,
13
elite actors, 153, 171, 174, 187n1; common
land, control of, 150; state actors,
control of, 151–52; and women, 182
enclosure, 188–89n9; of commons, 18;
and gender, 18; women's role in public
life, 18
England, 13–14, 78–79; enclosures
movement, 188–89n9; Speenhamland
system in, 193–94n3. *See also* Britain
Enlightenment, 190n16
ethical life, 144, 150–51, 153, 175, 197n4;
of bazaar actors, 130, 139, 146; in

bazaar economy, 131–34, 148–49, 152; competitive market economy, as shock absorber of, 35; as momentary relief, 128

ethics, 6, 36, 144, 150, 152–53, 174–76, 198n9; bargaining ritual, 132; boundaries of commerce, creating of, 147; economic behavior, 130–31; as mitigator, 134; v. morality, 197n1; profit, relationship between, 147–48; sense of purpose, 133

euergetism, 198n10

Europe, 11–13, 18, 39, 47, 7`, 111, 131, 133–34, 150, 188n6, 188–89n9, 193n2; tinkers in, 116

exchange relations, 175, 183

Facebook, 68, 157, 163

face-to-face trade, 4

Fanselow, Frank S., 59, 73

fascism, 38

fast fashion, 182

Federici, Silvia, 18

Fernandes, Leela, 65–66, 138

Fernandes, Leela, 65–66

feudalism, 12

flaneurs, 192–93n10

Florence (Italy), 11

Forest Charter, 188–89n9

Fox, Richard G., 59

France, 15–16

Frankfurt School, 38 39

Frankopan, Peter, 11

free riding, 18

free software culture, 127

French Annales School, 15

frugal innovation, 101–2

frugality, 144–46

games, 23, 49, 57–58, 61, 64, 78, 80, 82, 90, 93, 108, 110, 116, 155, 169, 175, 194n6; arcade, 91, 106; counterfeited, 81; modifying of, 111–12; pirated, 26, 89,

105–6, 109, 114, 140, 142; secondhand, 79, 113, 162, 168. *See also* TV games, video games

gaming economy, 8, 109, 114

Gandhi, Ajay, 47, 153, 192–93n10

Gandhi, Mahatma, 51, 65, 119, 176, 190n16; *swaraj* (autonomy achieved through sustainable local manufacturing), vision of, 120

Gao, Bai, 104, 190–91n1

Geertz, Clifford, 59, 73, 93, 132, 146

Geertz, Hildred, 59, 146

gender politics: intersectionality of, 34

General Public Licenses (GPLs), 127

Genoa (Italy), 11, 16

Gestalt psychology, 195n1, 101

Ghana, 43–44

Ghertner, David Asher, 191n2

Gibson-Graham, J. K., 16

Gidwani, Vinay, 41

global goods, 24

globalization, 14–15, 190–91n1; of consumer culture, 39

globalization from below literature, 14–15

Global North, 111–12, 124, 172, 184

Global South, 41, 54, 111–12, 170, 177, 184, 196–97n16; residual savagery of ordinary life, 178

global urbanism, 69

"Goblin Market" (Rossetti), 12

Goffman, Erving, 77

Gopalkrishnan, Shankar, 137–38

Graeber, David, 16

Gramsci, Antonio, 43, 151

Grand Bazaar, 85–86

Grand Theft Auto (video game), 51

Granovetter, Mark, 178–79

greed, 145–47

Gréine, Pádraig Mac, 24

Guattari, Felix, 165

Guru, Gopal, 118

gutka (tobacco-infused betel nut), 140

hackers, 7, 101, 109, 127; and bazaars, 187n3; digital commons of, 19; piracy, skepticism toward, 196–97n16
hafta (protection money), 76
Haiti, 86
Halberstam, Jack, 19–20
Han, Byung-Chul, 199n5
Han dynasty, 11
Hanoi (Vietnam), 44
Haraway, Donna, 173
Hardin, Garrett: tragedy of commons, 18, 189n10
Harney, Stefano: undercommons, 19–20
Hart, Emma, 188n5
Haug, Wolfgang Fritz, 38
hawala network, 8, 76
Heath, Deana, 193n14
Hegel, Georg Wilhelm Friedrich, 31, 190n16
Heidegger, Martin, 158
Heller, Patrick, 138
Hennessey, William, 39
Heslop, Luke, 75
heterogeneity, 138, 183–84
Heterologies: Discourse on the Other (de Certeau), 31
Hill, Sarah, 25, 61–62
Hinduism, 134, 198n8, 198n9; everyday ethics of, 136, 138; experimental nature of, 136–38; flexibility of, 136; as Hindutva ideology, 137; modern technology, interaction between, 136–37
Hindu movies, 115–16
Hindutva ideology, 137; new middle-class (NMC) white collar professionals, links between, 138
Hobbs, Dick, 170
Hoek, Lotte, 47
Holmes, Elizabeth, 196n14
homo economicus, 8
Hong Kong (China), 2
Horkheimer, Max, 39

Hotz, George, 196n13
Hui, Yuk, 198n3
Hüwelmeier, Gertrud, 44–45

identity politics, 20
Ilahiane, Hsain, 146, 198n7
illegal distribution networks, 4
India, 11, 14, 21, 25, 43, 52, 59, 65, 67, 101, 105, 116, 119, 129–30, 133, 135, 154–55, 161–62, 168, 171, 189, 190n16, 191n4, 197–98n5; brahminical knowledge, 118; caste system, 118, 134; demonetization measures in, 194n5; developmentalism, 193n14; e-commerce market, 156; elites, 187n1; gaming industry, and TV games, 194n6; Hindu nationalism, 137; illegal and semi-legal dealings, with state, 152; Indian customers, as miserly, 89–90; Indian weddings, extravagance of, 194–95n8; Indian way of thinking, 134; information technology (IT), 122; land control, 18; "Make in India" program, 122–23, 196n12; media modernity in, 23–24; moral thoughts, 136; popular knowledge, and British colonialism, 121–22; *sati*, glorification of, 18; secularism, 176; street performers, 124; widows, 18
India Human Development Survey (IHDS), 90
Indian Institute of Technology (IIT), 25, 122
Indian Statistical Institute, 122
Indonesia, 1, 84, 132
Indra, 142
industrialization, 172
Industrial Training Institutes (IITs): as left outs, 115
informal economy, 148–49, 154, 167–68, 179; COVID-19 pandemic, long-term impact, 199n3
informal knowledge systems, 116

information communication technolo-
     gies (ICTs), 43–44, 104
information society, 2
innovation, 101–3, 106, 120, 122, 168;
     bazaar-level, 124; of bodies, 117–18;
     copying of, 127–28; do-it-yourself
     (DIY) approach to, 175; explicit
     knowledge, crucial for, 195n2; *jugaad*-
     style, 196n9; marginalization, 105; of
     street performers, 117; and tinkering,
     105, 112; with video games, 112
Instagram: aesthetic of, 67–68; Reels, 67
intellectual property rights, 103, 126–27,
     190n19, 190–91n1, 191n5
Islam, 176–77
Istanbul (Turkey), 85–86
Italian Marxism, 16–17
Italy, 120

Jackson, Steven J., 62, 105
Jahan, Shah, 22
Jain, Kajri, 42
Japan, 111, 121
Jeffrey, Craig, 192n9
Jerrold, Douglas, 188n6
JJ colony Madanpur Khadar, 26
Jhabvala, 51
Johannesburg (South Africa), 68
Joseph, Manu, 101
Joutia, 198n7
jugaad (frugal innovation), 36, 101,
     119–20, 196n9; bazaar-style tinkering,
     123
Jullien, Francois, 103

Kabbani, Rana, 12
kalapila (black and yellow taxis), 154
Kali (goddess), 157
kanjus, 90
karma (duty), 139, 198n9
Karol Bagh marketplace, 25–26, 169,
     189n14
Karrar, Hasan, 44, 97, 192n6

Kavango, 62
Kazakhstan, 97, 192n6
khalbali, 47–48
Khan, Genghis, 165
Khan Market, 89
Kharagpur (India), 122
kinship networks, 179; and bribes, 194n7
kirana stores (neighborhood grocers), 156
Knight, Frank, 95
knowledge: access to knowledge move-
     ment, 127; as copied and circulated,
     128; embedded, 195n1; embodied, 116;
     exchange of, as interpersonal, 128; ex-
     plicit, 195n2; hide-and-seek approach
     to, 126; *jugaad*-style, 196n9; keeping
     to oneself, 126; knowledge-sharing
     systems, 127; marginalized, 117; peer
     to peer, 127; personal, 195n1; popular,
     119–21, 125; scientific, 118, 195n1; tra-
     ditional, 195n1, 196n9; transmission
     of, 125, 128
knowledge production, 125; copyleft
     culture of, 196–97n16
Koons, Jeff, 199n5
Kracauer, Siegfried: tiller girls, reference
     to, 38
Krieshok, Gabriel, 62, 105
Krishna, 198n9
Krishnamurthy, Mekhala, 83
Kumar, Akshaya, 69
Kyrgyzstan, 97, 192n6

laissez-faire economy, 13–14
Lajpat Rai marketplace, 6, 22, 24–25,
     28–29, 31, 48, 51, 52, 57, 61–62, 69, 71,
     80–81, 83, 90–91, 93–94, 113, 126, 128,
     130, 154, 156–57, 169, 171, 184, 194n6;
     innovation in, 106; Jain and Hindu
     traders, 26; repair persons, 109
Lagos, 170
lal dora, 22
Laozi, 103–4
Lara Croft (video game), 80

Larkin, Brian, 14
Ledeneva, Alena, 194n7
Legg, Stephen, 193n14
Lemire, Beverly, 78–79
Lessig, Lawrence, 196–97n16
living on the margins, 1
Lobato, Ramon, 196–97n16
lobh (greed), 145
lokavidya, 119–20, 196n9
London (England), 12, 55–56, 189–
    90n15
longue durée, 8, 10–11, 16
Lord Krishna, 139
Louis XVI, 193n2
Lu, Miao, 43–44, 104
Lucknow (India), 103, 125
Lutyens, Edwin, 189n14
Lysack, Krista, 12

Madanpur Khadar colony, 55
Madhya Pradesh, 83
Magna Carta, 188–89n9
Mahalanobis, P. C., 122
Mali, 1
Manchester (England), 121
Mansion, Chungking, 15
Manuel, Peter, 14
Manushi (NGO), 33
Maori, 40
marginalization, 26, 43–44, 119–20, 123,
    153; of women, in urban bazaars,
    180–81
marginalized communities, 125, 134
Maringanti, Anant, 41
market anarchism, 188n8
market economy, 35, 150, 164, 178; as
    face-to-face exchanges, 16
market exchanges, 8, 11–12, 15, 17, 86
marketplaces, 48, 50–51, 54–55, 58,
    68–69, 101, 109–12, 142, 144, 148, 151,
    156, 158, 161, 165, 169; aesthetics of, 35;
    betrayal, 148; capitalism, as distinct

from, 188n8; caste groupings, 179;
    endurance of, 183; flow of, 57; kin
    networks, 179; lockdown economy,
    adapting to, 184; openness in, 126;
    physical experience of, 35; recycling,
    113; repair work, 114; sociality of, 46;
    terrorist attacks, 49; urban under-
    class, as spaces of, 182; young couples,
    hostility toward, 49; as women-led,
    180. *See also* bazaars
Marx, Karl, 63, 147, 190n16, 192n7,
    193–94n3; religion, as seductive possi-
    bility, 197n4
Massachusetts Institute of Technology
    (MIT), 122
Master Plan for Delhi, 193n12
Mathews, Gordon, 15
Mazzarella, William, 177–78
Mbembe, Achille, 68
mechanics, 114; as derogatory, 115; as
    redemptive figures, 196n6; trial-and-
    error method of, 115; as working-class
    icons, 115–16
Media Tek, 190–91n1
Meena Bazaar, 47, 51, 153
Mehra, Diya, 189n14
Mengzi, 103–4
Messias, José, 111
Microsoft Xbox, 77–78
Middle Ages, 11, 46–47; great exchange,
    of merchant networks, 16; medieval
    commons, 17
Middle East, 11, 85
Milan (Italy), 166, 195n3
mimicry, 47
mistriis (artisans), 102
modernism, 22–23, 52; ecumene of, 39
modernity, 11, 13, 23, 40, 185; aesthetics
    of, 38; consumer, 39
modernization, 44
Montaigne, Michel de, 31
Morocco: *suqs* in, 59, 146

Moten, Fred: undercommons, 19–20
Mughal, 193n14; Mughal bazaars,
    11, 22
Mumbai (India), 43, 54
Municipal Corporation of Delhi,
    26–27

Nakassis, Constantine, 63, 191n5
Namibia, 62, 105
Nandy, Ashis, 118, 176
naqsheband system: and secrecy, 125;
    trained weavers, 125
Naples (Italy), 43, 120–21
Narada (sage), 142
National Council of Applied Economic
    Research (NCAER), 90
Naya Bazaar, 82–83, 179
Negri and Hardt, 111
Nehru, Jawaharlal, 122
Nehru Place marketplace, 6–7, 23–26,
    28–29, 31, 33, 48, 52, 55–58, 69, 76–77,
    83, 87, 89, 97, 100, 105–6, 108, 126,
    139–41, 149, 169, 187n2
neoliberalism, 129, 183–85
networks, 3, 8–11, 14, 83–84, 86, 96, 98,
    110, 127, 147, 150–52, 170, 172, 180,
    189–90n15, 199n3; bazaar, 113; caste,
    179; distributive, 26, 104; e-com-
    merce, 165; familial, 4, 26; informal,
    187n3, 194n6, 194n7; interdependent,
    128; interpersonal, 6, 179; kin, 74, 99,
    178–79; kinship, 194n7; merchant,
    16; peer-to-peer, 36; semi-legal, 48;
    smuggling, 23–24
Neumann, Adam, 196n14
New Delhi Municipal Corporation
    (NDMC), 189n14
Niessen, Bertram, 128
Nigeria, 14
Nintendo Game Boy, 77–78
nomads, 165–66
Nonaka, Ikujiro, 195n2

non-elites, 2, 5, 9, 13–14, 21, 24, 47,
    119–20, 128, 150, 168, 174–75, 183, 187n1,
    189–90n15; and brandedness, 66–67;
    as invisible, 7; undercommons,
    concept of, 20; urban commons, use
    of, 43
North America, 111, 131

Obama, Barack, 103
Obeyesekere, Gananath, 135
"Of Cannibals" (Montaigne), 31
Ola, 154
Old Delhi, 51
open-source systems, 127; open-source-
    backed hacker and maker spaces,
    124
opium and gaming dens, 12
Ostrom, Elinor, 18
overproduction, 182

Pakistan, 14–15, 52, 86, 97
Palika Bazaar marketplace, 6, 23–26,
    28–29, 31–33, 45, 48–49, 52, 57, 69, 76,
    79, 83, 90–93, 104, 113, 126, 129, 142,
    145, 148, 152, 159–60, 162, 164, 169, 181;
    field notes from, 155–56; meditation,
    139; old consoles, reviving of, 105–6;
    repair persons, 109
pandemics, 6, 171
Pandian, Anand, 136
pan Indian Hinduism, 176–77
Parashuram Das, 137
Paris (France), 11, 192–93n10
Partition of India, 189n14
Patil, C. B., 21
peasant economies: communal lands, 98
peddlers, 4, 123
Philippines, 86
pilgrimages, 140
Pine, Jason, 43
Pinjra Tod (Break the Cage) movement,
    181

piracy, 24, 39; hackers' skepticism
toward, 196–97n16; pirated cassette
culture, Hindu films and folk music,
14; pirated games and software, 141–
42; pirated goods, 157; pirated video
games, 15; pirating of software and
video games, 87–88; radical potential
of, 128; of video format, 14–15
pirated DVDs/CDs, 114, 140; *keygen*
(serial number), 106, 108
pirate modernity, 174–75
Pisa (Italy), 11
platform economy, 154–56, 161–63,
166, 171–72, 176; "consumer is king"
phrase, 164
playbour, 8
Pocock, J. G. A., 135
poiesis, 158, 199n4
Poland, 187n3
Polanyi, Karl, 72, 193–94n3, 195n1
Pollock, Sheldon, 199n1
Pompe, Alex, 62, 105
popular commons, 39
popular knowledge: lack of patents, 125;
secrecy, 125
populism, 176–78
postcolonial media piracy, 14
prateek, 86
predestination, 131
Prometheus, 198n3
Protestant ethic, 131
Proudhon, Pierre-Joseph, 188n8
public spaces, 41, 54, 56–57, 67, 69, 181,
184
public spheres, 8; as masculine, 181; v.
private, 42
Punjab (India), 18
Puranas, 137, 146, 198n8

Rabelais, François: as antithetical figure,
46
racialization, 193n14
ragpickers, 123

Ramanujan, Srinivasa, 133–34
Ray, Purnima, 21
Ray, Rajat Kanta, 189–90n15
Raymond, Eric, 2
ready-made parts, 103; absence of, 112–13
reciprocity, 8
recycling, 41, 112, 124, 175, 182, 184, 196n5,
196n15; of secondhand games, 113
Redfield, Robert, 134–35
redistribution: and reciprocity, 8, 17
Reformation, 46
Renaissance: capitalist rationality of, 46
rentier system, 152, 154
Ricardo, David, 193–94n3
Rio Olympics, 52
Rosen, Lawrence, 59, 146
Rossetti, Christina, 12
Rothschild, Emma, 193n2
Roy, Ram Mohan, 18
Ruggiero, Vincenzo, 170
Rundu (Namibia), 62
Russia, 120, 192n6, 194n7. *See also* Soviet
Union

sabotage mentality, 149
Sadar Bazaar, 25–26
Said, Edward W., 12
Samurai (video game), 104
Sanskrit, 199n1
Santiago (Chile), 1
Santiago de Cuba (Cuba), 25, 61
Sarukkai, Sundar, 118
Sayeed, Mohammed, 51
scavenging, 62
science and technology studies (STS),
118–19
science, technology, engineering, medicine (STEM) disciplines, 180
Scott, Michael, 98
secondhand products, 3–4, 15, 24, 69, 73,
78–80, 92–93, 112–13, 124–25, 156, 157,
159, 162, 168, 182; economy, 39–40;
technologies, 43–44

secularism, 176

Serres, Michel, 185

sexuality, 199n2; and gender, 33

Sethi, Aman, 174

shanzhai, 39, 104–5; innovation, 103, 195n3; phones, widespread use of, 190–91n1; sumptuary laws, rebellion against, 39

shared codes of conduct, 87

sharing economy, 16

Shenzhen (China), 102–3, 195n3

Sherry, John, 146, 198n7

Silk Road, 11

slavery, 172

small-scale economies, 148

Smith, Adam, 150, 189n10, 193n2

Smith, R. V., 191n2

sociality, 2, 9, 50, 183–84, 192n8; of marketplaces, 46

social media, 157, 163; cultural clusters, creating of, 197n3

social theory, 178–79

Sohn-Rethel, Alfred, 120–21

Sony, 168, 196n13; Sony PlayStation, 77–78, 106, 109–11

Soroo, 80

South, Nigel, 170

Soviet Union, 64. *See also* Russia

Spivak, Gayatri, 18

Sri Lanka, 75, 135

Srinivas, Tulsi, 136

Srivastava, Sanjay, 66, 199n2

Stallybrass, Peter, 46

state actors, 151, 183–84

storytelling, 94, 99, 197n4; algorithmic governance of, 95; bazaar bargaining, 96–97

street-level commerce: tenacity of, 4;

street vendors, 4, 6–8, 25, 29–30, 49, 51, 54, 56, 59, 69, 74, 91, 112, 128, 136, 181; aging, concern of, 144; alienation, 144; astrological influence, 139; bank accounts, 28; as bazaar actors, 26; bazaar traders, 179; behavior of, as condemnable, 142, 144; body language, 76–77; cheating, claims of, 88; despair, state of, 141; digital payments, 28; DVDs/CDs, and assigned keys to customers, 87–88; e-commerce, 165; electronics, selling of, 23; ethics, 174; fear of persecution, 27; gossip, 169; jokes, as alternative knowledge system, 31–32; hedonism of, 142; *keygen* (serial number), 106, 108; liquidity, 97–98; male space of, 34; marginal status of, 116; marginalization, sense of, 28; and mechanics, 115–16; mobility, lack of, 145; monthly earnings of, 26; as moral agents, 89; as nomads, 165–66; platform economy, 155; police raids, fear of, 145; popular meeting points, in cities, 169–70; precarity of, 153; religious identity, 177; repairing skills, 116; risk-taking, 149; security, 97; shouting and chewing of *gutka*, repetitive nature of, 140–42; slow business hours, 145; sociality, dependence on, 99; status quo, maintaining of, 149; tinkering, 109; tinkering, ingenuity of, 114; of video games, 26; as young men, 34

Suez Canal, 189–90n15

suki, 86

Sundaram, Ravi, 14, 137

survival income, 98

swadeshi, 65

Tamil Nadu, 63

Tarikh-i-Firishta, 21

Tarrius, Alain: poor to poor networks, 14

Tata Institute of Fundamental Research, 122

Tata, J. R. D., 122

team building, 101

techne, 157–58, 198n3

Theranos, 196n14

third space, 165, 191n4

TikTok, 66; banning of, 67–68

timepass, 192n9

tinkers, 4, 175; bazaar, 122–23; on the fringes, 116; gladar box, 24–25; Irish, 7, Roma, 7, 24–25; soldering technique, use of, 117; as term, 7, 24–25, 116. *See also* travelers

tinkering, 25, 109, 121, 127; bazaar innovation, 102; class and geographical angle to, 111; as communitarian, 36; cosmetic, 113; creativity, challenging of, 36; embodied knowledge, 36; ingenuity of, 114; innovation, 105; intellectual property rights, challenging of, 36; Irish, 124; and poverty, 111–12; Scottish, 124; with video games, and innovation, 112

tirni, 18

Tomb Raider (DVD), 93

trade unions, 13–14

transnational commerce, 2

travelers: Irish, 116; Roma, 116; Scottish, 116

Tripathi, Dwijendra, 121

Tsing, Anna, 173

Turgot, Anne Robert Jacques, 193n2

TV games, 80, 90–91, 104, 106, 194n6. *See also* games, video games

Tyabji, Nasir, 189–90n15

Uber, 154

undercommons: of marginalized groups, 19; as wild space, 20

United States, 13–14, 19, 122

University of Maryland, 90

Upanishads, 118, 137

urban bazaars, 5–7, 10; displaced groups, 14; face-to-face commerce, 13; price-setting mechanisms, and intermediaries, 82, 83; as term, 13

urban commons, 17; bazaar actors, 21; bazaar economy, reliance on, 35

urbanism, 52; urban informal labor, 28; urban spaces, 14, 181, 199n2; urban spatialization, 54–55; urban underclass, 182–83, 196n5

ustaad, 145

Vedas, 118

Venice (Italy), 11, 16

Veyne, Paul, 198n10

Vidal, Denis, 82–83, 179

video games, 6–7, 9, 24–26, 30, 32, 50, 61, 74, 82, 91–93, 95, 104, 124; modifying of, 111–12; pirated, 15, 87. *See also* games, TV games

Vietnam, 44

Vigo videos, 66

Virno, Paolo, 192n7

Vishwakarma (Hindu god of craftsmanship), 157

Vishva Hindu Parishad, 137–38

Wall Street crash, 151

Wasiak, Patryk, 187–88n3

waste, 182

Wealth of Nations, The (Smith), 193n2

Weber, Max, 131–32

Wesley, John, 131

WeWork, 196n14

WhatsApp, 163, 184; WhatsApp university, as term, 197n3

White, Allon, 46

World Trade Organization (WTO), 44; Trade-Related Aspects of Intellectual Property Rights (TRIPS), 124, 190n19

World War II, 189n14

Xbox, 109–10

Yadav, Yogendra, 176

Yang, Anand A., 190n16

Zanjeer (film), 196n6

zombie media, 112

CULTURE AND ECONOMIC LIFE

_____

Making Sense: Markets from Stories in New Breast Cancer Therapeutics
Sophie Mützel
2022

Supercorporate: Distinction and Participation in Post-Hierarchy South Korea
Michael M. Prentice
2022

*Black Culture, Inc.: How Ethnic Community
Support Pays for Corporate America*
Patricia A. Banks
2022

The Sympathetic Consumer: Moral Critique in Capitalist Culture
Tad Skotnicki
2021

Reimagining Money: Kenya in the Digital Finance Revolution
Sibel Kusimba
2021

*Black Privilege: Modern Middle-Class Blacks
with Credentials and Cash to Spend*
Cassi Pittman Claytor
2020

Global Borderlands: Fantasy, Violence, and Empire in Subic Bay, Philippines
Victoria Reyes
2019

*The Costs of Connection: How Data Is Colonizing Human
Life and Appropriating It for Capitalism*
Nick Couldry and Ulises A. Mejias
2019

The Moral Power of Money: Morality and Economy in the Life of the Poor
Ariel Wilkis
2018

The Work of Art: Value in Creative Careers
Alison Gerber
2017

Behind the Laughs: Community and Inequality in Comedy
Michael P. Jeffries
2017

Freedom from Work: Embracing Financial Self-Help in the United States and Argentina
Daniel Fridman
2016

The authorized representative in the EU for product safety and compliance is:
Mare Nostrum Group
B.V Doelen 72
4831 GR Breda
The Netherlands

www.ingramcontent.com/pod-product-compliance
Lightning Source LLC
Chambersburg PA
CBHW030403270326
41926CB00009B/1248